AF840616

Corporations and Partnerships in Malaysia

Corporations and Partnerships in Malaysia

Aiman Nariman Mohd-Sulaiman
Halyani Hassan
Zuhairah Ariff Abd Ghadas

This book was originally published as a monograph in the International Encyclopaedia of Laws/Corporations and Partnerships.

Founding Editor: Roger Blanpain
General Editor: Frank Hendrickx
Volume Editors: Koen Geens

Wolters Kluwer

Published by:
Kluwer Law International B.V.
PO Box 316
2400 AH Alphen aan den Rijn
The Netherlands
E-mail: lrs-sales@wolterskluwer.com
Website: www.wolterskluwer.com/en/solutions/kluwerlawinternational

Sold and distributed by:
Wolters Kluwer Legal & Regulatory U.S.
7201 McKinney Circle
Frederick, MD 21704
United States of America
E-mail: customer.service@wolterskluwer.com

DISCLAIMER: The material in this volume is in the nature of general comment only. It is not offered as advice on any particular matter and should not be taken as such. The editor and the contributing authors expressly disclaim all liability to any person with regard to anything done or omitted to be done, and with respect to the consequences of anything done or omitted to be done wholly or partly in reliance upon the whole or any part of the contents of this volume. No reader should act or refrain from acting on the basis of any matter contained in this volume without first obtaining professional advice regarding the particular facts and circumstances at issue. Any and all opinions expressed herein are those of the particular author and are not necessarily those of the editor or publisher of this volume.

ISBN 978-94-035-4945-3

e-Book: ISBN 978-94-035-4585-1
web-PDF: ISBN 978-94-035-4595-0

© 2022 Kluwer Law International BV, The Netherlands

All rights reserved. No part of this publication may be reproduced, stored in a retrieval system, or transmitted in any form or by any means, electronic, mechanical, photocopying, recording, or otherwise, without the prior written permission of the publisher.

Permission to use this content must be obtained from the copyright owner. More information can be found at: www.wolterskluwer.com/en/solutions/legal-regulatory/permissions-reprints-and-licensing

The Authors

Prof. Dr Aiman Nariman Mohd-Sulaiman obtained an LLB (Hons) (First Class) from the International Islamic University Malaysia (1993), a Master's of Comparative Laws from the International Islamic University Malaysia (1994) and a Doctor of Legal Science (SJD) from Bond University, Australia (2000). She is presently a Professor in the Faculty of Law, International Islamic University Malaysia. She teaches company law and corporate governance at the undergraduate and postgraduate levels. Her areas of specialization are company law, corporate governance and securities regulation. She has published widely on company law and corporate governance in several academic journals and is the author of Malaysia Company law-Principles and Practices (Wolters Kluwer) which is in its third edition. She was a recipient of the Australian Endeavour Scholar Award from the Australian Government in 2012 and was a Visiting Professor at the School of Law, Bond University, Queensland, Australia in 2012 and Fakultas Hukum, Universitas Indonesia in 2017. She wrote the parts on corporations and Takeovers and Mergers.

Dr Halyani Hassan is an Associate Professor at the Ahmad Ibrahim Kulliyyah of Laws, International Islamic University Malaysia (IIUM). She obtained her LLB (Hons) (Second Class Upper) in 1991, LLB Shariah (Hons) (Second Class Upper) in 1992 and Master's in Comparative Law (MCL) in 1993 from IIUM. In 2004, she obtained her PhD in Business Law from Universiti Putra Malaysia (UPM). Dr Halyani is a faculty member of Ahmad Ibrahim Kulliyyah of Laws since 1993. Her areas of interest are company law, law of partnership and law of contract. She taught business laws and law of meeting for other programs at IIUM. She is also a member of the Board of Examiners Committee for the Malaysian Association of Company Secretaries (MACS) since November 2012 and an external examiner for Open University Malaysia (OUM). Dr Halyani has presented papers at local and international conferences.

The Authors

Prof. Dr Zuhairah Ariff Abd Ghadas is currently Dean Faculty of Law, Accountancy and International Relations (FLAIR), University Sultan Zainal Abidin (UNISZA) in Malaysia.

Prof. Dr Zuhairah graduated with LLB (Hons) in Business Law from the University of Huddersfield, United Kingdom, and later obtained her Master's in Comparative Laws from the International Islamic University Malaysia. She obtained her PhD in Business Law from the Graduate School of Management, University Putra Malaysia. Prof. Dr Zuhairah's area of specialization is Business Law and Construction Law. She has published many articles and academic books related to Business Law.

Amongst articles she published are 'Real or Artificial, Jurisprudential Theories on Corporate Personality', *US–China Law Review* (2007), 'Participation in Business as Part of Matrimonial Property', *International Islamic University Malaysia Law Journal* (2007), 'The Development of Business Vehicles in Asia: A Convergence or Divergence', *US–China Law Review* (2007), 'Limited Liability in Business Vehicles and the Application to Malaysian SMEs', *International Islamic University Malaysia Law Journal* (2006), 'The Concept of Sharikah and its Benefit to the Society', *International Islamic Digital Library* (2006), 'Registration of Companies: An Overview from the Malaysian Law and the Islamic Law Perspectives', *Journal of Islamic Law Review* (2005). In the Midst of Malaysian Limited Liability Partnership (LLPs): The Issue of Moral Hazards' (2005). She is also a contributing editor for 'Annotated Statute of Malaysia – Companies Commission Act 2001', *Malayan Law Journal*, 2003.

Table of Contents

Table of Contents

List of Abbreviations

AGM	Annual General Meeting
BMLR	Bursa Malaysia Listing Requirements
CA	Companies Act 2016
CEO	Chief Executive Officer
CMSA	Capital Market and Services Act of 2007
EGM	Extraordinary General Meeting
ESOS	Employee Stock Ownership Scheme
IBFC	International Business and Financial Centre
IOFC	International Offshore Financial Centre
IPO	Initial Public Offering
KLSE	Kuala Lumpur Stock Exchange
LFSA	Labuan Financial Services Authority Act 1996
LFSSA	Labuan Financial Services and Securities Act 2010
LIFSSA	Labuan Islamic Financial Services and Securities Act 2010
LLP	Limited Liability Partnerships
LP and LLPA	Labuan Limited Partnerships and Labuan Limited Liability Partnerships Act
LOBATA	Labuan Offshore Business Activities Tax Act of 1990
LOFSA	Labuan Offshore Financial Services Authority
LPA	Labuan Offshore Limited Partnerships Act of 1997
MASB	Malaysian Accounting Standards Board
MCCG	Malaysian Code on Corporate Governance
MIA	Malaysian Institute of Accountants
PA	Partnership Act of 1961
PCC	Protected Cell Company
RBA	Registration of Businesses Act
SC	Securities Commission
SCA	Securities Commission Act of 1993
SCORE	System on Computerized Order Routing and Execution

List of Abbreviations

General Introduction

§1. General Background of the Country

I. Geography

1. Geographically, Malaysia consists of Peninsular Malaysia and East Malaysia which are divided by the South China Sea. Peninsular Malaysia is surrounded by the Straits of Malacca on the west and the South China Sea on the east and the Tebrau Straits in the south. Peninsular Malaysia comprises the following states: Johor, Melaka, Negri Sembilan, Selangor, Perak, Kedah, Pulau Pinang, Perlis, Kelantan, Trengganu, Pahang, the Federal Territory of Kuala Lumpur and the Federal Territory of Putrajaya. East Malaysia comprises the following states: Sabah, Sarawak and the Federal Territory of Labuan.

The capital city of Malaysia is Kuala Lumpur. The administrative capital is the Federal Territory of Putrajaya.

II. Cultural Composition

2. Malaysia has multicultural citizenship comprising Malays and indigenous tribes such as the Orang Asli who are an indigenous minority in Peninsular Malaysia and Orang Asal who are natives of Sabah and Sarawak (68% of the total population), Chinese (23% of the total population) and Indians (7% of the total population). The Malay-speaking Malays and the indigenous people (collectively known as the Bumiputera) were the initial inhabitants in Tanah Melayu (as it was known, i.e., Peninsular Malaysia) before the arrival of European colonists such as the English, Portuguese and Dutch during the thirteenth and the fourteenth centuries. In East Malaysia, there are approximately twenty-eight indigenous groups making up 71% of the total population of Sarawak and forty-three ethnic groups making up 62% of Sabah's total population; some of the indigenous people are Iban, Bidayuh, Kadazan-Dusun, Bajau and Murut. Data in 2017, indicated that the Indigenous Peoples of Malaysia make up 13% of the national population. Although Malays are Bumiputera, they constitute the majority and have political and social dominance. There are other ethnicities making up 0.7% of the national population.

Malaysians are generally bilingual as, in addition to the respective mother tongues of Malay, Chinese, Indians and indigenous tribes, English is widely spoken.

III. Political System

3. Malaysia has a parliamentary democracy and a bicameral legislature with a constitutional monarchy. The legislative power is divided between a federal legislature and state legislatures. The federal legislature is bicameral in nature, i.e., comprising the Senate (Upper house) of appointed senators as well as representatives elected by the State legislatures and the House of Representatives (Lower House) that is entirely elected. The election of the 222 members of the Lower House must be held every five years. The State legislature is made up entirely of elected representatives.

Each state has its own head of state, with the nine Malay States (Johor, Negri Sembilan, Selangor, Perak, Kedah, Perlis, Kelantan, Trengganu, Pahang) each having its own ruling sultan, who is a descendant of the original sultans (rulers) of Tanah Melayu. Pulau Pinang, Sabah, Sarawak and Melaka have their respective head of states. There is also a constitutional monarch for Malaysia who is the Yang Dipertuan Agong, elected from the nine ruling sultans of the Malay States on a five-year rotation basis.

There is also a clear demarcation of authority between the federal and state legislatures which is to be found in the Federal Constitution clarifying matters which fall under the legislative authority of the states and the Federal government. The states can pass a law which will be applicable within the states, but the statutes enacted by the federal legislature are applicable throughout Malaysia.

IV. Population and Employment Statistics

4. In 2021, the population in Malaysia is estimated at 32.7 million where 26.0 million are non-citizens (comprising permanent residents, foreign workers with work permits, expatriates and foreign students). Of the population, 69% are within the 15–64 age group, 23% are below 14 years old and 7.5% are aged 64 and above.

The Labour force comprises those persons between the working age of 15 to 64 and as of November 2021 were at 16.3 million. The number of people employed during the same period was 15.6 million and the unemployment rate was 4.3%. The labour force comprises employees as well as own-account workers category defined by the Malaysian Department of Statistics as daily income earners working as small business operators such as retailers, hawkers, sellers in markets and stalls as well as smallholders involved in the agriculture sector. There are also persons categorized as outside the labour force who were not working due to schooling or training commitments or family or housework responsibilities (7.36 million persons). The ratio of employment to population has been on the increase since 2020. This ratio indicates the economy's ability to create employment. The number of employed persons is also on an increasing trend since 2020.

V. Enterprise, Corporations and Partnership Statistics

5. As of December 2021, there were approximately 1,434,326 registered companies in Malaysia of which 4930 are foreign companies. 45,419 new companies were registered in 2021 with the Suruhanjaya Syarikat Malaysia (SSM), i.e., the Companies Commission of Malaysia. As of December 2021, there were approximately 948 companies listed on Bursa Malaysia. These are the companies in which public investors can buy and sell shares on the Malaysian bourse or the stock exchange. Companies may also be formed for charitable purposes, i.e., with not-for-profit purposes and these are incorporated as companies limited by guarantee. There were 1135 companies limited by guarantee as of January 2021. The number of companies being wound up between 2009 to September 2021 was 43,337 and statistics from the Insolvency Department of Malaysia showed that there were approximately 1598 winding-up petitions filed in court in 2021. For September 2021, there were 609 petitions for liquidation of companies and all were due to insolvency. Of interest is the data for 2020 and 2021 reflecting the liquidation during the COVID-19 pandemic which is 2157 companies. The relatively low number of liquidated companies could be due to the various business recovery assistance plans that the government had put in place including the debt moratorium.

As of December 2021, there were 30,247 Limited Liability Partnerships (LLPs) registered with SSM, with 3,646 newly registered in 2019.

VI. Social and Cultural Values

6. Academic literature summarized Malaysian values as family-oriented, faith in God, humility, respect for the elderly and politeness, confrontation avoidance, respect for authority figures and collectivism. As the Malays make up the majority and they subscribed to Islam as their religion, Islamic values are also embedded in Malay culture, as reflected in the constitution which provides that Islam is the religion of the land. The result is that activities that are morally reprehensible in Islam would be frowned upon. For Malays, the word Adab reflects a person's good breeding, demonstrating courtesy in words and deeds and mastery over emotion. Because of the significance of faith amongst the races (Islam for Malays, Hinduism for Indians, Buddhism for Chinese, Christianity and indigenous beliefs), there is shared value in believing that success, failures, opportunities and misfortune are influenced by the power and the will of God. Islam is the official religion while Bahasa Melayu is the official language. Other faiths are guaranteed the right to practice their religion and religious festivities and practices. This can be clearly seen from the many national-level public holidays centred around the different faith festivities. Rituals and traditions are also important cultural components. Although a collective mindset seems to prevail in the sense of working towards a common goal and social harmony, values such as being ambitious and self-improvement are not alien concepts and are being demonstrated due to competitiveness in society.

For the business sector, the notions of saving face and losing face are significant to business dealings, where the relationship is built on trust and harmony. Direct answers or rejection are often avoided so as not to cause embarrassment, to prevent disagreement and preserve harmony.

VII. Privatization Efforts and Golden Shares

7. Privatization in Malaysia occurs in the following manner:

- the government disposes of its controlling or majority stake in a company or issues shares to the private, non-government party either by public share offerings or in the private market;
- the government transfers assets of a government department or a government operated entity to the private, non-government party;
- the government contracting out the services provided by government entities to private parties.

In some privatized companies, the government is able to retain control without being a majority or controlling shareholder via the creation of a 'golden share'. Some of the rights that may be attached to the golden share include the right to veto over specific corporate transactions, absolute veto right or the right to appoint or veto the appointment of directors and management as well as to prevent foreign ownership of strategic companies and strategic assets. The golden share gives the government control of companies in strategic sectors such as telecommunications, utilities, energy production, postal industries, transportation, etc., to ensure the achievement of social goals and for public interests. However, its presence is considered as creating an imbalance between ownership and control rights, especially in public listed companies as well as the possible abuse of the golden shares solely for political ends. As of 2020, the Malaysian government has golden shares in thirty-two companies, seven of which are public listed companies. Nonetheless, industry observers indicated that the rights under the golden share have not been exercised often.

§2. Historical Background of Corporations and Partnerships

8. The legal history of Malaysia was greatly influenced by English law, which was first introduced in one of the Malay States, Penang, in 1807 by the Royal Charter of Justice. A Second Royal Charter of Justice was introduced into Penang, Melaka and Singapore (which was then part of the Malays States) in 1826. The Civil Law Ordinance of 1878 introduced a considerable amount of English commercial law into Tanah Melayu/Malaya (as Malaysia was known then). Section 6 of the Civil Law Ordinance of 1878 provided that in all questions or issues arising in specific areas of commercial law as well as in all respects of mercantile law, generally, the law to be administered would be the same as that administered in England in the corresponding period. The Civil Law Ordinance of 1909 which replaced the

Civil Law Ordinance of 1878 retained this section and the same provision was also retained in the Civil Law Enactment of 1937 of the Federated Malay States.

9. In 1956, a Civil Law Ordinance was introduced into the Federation of Malaya and in 1972 the Civil Law Ordinance of 1956 was revised and extended to Sabah and Sarawak. Section 3 of the Civil Law Ordinance provides that English Common Law, rules of equity and statutes of general application may apply in Malaysia subject to such qualifications as local circumstances render necessary. However, section 5 of the Civil Law Ordinance of 1956 introduced English law with respect to the law of partnership and corporations, amongst others, that were administered in England at the date of coming into force of this Act, unless in any case, other provision is or shall be made by written law.

Although the Civil Law Ordinance of 1956 allowed the reception of English law relating to corporations in Malaya, prior to this, most of the Malay States already had their specific corporation legislation in the form of Enactments or Ordinances. However, after the Second World War, the move to unify the Malay States under one administration was also emulated in the unification of corporation legislation where the Companies Ordinance of 1940 was enacted. This was later replaced by the Companies Act of 1965. The Companies Act of 1965 was modelled after the UK Companies Act of 1948 and the Australian Uniform Companies Act of 1961. Where the law on corporations is concerned, the primary source for corporation law in Malaysia is the Companies Act of 1965 but decisions from these other jurisdictions are relevant. Based on the Civil Law Act, the law in England relating to corporations would be referred to where there is no legislation and the cut-off date for reception of the English law is 1956.

In 2016, as a result of the effort to modernize and reform company law, the Companies Act 2016 was introduced. The Companies Act 2016 is the result of a comprehensive law reform programme which was conducted by the Corporate Law Reform Committee (CLRC) between 2004 and 2008. The CLRC was established by the Companies Commission of Malaysia. This reform programme was followed by the establishment of the Accounting Issues Consultative Committee in 2012. In 2013, the government released an exposure draft of a new Companies Bill. After a period of public consultation, the Companies Bill 2015 was presented to Parliament and was passed as the Companies Act 2016. The Companies Act 2016 repealed and replaced the Companies Act 1965. The Companies Act 2016 is applicable to all types of the company and is the primary legislation dealing with the formation and incorporation rules and procedures, the management of the company which includes statutory provisions covering directors' duties, members' rights and remedies, statutory provisions dealing with share issuance, increasing and reducing share capital, debt capital, reporting and disclosure obligations and audit requirements and administration of companies in financial difficulties including a winding-up or liquidation of a company. Apart from the statutory provisions, the Companies Act 2016 also includes thirteen Schedules.

10. Partnership matters are regulated by the Partnership Act (PA) of 1961. The Act was modelled after the English PA of 1890. Before the PA of 1961 came into effect, partnership matters were regulated by the Contract Ordinance (Malay States) of 1950. For the Strait Settlement of Penang and the Strait Settlement of Malacca, the law applicable for partnership matters was the English PA of 1890. As for Sabah and Sarawak, prior to 1974, all partnership matters were regulated by the Partnership Ordinance of 1961.

11. Another business form is the LLP introduced via the Limited Partnership Act 2012. In addition, the Labuan Limited Partnerships and Labuan Limited Liability Partnerships Act 2010 (Labuan LP and LLPA 2010) govern LPs and LLPs in the Federal Territory of Labuan.

§3. Definitions and Structure of Corporations and Partnerships

I. Different Forms of Corporations and Partnerships

12. There are several types of business vehicles or structures in Malaysia:

(a) a general partnership;
(b) an LP;
(c) a private limited liability company limited by shares;
(d) a public company limited by share;
(e) an LLP.

II. Distinction Between Structures and Consequences

A. Partnerships and Corporations

13. The main difference between partnerships and corporations is that a corporation is a separate legal entity from its members and is a legal person. A partnership, on the other hand, does not have a separate legal personality. The individual partners in a partnership share and own the assets of the business. Unlike members of a corporation who have limited liability, all the partners in a firm are jointly and personally liable for any contractual obligation incurred by one partner in the course of the partnership's business. Under the partnership law, a firm can exist without being registered and there is no obligation for the firm to file documents at any central registry. All business needs to be registered under the Registration of Businesses Act (RBA) 1956 to ensure that the firm is able to enforce third-party obligations owed to the firm. However, non-registration does not affect the rights and duties that partners owed to themselves. A third party may also enforce any obligations incurred by the firm against it.[1]

A partnership is actually an association of persons who agree to carry on a business in common with a view to profit. Unlike a corporation that only comes into existence through an incorporation or registration process, a partnership is set up

1. Sections 6 and 8 of the RBA of 1956 (revised in 1978).

through the agreement of the partners, either verbally, in writing or by conduct. All the partners are entitled to be involved in the management of the partnership unless the partners agree to limit the authority of any one of them or any one of them agrees not to be involved in the management. However, in an LP, there are partners who can limit their liability up to a certain amount. The limited partners are not liable for debts and obligations of the firm and they cannot participate in the management of the firm.

In contrast, a company is usually managed by the board of directors where the Companies Act specifies the division of authority between the board of directors and members. Whenever there is any change in the identity of the partners, the partnership is considered dissolved and a new partnership is established. This is unlike a company that continues as an entity even though the membership changes.

In Malaysia, apart from the partnership and corporation business structure, a business can also be conducted via an LLP. The internal governance structure of an LLP is based on the contractual agreement between its members with less stringent procedures, unlike a company. The tax regime of LLP is also totally different from a company as LLP is taxed similar to a partnership. An LLP also has a separate legal entity distinct from its members and enjoys attributes as a legal person, such as ability to own property, enter into legal proceedings and perpetual succession. The partners of an LLP are not personally liable for the business's debts and liabilities. Creditors of the LLP cannot sue the partners and apply the partner's personal assets to pay off the LLP's debts. The liabilities of the partners in an LLP are limited to the agreed contribution. This is in contrast to the liability of partners in a partnership structure where all partners have unlimited liability for the business debts to the extent that their personal assets could be claimed by the creditors if the business assets are not sufficient to pay the creditors. In addition, due to its legal entity, partners of the LLP are the only agents of the LLP and not one another. As such they are not liable on account of the independent or unauthorized acts of other partners, thus allowing individual partners to be shielded from joint liability created by another partner's wrongful acts or misconduct.

However, for both LLPs and general partnerships, the internal affairs are regulated via an agreement between the partners or members. There is no formal constitution such as the Memorandum and Articles of Association (now called the company's constitution under the CA 2016) which determined how the internal relationships should be governed. Members and partners in an LLP enjoy internal flexibility similar to partners in a general partnership.

B. *Private and Public Companies*

14. As incorporated entities, private and public companies have a legal personality and the members enjoy limited liability. The Companies Act of 2016 categorizes a private company according to the following criteria:

(a) The number of members in a private company must not be more than fifty.
(b) The private company must have a share capital and shall restrict the right of shareholders to transfer their shares.

(c) A private company is prohibited from raising capital from the public.
(d) A private company is prohibited from inviting the public to lend money to the company.

The main difference between private and public companies limited by shares is the ability of a public company to raise capital from the public. While a private company cannot raise its capital from the public or make a public offer of its securities, public companies may do so. Public companies may also choose to have their company shares quoted on the stock exchange.

15. The use of the private or public company structure is often based on several considerations such as whether public funding is required, whether the shareholding structure is dispersed or closely held or whether the company is to be managed as if it were an unincorporated association internally. The Companies Act of 2016 contains several statutory provisions that distinguish a private from a public company. An example is the restriction for public companies to give loans to directors or persons connected to the directors.

III. Difference Between Commercial and Civil Corporations

16. Malaysia's company law does not categorize corporations based on whether it is a civil or commercial corporation. Unlike some countries where a civil company is defined as a company involving professionals, there is no specific provision or recognition of this distinction under the Companies Act 2016 framework. Where a group of professionals want to establish a business, these professionals may register a company limited by shares, a partnership or an LLP. However, other legislation may apply to restrict the ability of some professionals from operating in Malaysia under the corporate form. For example, the advocates and solicitors under the Legal Profession Act 1976 are not yet able to establish their business via an LLP or a company as the Bar Council which is the professional body regulating advocates and solicitors in Peninsular Malaysia, only recognizes a sole proprietor or a partnership as a business form for lawyers.[2]

IV. Non-profit Associations and Other Corporate Legal Persons

17. The charity sector or non-profit associations or bodies may be carried out to meet charitable purposes under the following legislation:

---

2. *See* Bar Council Rulings 7.06

> (1) Any individual or individuals who wish(es) to set up a legal firm either as a sole proprietor or partnership shall inform the Bar Council in writing of his/her (their) intention to do so. This notice in writing must be executed by the intending sole proprietor or all the intending partners.

(a) the establishment of a company limited by guarantee under the Companies Act 2016;
(b) the establishment of societies or organizations under the Societies Act 1966;
(c) the establishment of a trust company under the Trust Companies Act 1949 applicable to a public company whose business is to be a trustee for any business related to those authorized to be conducted by a trust company;
(d) the incorporation of a trustee as a body corporate under the Trustee Incorporation act 1952 which applies to bodies of persons. The trustee corporation is an incorporated trustee which has the responsibility of managing the trust;
(e) the establishment of Trust Company and Labuan Foundation under the Labuan Trusts Act 1996 and the Labuan Foundation Act 2010.

18. There are also corporate legal entities established under their own incorporating legislation. These are known as statutory bodies.

§4. Sources and Hierarchy of the Law on Corporations and Partnerships

I. National Sources of Law for Corporations

A. Legislation and Hierarchy of the Law on Corporations

19. The law relating to companies is found in the Companies Act 2016 (CA). The Act provides for the formation of Malaysian companies and the registration of foreign companies operating in Malaysia. It also regulates fund-raising activities, company management, the reorganization, winding-up and liquidation of companies. There are also other sources of law relating to corporations such as case law. This is because Malaysia has a common law system in which recorded decisions of the judges operate as binding statements. Under the common law system, if a decision is made by a higher court, then the courts that are lower in the court structure are obliged to follow the decision of the superior courts.

20. For corporations, the Companies Act 2016 must be complied with by all corporations incorporated in Malaysia under the Companies Act 2016 and under the previous Companies Act 1965.

There are also other regulations or statutes that are relevant to a company. These legislation apply to a public company whenever the company issue securities. These include:

(a) the Securities Commission Act (SCA) of 1993;
(b) the Capital Market and Services Act of 2007 (CMSA), which is a consolidating act. The CMSA consolidated the following statutes which have now been repealed, i.e., the Securities Industry Act of 1983 and the Futures Industry Act of 1993. The CMSA also incorporates some statutory provisions previously found in the SCA of 1993 that relate to fund-raising activities.

Some legislation applies specifically to certain types of companies such as the:

(a) the Offshore Companies Act of 1990;
(b) the Trust Companies Act 1949 applicable to a public company whose business is to be a trustee or any business related to those authorized to be conducted by a trust company.

There are also non-statutory guidelines and rules that apply to public listed companies such as:

(a) the Bursa Malaysia Listing Requirements (BMLR);
(b) the Code on Corporate Governance (revised 2017);
(c) the Code on Take-overs and Mergers of 2016 and the Rules on Take-Overs, Mergers and Compulsory Acquisitions 2016 (revised 2017); and
(d) the accounting standards.

B. Company's Constitution

21. A newly incorporated company limited by shares may be registered under the Companies Act 2016 without a constitution although it may adopt a constitution later if it wishes to do so. Under the former CA 1965, the constitution refers to two separate documents which are the Memorandum of Association and the Articles of Association which each company must have. However, the CA 2016 provides that a company limited by shares may also operate without having a constitution. However, if the company does not adopt a constitution later, there could be certain things that the company may not be able to carry out, for example, issuing redeemable preference shares under section 72(2), Companies Act 2016. In contrast, a company limited by guarantee must have a constitution at the point of registration and throughout the company's business life cycle.

Under the Companies Act 2016 framework, companies registered under the former Companies Act 1965 are deemed to have adopted their existing memorandum and articles of association which would be known as the company's constitution. These companies would be able to alter or delete the constitution subsequently.

C. The Relationship Between the Constitution and Legislation

22. The Companies Act 2016 expressly and specifically provides that the constitution has no effect to the extent that it contravenes the legislation: section 32(2). For example, there are several sections in the Companies Act 2016 that contain the phrase 'Notwithstanding anything to the contrary in the constitution … .' This means that any clause in the constitution that is not in line with the statutory provision is invalid. The Companies Act 2016 also explicitly provides that certain clauses cannot be included in the constitution. An example is section 38(5), Companies Act 2016 which states that any provision in the constitution of a company limited by guarantee that purports to give any person a right to participate in the divisible profits of the company shall be void.

The Companies Act 2016 however does provide priority to the constitution on certain matters. Certain sections of the Companies Act 2016 provide that the legal principle in the legislation is subject to the constitution. In this matter, the default provision is the Companies Act 2016 where, in the absence of a clause in the constitution addressing the matter, the rule as laid down in the Companies Act prevails.

II. National Sources of Law for Partnerships and LLPs

23. The law relating to partnerships is found in the PA of 1961 which is in *pari materia* with the English PA. Thus, English case law is always referred to by the Malaysian court in assisting the courts to interpret provisions of the local Act. In fact, under section 47(1) of PA of 1961, it is clearly stated that the rules of equity and common law applicable to the partnership shall continue in force, except so far as they are inconsistent with the express provisions of the Act. Nonetheless, the application of the English law for partnership and other matters generally is subject to the application of sections 3 and 5 of the Civil Law Act of 1956 (revised in 1972).

24. The Limited Liability Partnership 2012 governs LLPs in Malaysia.

III. National Sources of Law for Corporations and Partnerships in the Federal Territory of Labuan

25. In addition to these corporate and securities legislation and regulations, there are special corporate, securities and partnership legislation which are formulated for the Federal Territory of Labuan. Labuan is located about ten kilometres off the coast of Sabah. It is located on the major shipping and air routes of the Asian region and roughly halfway from the major cities of Bangkok, Hong Kong, Jakarta, Kuala Lumpur, Manila and Singapore. On 16 April 1984, Labuan was declared a Federal Territory and subsequently on 1 October 1990, the Government of Malaysia declared the Federal Territory of Labuan as an International Offshore Financial Centre (IOFC).[3] As an integrated IOFC, Labuan offers a wide range of offshore financial products and services to customers worldwide, including banking and investment banking, insurance, captives, trust business, fund management, investment holding, company management and Islamic financing.[4] This special status as an Offshore Financial Centre enables the formulation of laws which were introduced in 1990 to promote Labuan as an IOFC.

In 1996, the Labuan Offshore Financial Services Authority (LOFSA) was established as a one-stop agency and sole independent authority responsible for the administration of the offshore industry in Labuan. The main tasks of LOFSA are to

3. Retrieved from allmalaysia.info/state/labuan/labuanintro.asp on 25 Jan. 2007.
4. *Ibid.*

focus on business development and promotion, process the application and supervise offshore activities, develop national objectives, set policies and priorities and administer and enforce legislation.[5]

At present, statutes which are applicable in Labuan are as follows:

(a) The LOFSA Act 1996.
(b) Labuan Companies Act 1990.
(c) Labuan Trust Act 1996.
(d) Labuan Business Activity Tax Act 1990.
(e) Labuan LP and LLPA 2010.
(f) Labuan Financial Services and Securities Act 2010 (LFSSA).
(g) Labuan Foundations Act 2010.
(h) Labuan Islamic Financial Services and Securities Act 2010 (LIFSSA).

Amongst the highlights of the LFSSA enacted in 2010 is the name change from LOFSA to Labuan Financial Services Authority Act 1996 (LFSA). This is in line with the strategic direction to reposition Labuan as an international business and financial centre (IBFC). The FSA now has powers to investigate as well being given wide enforcement powers. Consequently, all reference to the term 'offshore' was deleted from Labuan laws and the distinction between Labuan and domestic markets was made through the term 'Labuan' with clear provisions on the applicability of relevant law, domestic or otherwise. The new laws allowed for a wider range of entities that may be established in Labuan IBFC, such as Labuan Protected Cell Companies (PCCs), Labuan Special Trusts and Labuan Foundations. The amended Labuan Companies Act 1990 (which was formerly known as the Offshore Companies Act) allows for the conversion of an existing Labuan company into a PCC for the conduct of insurance and mutual fund business. A PCC is allowed to ring-fence each of its cell's assets from the others while having one separate legal entity. A notable development is the introduction of the LIFSSA. This legislation is designed to cater to the demands of Islamic finance, one of the fastest-growing industries globally. It complements the conventional law for financial services that is the LFSSA by providing the platform to create Shariah-compliant entities and the enhanced roles and functions of the Shariah Supervisory Council.

LP in the Federal Territory of Labuan was regulated by the repealed Labuan Offshore Limited Partnerships Act of 1997 (LPA 1997). In its place, the Labuan LP and LLPA 2010 was introduced to regulate LPs and LLPs.

§5. The Labour Law Connection: Co-determination and Corporate Structure

26. Malaysian company law does not provide for labour force direct involvement in either the board or representation in the general meeting. However, as part of the duties of directors in managing the company's affairs, directors may take into

5. Retrieved from http://labuanibfc.com/ on 16 Mar. 2015.

consideration stakeholders' interests, including the employees' interests, in deciding what would be in the company's best interests. Labour law issues are based on the employment contract and legislation intended to protect employees, primarily via the Industrial Relations Act 1967.

Part I. Corporations

Chapter 1. The Public Company Limited by Shares

§1. CHARACTERISTICS OF THE PUBLIC COMPANY

I. Separate Legal Entity

27. When the incorporation process has been completed and the certificate of incorporation has been issued by the Registrar of Companies, the company is a legal entity or person as from the date stated on the certificate of incorporation.[6] The effect and consequence of incorporation and separate legal entity are that the members are separate from the company.[7] This means that:

(a) The company can own property in its own name.
The company's property is not the property of the members; thus members have no claim over the company's assets.[8]

(b) The company is able to enter into contractual obligations or to incur obligations and liability.
The company can sue and be sued in its own name. Where there is a breach of an obligation owed towards the company, this may only be enforced by the company in its own name. Any compensation is payable to the company and not to the members as it is the company's rights which have been infringed. This also means that the company may enter into contracts with its members as the members and the company are separate legal entities.

(c) Limited liability of members and directors
Once a company is registered, the members cannot be held liable for the company's debts or contractual obligations. The creditors will not be able to make the members or the directors personally liable for the debts and contractual obligations incurred by the company. Even if the shareholder is a majority shareholder, the shareholder cannot be sued for the company's debts and contractual obligations. The member's liability is limited to the amount of shares that the

6. Sections 18 & 20, Companies Act 2016.
7. Sections 20 & 21, Companies Act 2016; *see Abdul Aziz Atan v. Ladang Rengo Malay Estates Sdn Bhd* (1985) 2 *MLJ* 165.
8. *Ta Chai You & Syarikat Tingan Lumber Sdn Bhd* (1998) 4 *MLJ* 275; *Macaura v. Northern Assurance Co. Ltd* (1925) *AC* 619.

member has agreed to subscribe to but has not paid for. The creditors of the company cannot sue the members for the company's debts.

(d) Perpetual succession

A company has perpetual succession which is defined as the ability of the company to continue to exist until it is liquidated or wound up. Once a company is incorporated, it can only be dissolved by a process known as winding-up. Therefore, even if there is a change in the identity of the members, the company still remains the same. This 'perpetual succession' enables the shares to be transferable without having to wind up the business. Where all the members of the company have died, the company continues to exist until and unless the company is wound up.

II. Exception to Separate Legal Entity

28. The separate legal entity doctrine has been the catalyst for the growth of business. However, the separate legal entity doctrine has been abused. In these circumstances, the courts have relied on their inherent jurisdiction to overlook the separate legal entity of the company. Petition for the court to do this, i.e., for the court to 'lift the corporate veil' often involves creditors or third parties. Often, the court is asked to declare that the member and the company are the same person and therefore, the company is liable for the member's obligation or that the member is to be held liable or responsible for the company's conduct or obligation. The following are several situations where the court has lifted the corporate veil:

(a) If the company is incorporated by a person to evade his existing legal obligations. Cases under this category often showed that a company was incorporated by a person subsequent to the person incurring an obligation which he tries to avoid complying with. It must be shown that the person is someone who has control of the newly incorporated company usually by the fact that he is a majority shareholder.[9] However, in *Gilford Motor Co. Ltd v. Horne*[10] where the defendant breached his contractual obligation not to compete with the employer, he incorporated a company where the only shareholders were his wife and one of his business associates, and the court lifted the corporate veil.
(b) If the company was incorporated as a sham or façade for unlawful purpose or conduct.[11]
(c) Where the company was incorporated to be the alter ego or agent of the members. Cases under this category often involve situations where the company is managed or treated not as a separate legal entity but merely as an 'extension' of the members.[12]

9. *See Win Line (UK) Ltd v. Masterpart (Singapore) Pte Ltd* (2000) 2 *SLR* 98.
10. (1933) Ch. 935.
11. *Jones v. Lipman* (1962) 1 *WLR* 832.
12. *Tiu Shi Kian & Anor v. Red Rose Restaurant Sdn Bhd* [1950–1985] *MSCLC* 309.

29. The court has been asked to ignore the separate legal entity where there is a holding-subsidiary relationship. In most cases, the holding company is a separate entity from its subsidiary even though the subsidiary company is a wholly owned subsidiary.[13]

The corporate veil will only be lifted in a corporate group structure if certain criteria are found to exist. In *Edmund Charles Liebenberg v. ICG-Griffin Manufacturing Sdn Bhd & Ors*,[14] Instantgreen was the holding company of machinery, which in turn owned 51% shares in two other companies. The subsidiary companies were incorporated to manufacture and market motorcycles and acquired the intellectual property over the design of the motorcycles from the petitioner. In an action by the petitioner that there was oppression of his rights as a member of the two subsidiary companies, the petitioner applied for an order that the majority shareholder purchases his shares in the company or alternatively, for the ultimate holding company, i.e., Instantgreen, to purchase his shares. This would require the court to lift the corporate veil to show that the subsidiary companies were the alter ego of the holding company. It was held that the subsidiaries were incorporated to be the alter egos of the holding company, and thus the holding company is liable for the harm done against the petitioner and is jointly and severally liable to purchase the petitioner's shares in the two subsidiary companies. Machinery and the two subsidiaries shared common directors and any decisions made by the two subsidiaries can only be carried out with the approval of Instantgreen. The two subsidiaries were incorporated to be the nominees of the holding company in relation to a joint venture agreement with the petitioner. The intellectual property rights belonging to the petitioner were purchased in the name of the subsidiaries but the funds came from Instant green. These facts justified the lifting of the corporate veil.

30. The separate legal entity will not be applied in the context of certain statutory provisions that were intended to avoid the effect of a separate legal entity. There are statutory provisions in the CA 2016 and other statutes that apply in relation to the members of a company so that the members may be held liable for the company's debts and obligations. Section 540 of the CA also states that an officer of the company may be personally liable to creditors for debts incurred by the company at a time when the company is solvent and the officer is aware of this but allows the company to continue trading with intent to defraud creditors. Under the former CA 1965, if the company carries on trading for more than six months with only one member (except if the company is a wholly owned subsidiary), section 36 states that the sole member who is aware of this situation will be personally liable for debts contracted after the six-month period. However, with the CA 2016's recognition of a minimum member of one person to register a company, the personal liability of a sole member for the company's debts under the former section 36, CA 1965 is no longer applicable.

---

13. *People Insurance Co. (M) Sdn Bhd v. People's Insurance Co. Ltd* (1986) 1 *MLJ* 68; *Adams & Otr. v. Cape Industries PLC & Anor.* (1991) 1 *All ER* 929, followed in *ATA Management Consultants Sdn Bhd v. Makmuran Sdn Bhd* (2004) 3 *CLJ* 53.
14. (2005) 3 *CLJ* 613.

§2. FORMATION OF A COMPANY

31. A company, regardless of its type as a public or private company, comes into existence when the formal incorporation process and procedures have been complied with. Once the incorporation process has been completed, the company will be issued a certificate of incorporation. The incorporation process for a public company does not differ significantly from the incorporation of a private company. A company may be originally incorporated as a public company or be converted into a public company.

The registration process requires submission of certain information and documents to the SSM (i.e., the Companies Commission of Malaysia). These include the proposed name, the business to be carried out, names and details of members/ subscribers, directors, company secretary if any and any other information the Registrar may require subscribers. Each promoter and director must also state that he consents to act as promoter or director and that he is not disqualified to act in that capacity. There is no requirement for documents to be certified by any notary public. There is no requirement to make a statutory declaration by any director or promoter relating to anything that could disqualify the person from being appointed as director. This is unlike under the former CA 1965 which required a statutory declaration by the directors for registration purposes.

I. Formal Requirements for Incorporation

A. *Company's Constitution*

32. Under the Companies Act 2016, a company limited by shares has the option of adopting a constitution either at the time of incorporation or subsequently. A company may also be formed without any constitution. This changes the law under the former Companies Act 1965 where every company is required to have its Memorandum of Association and a separate Articles of Association: section 18 of the Companies Act of 1965. The Companies Act 2016 allows a company to adopt a constitution after incorporation and this may be done by the company passing a special resolution to do so. For most existing companies which were incorporated under the former Companies Act 1965, the existing memorandum of association and articles of association become the company's constitution on the date the Companies Act 2016 came into effect (31 January 2017) unless the company resolves otherwise by passing an ordinary resolution: section 32(c) and section 619(3), Companies Act 2016. Since the Companies Act of 1965 provided for a model Articles of Association in the Fourth Schedule, i.e., Table A, most existing companies will have this Table A as their model constitution with modifications. Section 35, Companies Act 2016, provides that the constitution *may contain* the following:

(a) the objects of the company;
(b) the capacity, rights, powers or privileges of the company if the provision restricts such capacity, rights, powers or privileges;
(c) matters contemplated by this Act to be included in the constitution; and

(d) any other matters as the company wishes to include in its constitution.

33. Amending the constitution. The provisions in the constitution may be altered by a special resolution of the general meeting of shareholders unless the constitution itself prohibits the alteration.[15] A member or a director of a company may also make an application to the court for the constitution to be amended if it is not practicable to amend the constitution in accordance with the procedures under the Companies Act 2016 or the constitution itself.

II. Notification, Registration, Incorporation and Publicity

34. Once registered, the company's name will be included in the list of companies maintained by SSM. A company is subjected to reporting obligations where information regarding the company must be lodged with the SSM periodically and upon the occurrence of certain events. Information regarding directors and company secretaries are also subject to disclosure obligations.

Apart from the requirement to submit certain information both of a financial and non-financial nature as specified by the Companies Act 2016 with SSM during the company's lifetime, a public company must also comply with disclosure obligations as required under the CMSA 2007 which must be made to the Securities Commission. A public listed company also has additional disclosure obligation under the stock exchange listing rules i.e., BMLR for purpose of the initial listing and to continue to be listed on the stock exchange.

III. Contracts Made on Behalf of a Company in Formation/Pre-incorporation Contracts

35. Prior to incorporation, the promoters may enter into a contract on behalf of the company. A contract entered into by any person on behalf of a company which is yet to be incorporated is known as a pre-incorporation contract. An important legal issue is who is liable for the pre-incorporation contract. A pre-incorporation contract may be ratified by the company after it has been incorporated. The company has no obligation to ratify the pre-incorporation contract. Ratification takes effect by a resolution of the general meeting of shareholders as soon as is reasonable. If the company has ratified the pre-incorporation contract, the company is entitled to all the benefits of the contract and is also liable for the contract from the date the pre-incorporation contract was entered into. If the company does not ratify the pre-incorporation contract, the person who enters into the contract will be liable for the contract unless he has expressly excluded liability at the time the pre-incorporation contract was entered into.[16]

15. Section 36.
16. Section 65.

36. It is the norm that the subscribers or the initial members are directly involved in the incorporation of the company as they are usually the persons who want to incorporate the company and use the company as a vehicle to carry on business. The persons who incorporate the company are known as promoters although persons who are employed to carry out the incorporation process such as lawyers or incorporations agents are not promoters.[17]

Not all of the subscribers will be considered promoters and it is usually a question of fact to determine who are the promoters of a company. The identification of persons as promoters is important as promoters owe certain duties towards the company arising out of the formation and incorporation of the company. A promoter must not make any secret profit in relation to the promotion, formation and incorporation of the company and has to make full and frank disclosure of any profit that he makes during this period.[18] Normally, a promoter may have acquired property on behalf of the company that is being formed and will transfer that property to the company when the company has been incorporated. The promoter must ensure that disclosure of this fact and any profit arising out of the transfer of property must be made to either an independent board of directors or the shareholders. The board is independent if the members are not the promoters themselves or persons who are their associates.[19] If there is no independent board, then the promoters must ensure that disclosure is made to the shareholders either by making a disclosure at the general meeting of shareholders or in the constitution or in the prospectus of the company.[20] If the promoters fail to do so, the company may set aside the contract provided that the parties may be returned to their status quo and that the property can be returned to the promoters.[21] This will not be possible if the company has made use of the property. Alternatively, the company may accept the contract and claim compensation or an account of profits from the promoters.[22]

IV. Number of Subscribers

37. Each company must have at least one person as a subscriber. There is no maximum number of subscribers for a public company, unlike a private company that must have not more than fifty members. In general, where a company is to be listed on the main market of the Stock Exchange, the company must have at least MYR 500 million issued paid-up share capital and 25% of the shares listed must be held by not less than 1,000 public shareholders. Public shareholders are generally shareholders who are not directors, substantial shareholders, promoters or associates of the directors or substantial shareholders of the public listed company.

---

17. *Twycross v. Grant* (1877) 2 *CPD* 469.
18. *Erlanger v. New Sombrero Phosphate Co.* (1873) 3 *App Cas* 1218.
19. *Gluckstein v. Barnes* [1900] *AC* 240.
20. *Ibid.*; *Lagunas Nitrate Co. v. Lagunas Syndicate* (1899) 2 *Ch.* 392.
21. *Ibid.*; *Lagunas Nitrate Co. v. Lagunas Syndicate* (1899) 2 *Ch.* 392.
22. *Re Leeds & Hanley Theatres of Varieties Ltd* [1902] *Ch.* 809.

A. Consent of Initial Subscribers and Directors

38. The CA 2016 requires that there be at least one initial subscriber who is the promoter for a company. As for directors, a private company must have at least one director and a public company must have at least two directors. Their consent is required as part of the incorporation process. The consent must be given by the initial subscribers and directors by making a statement consenting to being a promoter or to the appointment as director. There have been cases where the initial subscribers and directors subsequently announced that they have never consented to the appointment despite their signatures appearing on the form. In such a situation, criminal action may be taken against the person who forged the signature. However, the fact that the initial subscribers or directors had consented to the appointment but are mere puppets does not mean that the consent was invalidly given.

V. Initial Share Capital

39. There is no minimum capital requirement for incorporation. Consideration for the shares may be in cash or in kind, i.e., in money or money's worth. The price for the shares is determined by the directors although in exercising this power directors are bound by their duty to ensure that their power is exercised for a proper purpose and in the best interests of the company. The shareholders are obligated to pay the full issued price for the shares either immediately or at a later time. The members will be liable to pay for the shares that they have agreed to take up. The consideration agreed upon cannot be increased without the members' consent.

Public companies usually issue shares that are payable in full if the shares have been successfully applied for by the subscribers. Section 83, CA 2016 enables the directors to forfeit the shares if a call has been made to pay for the shares that have been issued. The Constitution may contain a provision authorizing the payment of the shares to be made in instalments upon request by the company.[23] The constitution may also contain a provision authorizing the forfeiture of shares if the shares are not paid for by the shareholders upon request by the company.[24] An unlimited liability company may, upon re-registration as a limited company and by passing a resolution, provide that a specified portion of its uncalled share capital shall not be capable of being called up except in the event and for the purposes of the company being wound up.[25]

VI. Contributions in Kind

40. A company is authorized to accept payment for the shares in money or 'money's worth' such as any property or anything which is of value. There is also no requirement in the Companies Act of 2016 for a statutory valuation procedure if

23. Section 56(1)(a).
24. Article 29, Table A of Fourth Schedule.
25. Section 84(3)(b).

shares are not paid in cash. The concern here is that if the property that is used as consideration for the shares issued is not properly valued, this may result in shares being issued at a discount or at less than the equivalent value of the shares. Shares which are issued in exchange for property where no proper valuation is done may also cause a dilution of the capital or results in the capital being only illusory, i.e., not truly reflecting the capital that the company actually has. In common law, it has been held that while the court will not interfere with the question of whether the consideration is adequate, the view is that the consideration 'moving from the company must be at least of equal value to the par value of the shares and must be based on an honest estimate by the directors of the value of the assets acquired'.[26] The challenge to the adequacy of consideration for the shares may be made in accordance with the principles in relation to the law of contract but this challenge is usually mounted between the parties to the transaction. Members may challenge the directors' authority in accepting the consideration as a breach of the director's duties in the best interests of the company, breach of duty to avoid conflict of interests or breach of duty of care, skill and diligence.

While the Companies Act 2016 does not contain any provision dealing with the valuation of the non-cash consideration, public companies must comply with the Securities Commission's guidelines 'Policies and Guidelines on the Issue/Offer of Securities' relating to the issue of shares for non-cash consideration. The Securities Commission (SC) through its 'Policies and Guidelines on the Issue/Offer of Securities' provides guidelines that each public company must comply with in relation to valuations to be carried out in respect of assets or investment that is to be acquired by a public company.

There is no restriction in the CA 2016 to authorize the issue of shares for services that have been performed.[27]

§3. Essential Elements of the Legal Person

I. Company's Name

41. Prior to registration, the promoters or incorporators of the company must reserve a name to be used for the company.[28] The name reservation is effective for thirty days and during this period no other company that is yet to be incorporated may use the name which has been reserved and no existing company may change its name to the name that has been reserved.[29] A public company must have the word '*Berhad*' or its abbreviation, '*Bhd*' as part of the company's name. The registrar has the discretion to refuse to register a name if it is found to be undesirable or if the Minister directs the registrar not to accept the name for registration. If a company is registered using a name under which it could not be registered because it contravenes section 26 or 29, the company may change the name by passing a

26. *Osborne v. Steel Barrel Co. Ltd* (1942) 2 *All ER* 634.
27. *See* the former s. 54, Companies Act 1965.
28. Sections 26 & 27.
29. Section 27(5).

special resolution, and the registrar may also make an order requiring the company to change its name.[30] The company may also change its name for any other reason by passing a special resolution.[31]

The name reservation process does not mean that the registrar is guaranteeing that the name of the company is the exclusive property of the company. It is possible that a company that reserves a name and subsequently uses it may be liable for an action of passing off. This must be resolved between the businesses. The Registrar is also not liable for any loss arising out of the reservation or registration of a name.

II. Corporate Capacity, the Objects Clause and Ultra Vires

42. The Companies Act 2016 confers on a company the capacity and powers to carry out any business or activities. Under the Companies Act 2016, a company has unlimited capacity unless the constitution specifies any limits on the capacity and powers of the company. A company may specify the objects, i.e., the business purpose for its incorporation or the business to be conducted after its incorporation and this will be stated in the constitution.[32] For companies that decide to have an objects clause, the courts have distinguished between an objects clause from a powers clause. In common law an act which is unauthorized by the objects clause is ultra vires and is illegal and unenforceable. However, whether a transaction is ultra vires depends on the court's interpretation of the objects clause. Thus, a transaction entered into by a company that is beyond the objects clause is ultra vires but an act that is authorized by the objects clause but is an abuse of directors' powers is not void but is voidable, i.e., could be set aside.[33] However, under the Companies Act 2016, 'the ability or capacity of these companies to enter into transactions may be limited by what is stipulated by the objects clause: section 35(2)(a), Companies Act 2016'.

These companies, however, shall have full capacity and powers to achieve such objects unless the constitution provides otherwise: section 35(2)(b), Companies Act 2016. Where the constitution contains the objects clause and the directors have caused the company to act beyond its objects, the director would be liable for acting in breach of duties under section 213(1), Companies Act 2016.

30. Sections 28 & 29.
31. Section 28.
32. Sections 21 & 35.
33. *Rolled Steel Products (Holdings) Ltd v. British Steel Corporation* [1984] *BCLC* 466.

§4. Capital and Shares

I. Different Concepts of Capital

A. Issued Share Capital

43. The issued share capital reflects the number of shares actually issued by the company. Any voting in a company is based on the issued share capital. The power to issue shares is given to directors who must obtain the prior approval of the shareholders at a general meeting.[34]

B. Paid-Up Capital

44. This is the capital which has been issued by a company and for which payment has been made by the subscribers. Sometimes, a company allows a subscriber to make a partial payment for the shares issued by the company to the subscriber. The portion of the payment for the shares that have not been paid for is called the 'unpaid capital'. In practice, a company requires full payment for the shares to be made upon successful application for the company's shares. If shares are issued partly paid for, the company may subsequently request for full payment to be made. The call for the shares must be done in accordance with the procedures under section 82, CA 2016 and the constitution. If the subscriber is not able to pay for the shares when a call is made, the company may forfeit the shares. The shares forfeited may be sold by the company and the excess, if any is returned to the subscriber.[35]

There is no minimum issued paid-up capital required for a company but for the purpose of listing on the stock exchange, a company must have at least a market capitalization of not less than MYR 500 million.

C. Abrogation of the Authorized Share Capital Requirement and Nominal/Par Value

45. The Companies Act 2016 has done away with the requirement that a company must specify what is its authorized share capital in its constitution.[36] The former CA 1965 framework considers that the authorized share capital reflects the maximum amount of capital and the maximum number of shares that may be issued by a company at any one time. A company cannot issue shares exceeding the authorized share capital as the issue of these shares is invalid. The company, however, may increase its authorized share capital. This may be carried out if the general meeting of shareholders approves the amendment to the authorized share capital.

---

34. Section 75.
35. Section 83(8) & (9). *See also* the former Art. 29, Table A of Fourth Schedule, Companies Act 1965.
36. *See* the former s. 18, CA 1965.

Prior to the CA 2016, the law also required that the constitution must state the nominal value of the shares.[37] The company is given the discretion to decide what is the nominal value for each share that the company issues. The nominal/par value is the minimum value for each share that can be issued by the company. Shares cannot be issued at less than the nominal value. Nonetheless, shares may be issued at more than the nominal value, i.e., *issued at a premium*. When a company issues its shares at a premium, i.e., at more than nominal value, the premium must be kept in a share premium account.

With the introduction of the CA 2016, all shares issued before or upon the commencement of the Companies Act 2016 shall have no par value. The shares are issued at the issue price as determined by the directors.

Nonetheless, as a legacy of the CA 1965, there are some companies that may have an amount in their share premium account. These companies are given up to twenty-four months from the date of the implementation of the no par value environment to utilize the amount in their share premium account: section 618, Companies Act 2016 for the following purposes:

(i) provide for the premium payable on redemption of debentures or redeemable preference shares previously issued;

(ii) write off—
   - the preliminary expenses of the company incurred prior to the NPV regime; or
   - expenses incurred, or commissions or brokerages paid or discounts allowed, before or upon the commencement of the NPV regime, for any duty, fee or tax payable on or in connection with any issue of shares of the company;

(iii) pay up, under an agreement made before the commencement of the NPV regime, shares which were unissued before that date and which are to be issued upon that date to members of the company as fully paid bonus shares.[38]

(iv) pay up in whole or in part the balance unpaid on shares issued before the commencement of NPV regime to members of the company; or

(v) pay dividends declared before the commencement of NPV regime, if such dividends are satisfied by the issue of shares to members of the company.

At the end of this period, the funds in the share premium account will be part of the company's subscribed capital and cannot be used except in accordance with the Companies Act 2016.

---

37. *See* the former s. 18, CA 1965.
38. Practice Note N01/2017 that SSM has issued regarding this explained that any power of the board of directors to recommend the issuance of bonus shares in the Constitution (Memorandum & Articles of Association) of the company or in any written agreement made, or resolution passed by the company is sufficient. In addition, the right to use the credit standing in the share premium account must be exercised within twenty-four months after the commencement of the Companies Act 2016 irrespective of whether the decision to pay up any unissued shares as fully paid bonus shares is made before or after the commencement of the Companies Act 2016.

II. Alteration of Capital Requirements

A. *Capital Increase: Formal Requirements*

46. There are several ways that a company may alter its capital. A company may:

(a) increase its capital by issuing new shares;
(b) consolidate and divide all or any of its share capital into shares of a larger denomination;
(c) convert paid-up shares into stock or re-convert stock into paid-up shares of any denomination; or
(d) subdivide its shares or any of them into a smaller denomination.

47. The above can be carried out by the passing of an ordinary resolution. Any alteration of the capital as stated above may sometimes require compliance with specific sections of the Companies Act 2016. An increase in the issued capital could involve the issuance of new preference shares which may require the company to comply with the procedure set out for variation of class rights.

III. Preferential Right of Subscription

48. A pre-emption right in a company is intended to protect existing shareholders from any dilution of their shareholding that will affect the voting powers or control rights of the shareholders. A pre-emption right confers on the existing members the right to be given the first right of refusal for all new issues of shares. Section 85, Companies Act 2016 requires that for any new issues of shares, the shares must first be offered to existing shareholders in a way that will maintain the relative voting and distribution rights of those shareholders. This section is subject to the constitution which means that unless the constitution provides otherwise, existing shareholders have pre-emption rights for any new issue of shares. If the company chooses not to follow section 85, this must be expressly stated in the constitution. Although a company cannot issue new shares without offering them first to existing shareholders, the existing shareholders are not obliged to exercise their pre-emption rights.

IV. Forbidden Reductions of Capital and Acquisition of Shares by the Corporation Itself

A. *Capital Reduction*

49. A capital reduction involves an alteration of the existing authorized share capital. A capital reduction may occur where the company:

(a) extinguishes or reduces uncalled capital;

(b) cancels its paid-up capital that is lost or not represented by available assets; or
(c) pays off capital in excess of the company's needs: section 116(1).

Where the company wants to cancel its paid-up capital that is unrepresented by available assets or extinguish or reduce its uncalled capital, there is no return of capital to the shareholders. However, if a reduction is for paying off capital which is in excess of the company's needs, the capital is returned to the shareholders.

A company may reduce its capital unless the constitution prohibits any reduction: section 115.

Capital reduction may be carried out in the following two ways:

(a) capital reduction by court's confirmation. The company must obtain the approval of the general meeting of the shareholders who must pass a special resolution approving the proposal to reduce capital. The company must then obtain the court's confirmation. The court's role is to ensure that the reduction will not prejudice the creditors' interest which essentially means that the court must be satisfied that the reduction of capital will not affect the company's ability to settle its debts. The creditors can contest the reduction. For this purpose, the company has to prepare a list of creditors who are entitled to make a claim against the company. Normally, the creditors consent is obtained prior to the confirmation by the court. The reduction is unlikely to be approved or sanctioned by the court if the debt has not been secured and the company did not provide any other adequate safeguards for the debt: section 1115(a);
(b) capital reduction by solvency statement. The company must obtain the approval of the general meeting of the shareholders who must pass a special resolution approving the proposal to reduce capital. This must be supported by a solvency statement to be made by all the directors of the company. The solvency statement is made prior to the special resolution. For a private company, the solvency statement must be made within the period of fourteen days ending with the date of the special resolution. The *solvency* statement for a public company must be made within the period of twenty-one days ending with the date of the resolution. The solvency statement must be made available for inspection by members at a general meeting to pass the special resolution to approve the reduction of capital. Alternatively, if a private company relies on the written resolution procedure to approve the reduction of capital the solvency statement must be circulated with every copy of the written resolution sent to all members entitled to vote on the resolution.

The solvency statement must state that each director has formed the opinion that the company satisfies the solvency test. The directors' evaluation must be:

(i) based on the directors' inquiry into the company's state of affairs and prospects; and
(ii) must take into account all of the company's liabilities including contingent liabilities.

The directors must satisfy themselves that the company is able to comply with the *solvency test* in relation to the reduction. The test is that:

(i) immediately after the transaction, there is no ground for the company to be unable to pay off its debts;
(ii) either –
  – if the intention is to wind up the company within twelve months of the date of transaction, the company will be able to pay its debts in full within twelve months after commencement of winding-up;
  – in other cases, the company will be able to pay off its debts as they fall due twelve months from the date of transaction;
(iii) the asset of the company is more than the liability of the company at the date of the transaction.

However, a company need not meet the solvency requirements if the reduction is solely by way of cancellation of any paid-up shares share capital which is lost or unrepresented by available assets.

Section 118 enables the company's creditors to challenge the reduction by making an application to the court to cancel the reduction. The application must be made within six weeks from the date of the resolution. To assist the creditors to decide whether or not to challenge the reduction, the company is required to make the solvency statement available for inspection by creditors for six weeks after the date of the resolution section 117 (6)(b).

The reduction is effective and can be carried out if there is no objection at the end of the six-week period after the resolution is passed, and after the Registrar records information lodged by the company in the register: section 119(3).

B. Acquisition of Shares by the Corporation Itself: Share Buy-Back

50. One of the fundamental common law principles under company law is the capital maintenance rule that requires the subscribed capital to be maintained by the company and should not be used except in the ordinary course of business and cannot be returned to the shareholders except upon winding up. In general, the capital maintenance rules prohibit a company from buying back its issued shares, giving financial assistance to any person to acquire the company's shares, declaring dividends unless there are available profits or reducing capital without the court's confirmation.

The maintenance of capital rules that were laid down in *Trevor v. Whitworth*[39] was accepted in Malaysia in *Mookapillai v. Liquidator, Sri Saringgit Sdn Bhd.*[40] It was held in *Trevor v. Whitworth* that:

> Paid-up capital may be diminished or lost in the course of the company's trading; that is a result which no legislation can prevent; but persons who deal with,

39. (1887) 12 *App. Cas.* 409.
40. (1981) 2 *MLJ* 114.

> and give credit to a limited company, naturally rely upon the fact that the company is trading with a certain amount of capital already paid, as well as upon the responsibility of its members for capital which has been paid into the coffers of the company has been subsequently paid out, except in the legitimate course of its business.

In *Trevor v. Whitworth*, the court stated that the common law rule against a company buying back its shares is very strict and that the share buy-back is invalid even though the purchase may be authorized by its Articles (i.e., constitution) or is sanctioned by a general meeting of its members.

This common law principle has been modified by the CA 2016 in relation to certain corporate transactions. Under section 127, a public listed company is allowed to buy back its own shares subject to certain conditions. In general, a public company must first ensure that the share buy-back is permitted by the constitution. The board must convene a meeting of shareholders and the share buy-back proposal must be presented to shareholders at the general meeting for their approval. The approval of the general meeting is needed *before* the shares can be repurchased.

C. Board Resolution and Declaration of Solvency

51. Prior to obtaining the general meeting's approval, the board must determine whether or not the company is solvent. It is the directors who are required to resolve whether or not the company is solvent and the directors are required to make a solvency statement. The solvency statement must be made by a majority of the directors of the company.

52. The solvency statement must state that each director has formed the opinion that the company satisfies the solvency test. The directors' evaluation must be:

(i) based on the directors' inquiry into the company's state of affairs and prospects;
(ii) must take into account all of the company's liabilities including contingent liabilities; and
(iii) must state that it is necessary for the company to buy back its own shares and the purchase is made in good faith and in the interests of the company.

53. A company cannot purchase its own shares unless it is solvent at the date of the purchase and will not become insolvent by incurring the debts involved in the obligation to pay for the shares so purchased. The Companies Act 2016 provides for a solvency test that must be fulfilled before the company may buy back its shares. For a share buy-back, the solvency test is that:

(i) the company will not become insolvent and capital not be impaired at the date of the solvency statement. A company shall be deemed to be solvent if it is able to meet its debts when they become due without any substantial disposition of assets outside the ordinary course of business, restructuring its debts, or externally forcing a revision of its operations. The company's capital is impaired if the value of its net assets is less than the aggregate amount of all shares of the company after the share buy-back: section 112(3)(a)&(b), Companies Act 2016; and

(ii) the company must remain solvent after each buy-back during the period of six months after the date the solvency statement was made by the directors: section 112(2)(a)&(b) and section 113(5), Companies Act 2016.

If any director, whether or not the director that signed the declaration, is of the opinion that it is likely that the listed company will not remain solvent at the time of the relevant purchase, the director must immediately notify the board of directors of the listed company in writing and lodge a copy of such notice with the Market Supervision Division of the Exchange. Service of such notice shall revoke the validity of the earlier solvency declaration.

D. Compliance with the Rules of the Stock Exchange

54. Section 127 allows a public company to buy back its shares which are listed on the stock exchange in accordance with the rules of the stock exchange, i.e., BMLR.

The on-market purchase must be in accordance with the relevant rules of the Stock Exchange. The public company is not permitted to purchase its own shares which are not listed. The BMLR imposes certain conditions and rules for an on-market share buy-back. However, an off-market purchase is allowed subject to the rules of the stock exchange. An off-market purchase takes place through a private agreement and not via the stock exchange. As of now, the stock exchange has not yet created rules to allow for an off-market purchase of a listed company's shares except for the purchase of odd lots (shares of a listed company held by a person which is less than the minimum number of one hundred shares that can be traded) and shares bought back by a Special Purpose Acquisition Company (SPAC).

A listed company seeking shareholders' approval for an on-market share buy-back should provide certain minimum information to its shareholders. A listed company may purchase its own shares on a stock exchange if the purchase or acquisition has been authorized in advance by the company in a general meeting. The ordinary resolution for a share buy-back must include the following:

(a) the total number or percentage and description of the shares authorized to purchase on the Exchange;
(b) the dates on which the authority conferred by the resolution will commence and determine;
(c) the maximum funds to be allocated by the listed corporation for the purpose of purchasing its own shares or a basis, other than a reference to any person's discretion or opinion, or a formula to determine the maximum fund that is to be allocated;
(d) whether the shares are proposed to be cancelled or retained as treasury shares, or both and, if available, information as to the percentage or number of shares

purchased which are to be retained and/or cancelled. Normally, the circular will contain information giving the directors discretion, and thus, the decision on the fate of the shares so purchased is to be made by the directors.

55. Such authority may only commence in force until:

(a) the conclusion of the first annual general meeting (AGM) of the company following the passing of the resolution at which time it shall lapse unless by ordinary resolution passed at that meeting, the authority is renewed, either unconditionally or subject to conditions;
(b) the expiration of the period within which the next AGM after that date is required by law to be held;
(c) revoked or varied by ordinary resolution of shareholders at a general meeting – whichever occurs first.

The BMLR specifies that the amount of listed shares that may be bought back by a listed company cannot exceed 10% of its issued and paid-up capital: paragraph 12.09, BMLR. The purchase price must not be more than 15% above the weighted average market price for the shares. This is to be calculated based on the five market days immediately before the share buy-back is carried out: Paragraph 12.17, BMLR. The resale price must not be less than the weighted average market price for the shares for the five market days immediately before the resale. This must not be at a discounted price of more than 5% to the weighted average market price for the shares for the five market days immediately before the resale. However, if the resale price is at this discounted price, the resale must take place not earlier than thirty days from the date of purchase; and the resale price is not less than the cost of purchase of the shares being resold: paragraph 12.18, BMLR.

Once the company completes its share buy-back and in the event that the shares are cancelled, it is possible that the company's public spread could be affected. Listed companies are required to maintain at least 25% of their total listed shares (excluding treasury shares) or listed units are in the hands of public shareholders. Bursa Malaysia may accept a percentage lower than 25% of the total number of listed shares (excluding treasury shares) if it is satisfied that such a lower percentage is sufficient for a liquid market in such shares.

E. Funds for the Share Buy-Back

56. The company may use its available profits, retained earnings, capital or borrowings provided this does not cause the company to contravene the solvency test. The share premium account which was capable of being used to fund the share buy-back under the CA 1965 no longer exists under the CA 2016. The BMLR states that the company must ensure that the proposed purchase(s) of its own shares is made wholly out of retained profits and/or the share premium account of the listed company. However, there are no restrictions on the types of funds which can be utilized so long as the buy-back is backed by an equivalent amount of retained profits and/ or share premium. The company may use borrowings as a funding source for effecting a buy-back.

F. Publicity and Disclosure Obligation

57. A listed company must immediately announce to the stock exchange any decision by the board of directors to submit to shareholders a proposal for the company to be authorized to purchase its own shares.

The company must also announce to the Exchange the outcome of the general meeting called to consider the proposed purchase of its own shares on the Exchange immediately following such a meeting taking place. Within fourteen days of the purchase of the shares, the company must lodge a notice of the purchase with the Registrar of Companies and the stock exchange. If there is default, the company and every officer of the company are guilty of an offence against the Act liable to a fine of not exceeding fifty thousand ringgit and a further fine not exceeding one thousand ringgit for each day during which the offence continues.

The notice of the purchase or acquisition must contain the information as requested by the Registrar and usually includes the following particulars:

(a) The total number of shares purchased.
(b) The minimum price paid for each share purchased.
(c) The maximum price paid for each share purchased.
(d) The total amount paid for the shares purchased.
(e) The name of the Stock Exchange through which the shares were purchased.
(f) Number of shares purchased retained in treasury.
(g) Total number of shares retained in treasury.
(h) Number of shares purchased which were cancelled.
(i) The total issued capital is diminished.

The Listing Requirements also require notification of purchase, resale or cancellation to be made to the Bursa Securities. Any purchase(s) of the listed company's own shares by the listed company must be announced to the Exchange no later than 6.30 pm on the day the purchase is made. The announcement must include the description of shares purchased, the number of shares purchased, the price of each share or, where relevant, the highest and lowest price paid, the total consideration paid and where all or any of the shares are proposed to be cancelled and the adjusted share capital.

A company must also include in its annual report, information with respect to the purchase of its own shares.

G. Treatment of Shares Bought Back

58. Where a company has purchased its own shares, the directors of the company may resolve:

(a) Distribute the treasury shares as dividends to shareholders, such dividends to be known as 'share dividends'. If this is done, the costs of the shares shall be applied in the reduction of the funds otherwise available for distribution of dividends: section 127(10), Companies Act 2016.
(b) Resell the treasury shares or any of the treasury shares in accordance with the relevant rules of the stock exchange. The BMLR requires the public listed company to make an immediate announcement to the Bursa of any resale of its treasury shares on the day the resale is made.
(c) Transfer the shares, or any of the shares for the purposes of or under an employees' share scheme.
(d) Transfer the shares or any of the shares as purchase consideration.
(e) Cancel the shares. If these are cancelled, they will automatically be de-listed from the stock market.
(f) Sell, transfer or otherwise use the treasury shares for such other purposes as the Minister may by order prescribe.

59. Where the directors resolve to cancel the shares so purchased or cancel any treasury shares, the issued capital of the company shall be diminished by the shares so cancelled. This cancellation of shares shall not be deemed to be a reduction of share capital within the meaning of the Act. This means that the company does not have to comply with the procedure under sections 116 and 117 to have the reduction effected. A notice of sale or cancellation of treasury shares must be given to the Registrar, the Stock Exchange and the SC. The notice contains the following:

(a) The number of treasury shares sold or transferred.
(b) The minimum price at which the treasury shares were sold.
(c) The maximum price at which the treasury shares were sold.
(d) Total consideration received for the treasury shares sold.
(e) The name of the Stock Exchange through which the treasury shares are sold.
(f) Total number of shares still in treasury.
(g) The number of treasury shares cancelled.
(h) Total issued capital as diminished.

Any resale(s) of treasury shares by the listed company must be announced to the Exchange no later than 6.30 pm on the day the resale is made. The announcement must include the description of shares resold, the number of shares resold, the resale price of each share or, where relevant, the highest and lowest resale price and the total consideration received.

Any cancellation of shares or treasury shares of the listed company must be announced to the Exchange no later than 6.30 pm on the day the cancellation is made. The announcement must include the number of shares cancelled, the date(s) of cancellation and the outstanding and paid-up capital of the listed company after cancellation.

While the shares are held as treasury shares, the rights attached to them as to voting, dividends and participation in other distribution are suspended and the treasury shares must not be taken into account in calculating the number or percentage of shares or of a class of shares in the company for any purposes.

H. Offences

60. If section 127 is contravened, the company and every officer of the company shall be guilty of an offence and may be liable to a fine of MYR 500,000 or imprisonment for five years or both.[41] A director who makes a declaration of solvency without having reasonable grounds for his opinion shall be guilty of an offence.[42]

V. Prohibition Against Giving Financial Assistance

61. Section 123 prohibits a company from giving financial assistance for the purpose of, or in connection with, an acquisition of shares in the company or in its holding company.[43] However, section 126 allows a non-listed company to provide financial assistance if a special resolution is passed and the financial assistance does not exceed 10% of shareholders' funds.

To determine whether the transaction is a financial assistance transaction, the court must consider the transaction as a whole. Where it can be shown that the transaction was not 'for the purpose' of or 'in connection with' an acquisition of shares, the transaction will not be in contravention of section 123.[44]

Examples of the transactions that may be considered as giving financial assistance include the provision of a loan or guarantee or the provision of security by a company for the purposes of enabling a person to acquire shares in the company. It has been held that there is financial assistance where a company uses its property as security for a charge given in favour of a bank, which provided the loan to a person who is using the loan to acquire the company's shares.[45]

There is also financial assistance where a company acquires an asset or property from the seller which will enable the seller to acquire the company's shares by using the purchase price and the acquisition of assets was not because of a genuine commercial need of the company, even though the price paid is at market value and is a fair price.[46] The Court had also held that a company had assisted in the purchase of its own shares when the company's shareholders transferred their shares to a developer in return for a number of houses the developer was planning to build using funds obtained on security of the company's land.[47] A company cannot reduce the liability of the members on unpaid shares or waive the payment for unpaid

41. Section 127(18).
42. Section 114.
43. *Cheah Theam Swee & Anor v. Overseas Union Bank Ltd & Ors*. In this case, the company did not pass any resolution which would result in the company giving financial assistance. The shares were used as security but this was done by the shareholders as owners of the shares.
44. *Lori (M) Sdn Bhd (Interim Receiver) v. Arab–Malaysian Finance Bhd* (1999) 3 *MLJ* 81.
45. *Chung Khiaw Bank Limited v. Hotel Rasa Sayang Sdn Bhd & Anor.*
46. *Belmont Finance Corpn v. Williams Furniture Ltd & Ors (No. 2)* (1980) 1 *All ER* 393.
47. *KL Sdn Bhd & Anor v. LGH & Ors*; *ALLS v. LGH & Ors* (1990) 1 *MSCLC* 90,402.

shares as this is giving of financial assistance.[48] The prohibition against the giving of financial assistance does not apply to a debenture with a floating charge over the assets of the company.[49]

62. Section 125, Companies Act 2016 identifies several transactions which are not considered financial assistance transactions. These are as follows:

(a) Where a company whose ordinary course of business is lending money lends money in the course of its ordinary business. This would enable banks and financial institutions to provide loans as part of their ordinary course of business and the loan must be provided on ordinary commercial terms.
(b) Where a company gives the financial assistance in accordance with any employee share scheme or share ownership scheme which is in force at the time for fully paid shares in the company or its holding company. These shares are purchased or subscribed by trustees and are to be held by or for the benefit of employees of the company or its subsidiary company.
(c) Where a company gives financial assistance to its employees (other than directors of the company) or to the employees of its subsidiary to enable them to purchase fully paid shares in the company or its holding company to be held by such persons by way of beneficial ownership.
(d) the making of a loan or the giving of a guarantee or the provision of security in connection with one or more loans made by one or more other persons by a company in the ordinary course of its business where the activities of that company are regulated by any written law relating to banking, insurance or takaful or which are subject to the supervision of the SC and where:
    (i) the lending of money or the giving of guarantees or the provision of security in connection with loans made by other persons is done in the course of such activities;
    (ii) the loan that is made by the company, or, where the guarantee is given or the security is provided in respect of a loan, such loan is made on ordinary commercial terms as to the rate of interest or returns, the terms of repayment of principal and payment of the interest or returns.

A. Consequences of Contravention

63. Sections 123(3) and 126(6) make the giving of financial assistance not in accordance with the Companies Act 2016 an offence. The officer in default will be guilty of a criminal offence which is punishable by a fine or imprisonment. In addition, the court may order the officer who has been convicted of the contravention to pay compensation to the company or another person who has suffered loss as a result of the contravention. Section 123(5) allows the company to enforce the transaction and enables a person to whom the company becomes liable in respect of any

---

48. *EH Dey Pty Ltd* [1966] *VR* 464; *Datuk Tan Leng Teck v. Sarjana Sdn Bhd & Ors* (1997) 4 *MLJ* 329.
49. *Yap Sing Hock Holdings Berhad & Ors v. Chuah Teong Hooi & Ors* (1990) 1 *MSCLC* 90, 538.

security or guarantee to enforce the transaction. Thus, a lender who obtains a security from the company to secure loans that are used to purchase the company's shares may enforce the security: section 123(5).[50]

VI. Distribution of Dividends

64. The right of members to be paid dividends is not an absolute right. Dividends are only payable if the company is solvent: section 131, Companies Act of 2016. The determination of a company's solvency must be made by the board of directors: section 132, Companies Act of 2016. Section 132(1), Companies Act of 2016 requires the board's authorization which is mandatory in nature. Section 132(2) Companies Act of 2016 indicates that directors are empowered to authorize a distribution at *such time* as the directors consider appropriate. What is important is that as long as the distribution is made out of profits and that the company is able to fulfil the solvency requirement under section 132, Companies Act of 2016, the directors may authorize the distribution of profits as interim dividends or finals dividends.

65. Under the Companies Act of 2016, the approval of the shareholders is not required for any payment of dividends. However, a company's constitution may specify that dividends can only be paid when it has been approved by shareholders, i.e., declared. In such a situation, a general meeting of shareholders must be convened and the resolution regarding the payment of the dividends needs to be passed at that meeting. The approval is known as 'declaration' of the dividends but the dividends cannot be more than recommended by the board of directors.

66. The rule for dividends is intended to ensure that the company's assets are not dissipated by members to the detriment of the creditors. If the company has available profit, then the dividends are the return given to shareholders for the use of their capital in the company's business. The contributed or subscribed capital is intact. Section 131(1) requires that distribution can be made only out of profits of the company available if the company is solvent. Section 132(2) and (3) then provide for rules to determine if the company is solvent.

Section 132(2) also enables the directors to authorize a distribution at such time and in such amount as the directors consider appropriate if the directors are satisfied that the company will be solvent immediately after the distribution is made. Furthermore, section 132(3) provides for the solvency test for the purpose of dividends distribution. Section 132(3) states that a company is regarded as solvent if the company is able to pay its debts as and when the debts become due within twelve months immediately after the distribution is made.

50. This is made possible by the amendment to the Companies Act of 1965 which came into effect on 10 Sep. 1992. Before that date, third-party lenders could not recover such loans, *see Chung Khiaw Bank Limited v. Hotel Rasa Sayang Sdn Bhd & Anor* (1990) 1 *MSCLC* 90,382. *See also Lori (M) Sdn Bhd (Interim Receiver) v. Arab–Malaysian Finance Bhd* (1999) 3 *MLJ* 81.

In *Hilton International Ltd (in liq.) v. Hilton & Anor.*,[51] the court laid down the relevant principles for the declaration of dividends:

(1) Dividends including capital dividends may be paid only out of profits, or putting the matter conversely, may not be paid out of paid-up capital without the Court's approval of a reduction of capital.
(2) The payment of a dividend out of paid-up capital will occur if the payment has the effect of reducing the company's net assets (often referred to as shareholders' funds) below the amount of its paid-up capital. The expression net assets for present purposes means the amount which remains after deducting all the company's liabilities both actual and contingent prudently assessed from the sum of all its assets prudently valued. Accounts should be taken to demonstrate the company's position overall. A capital or income transaction should ordinarily not be viewed in isolation.
(3) Whether there are profits and if so how much thereof should be paid out as dividends is essentially a matter of commercial assessment and judgment but that assessment and judgment must be made and exercised with these and the following propositions in mind.
(4) No dividend may be paid, whether out of capital or income profits, if the company is in a state of trading insolvency.
(5) No dividend may be paid, whether out of capital or income profits, if the company is in a state of balance sheet insolvency, or will enter that state as a result of the payment.
(6) No dividend may be paid, whether out of capital or income profits, if the company is in a state of doubtful trading or balance sheet solvency unless the directors can demonstrate, if later challenged, that they believed in good faith and on reasonable grounds that the payment of the dividend would not jeopardize the company's ability promptly to satisfy its creditors present and future and whether secured or unsecured.
(7) Even if the company is fully solvent in both the trading and balance sheet senses, no dividend may be paid whether out of capital or income profits if the directors ought to have appreciated that such payment was likely to jeopardize the company's balance sheet or trading solvency.

67. In *Chip Thye Enterprises Pte Ltd (in Liq.) v. Phay Gi Mo*,[52] the court held that when the company had not been generating sales for several years and where there was an auditor's report stating that there was a deficit in the company's accounts, the company was insolvent and did not have available profits to justify the payment of the dividends. It is not necessary for a company to make up the losses of fixed assets before treating a revenue profit as available for a dividend.[53]

51. (1988) 4 *NZCLC* 64,721 at p. 64,750.
52. (2004) 1 *SLR* 434.
53. Per Lindley, L.J. said in *Lee v. Neuchatel Asphalte Co.* (1889) 41 *Ch.D* 1:

> the [U.K.] Companies Acts do not require the capital to be made up if lost. They contain no provision of the kind … I cannot find anything in them which precludes payment of dividends

Under the common law as laid down in *Marra Development Ltd v. BW Rofe Pty Ltd* (1977–1978) 3 ACLR 185, the court has held that there should be profit at the time of declaration, and not necessarily at the time of payment.[54] As such, even if there are no profits available at the time of payment, the directors are not in breach of the former section 365, CA 1965.[55] Under section 132 (4), Companies Act 2016, if after a distribution is authorized and before it is made, the directors cease to be satisfied on reasonable grounds that the company will be solvent immediately after the distribution is made, the directors shall take all necessary steps to prevent the distribution from being made. This means that even if after a dividend is declared by shareholders, when section 132(4), Companies Act 2016 applies, the dividends must not be paid out. Because of section 132(4), Companies Act 2016, directors would then have to resolve to cancel the authorization.

Section 132(4) Companies Act 2016 replaces the common law position laid down in *Marra Development Ltd v. BW Rofe Pty Ltd* (1977–1978) 3 ACLR 185 that once the dividends are declared they cannot be revoked or cancelled. To proceed with paying out the dividends would be a breach of the section. It can be argued that the directors' solvency determination as originally made is no longer true and therefore the dividends are not authorized by the board.

The profit realized on the sale of the company's business can also be distributed as profit.[56]

VII. Stock Exchange Introduction Requirements

68. Public companies that intend to list the shares on the Stock Exchange, that is to have the shares admitted on the official list of the Stock Exchange, that is, Bursa Malaysia Securities Bhd, must inform and apply to the SC and the Bursa Malaysia for listing. A private company cannot list its shares and must first convert to a public company to enable the listing of its shares. The company must comply with the relevant provisions of the SCA, the SC's Policies and Guidelines on Issue/ Offer of Securities and the Listing Requirements of Bursa Securities.

---

so long as the assets are of less value than the original capital'. His Lordship concluded that since the Acts were silent on the question, and since to decide otherwise would 'paralyse the trade of the country', it should be held that 'so long as they pay their creditors there is no reason why they should not go on and divide profits, so far as I can *see*, although every shilling of the capital may be lost'. The Court of Appeal affirmed this decision in *Verner v. General and Commercial Investment Trust Ltd* (1894) 2 *Ch.* 239.

54. *See BSN Commercial Bank (M) Bhd v. River View Properties Sdn Bhd* [1996] 1 MLJ 872, (High Court).
55. However, the payment of dividends as a debt due to the shareholders may amount to an undue preference and subject to claw-back if at the point of distribution the company is insolvent and the distribution can appear to be in favour of one set of creditors i.e., the shareholders over other creditors: s. 53 of the *Bankruptcy Act 1967* read with s. 528, CA 1965.
56. *Verner v. General and Commercial Investment Trust Ltd* (1894) 2 *Ch.* 239; *Darvall v. North Sydney Brick & Tile Co. Ltd* (1989) 7 *ACLC* 81; *North Sydney Brick & Tile Co. Ltd & Anor v. Darvall* (1989) 7 *ACLC* 1,163.

The BMLR state what are the requirements that a public company must fulfil for listing. Prior to August 2009, the structure of the Stock Exchange is as follows: the Main Board, the Second Board and the Mesdaq Market. However, in August 2009, the new structure saw the creation of one Main Market merging the Main Board and the Second Board and the introduction of a new ACE market. In September 2017, a new market was introduced known as the Leading Entrepreneur Accelerator Platform (LEAP) market.

In general:

(a) There is a minimum capital requirement. The minimum amount of issued paid-up capital must be MYR 500 million for listing on the Main Market.
(b) The constitution of the public company must contain certain provisions that are required by the Listing Requirements to be included in the Constitution: Chapter 7 of the Bursa Securities Listing Requirements (BSLR).
(c) There must be a minimum of 25% public shareholding of the company's shares. This means that 25% of the company's shares must be held by public shareholders and there must be at least 1,000 public shareholders who each hold not less than one hundred shares. To continue to be listed on the stock exchange, this 25% public shareholding must be retained. However, there is no minimum number of public shareholders required for continuing listing.
(d) The public company must prepare a prospectus which must be in compliance with the CMSA, and the SC's Policies and Guidelines on Issue/Offer of Securities.
(e) There are also financial tests that must be met such as profit track record business operation and profit forecast.

VIII. Prospectus Requirements

69. A prospectus is required when a public company issues shares. The main intent is to ensure that any fund-raising exercise by a public company is accompanied by adequate disclosure of information. Section 4 identifies a prospectus as 'any notice, circular, advertisement or invitation inviting applications or offers from the public, or offering to the public to subscribe or purchase any shares in or debentures of a corporation or proposed corporation or interests in time-share schemes'. Section 226 of the CMSA 2007 defines a prospectus as any notice, circular, advertisement or document inviting an application to subscribe for or purchase securities, or offering any securities for subscription or purchase. This includes a supplementary prospectus, shelf and supplementary shelf prospectus, short form prospectus, profile statement and abridged prospectus unless expressly specified otherwise. The main criterion for ascertaining whether a document is a prospectus or not is by looking at the substance of the activities or intention of releasing the document.

The CMSA requires a prospectus to be issued unless the issue is part of 'excluded invitations' and 'excluded offers' as defined within Schedule 6 of the CMSA or 'excluded issue' under section 230 of the CMSA, and Schedule 7.

A prospectus must be registered with the SC under sections 231 and 232 of the CMSA and the SC will not register the prospectus unless:

(a) it is not misleading in form and context;
(b) it is signed by every director or persons who are proposed directors or by his agent who is authorized in writing to do so;
(c) it is lodged on or before the date of issue;
(d) it appears to comply with the requirements of the Act; and
(e) the consent of experts who have made statements in the prospectus and material contracts referred to therein are lodged.

70. The company has a duty to inform the recipients of the information in the prospectus of any changes which might have taken place between the date of the issue and the date of the proposed transaction.[57] If the prospectus does not comply with the CMSA, each director and other person responsible for the prospectus is guilty of an offence.[58] The directors are required to make a responsibility statement as stated under the Prospectus Guidelines on Public Offerings. A similar responsibility statement is required to be made by the principal adviser and managing underwriter.

Where a prospectus states or implies that an application has been made for permission for the shares or debentures offered in it to be listed for quotation on the Stock Exchanges, any allotment made or an application in pursuance of the prospectus will be void if:

(a) permission is not applied for in the form required by the Stock Exchanges before the third day on which the Stock Exchanges are open after the date of the issue of the prospectus;
(b) the permission is not granted before the expiration of six weeks from the date of issue of the prospectus or such a longer period.[59]

Any money received from applicants must be repaid if permission is not applied for or not granted.[60]

IX. Classes of Shares

71. A company may issue several types of shares with different rights attached. However, if the company issues more than one type of share, the constitution must state that the company's capital is divided into different types or classes of shares and must state the voting rights attached to the shares: section 90, CA 2016. If the shares are issued with no voting rights, the shares must be described as non-voting shares which must appear legibly on any share certificate, prospectus or directors' report issued by the company. The main types of shares are deferred, ordinary and preference shares. These shares have different rights which entitle the holders to

57. Section 42A and 47 of the SCA 1993.
58. Section 44(7) of the SCA.
59. Section 44(1).
60. Section 52(1) of the Securities Commission Act 1993.

exercise the rights attached to the shares. The rights are normally found in the constitution or alternatively in the terms of issue of the shares. Shares are classified into different classes or types depending on the rights and obligations of the holders of the shares. The rights normally attached to the shares normally relate to voting, participation at meetings and payment of dividends.

A. *Bearer Shares*

72. Bearer shares are shares which confer on the person who possesses the share certificate, i.e., the bearer, ownership of the shares. Section 73(1), CA 2016 prohibits the issue of bearer shares. Under the former section 57, CA 1965, the holders of such shares issued before 29 December 1967 may surrender the shares for cancellation and to have their names entered in the register of members: section 57(2), CA 1965. Section 73(2), CA 2016 requires that the bearer of these shares must surrender those shares to the company within twelve months upon the commencement of the CA 2016, i.e., 31 January 2017, for the shares to be cancelled. This person's name shall then be entered into the register of members. The person who has the bearer shares may also apply to the court to have his name be entered into the register of members. If the company enters the bearer's name in the register of members without having the bearer shares surrendered and cancelled, the company must compensate for any loss incurred by any person as a result of the company entering in the register of members the name of the bearer.

B. *Deferred, Founders or Management Shares*

73. These shares are usually taken up by or issued to the company's promoters or founders. They are called 'deferred' because the rights of the holders of them to receive a dividend are deferred until a dividend at a specified rate has been paid to other shareholders. However, after the dividend of a specified amount has been paid, the holders of the deferred shares might be entitled, e.g., to half of the remaining profits.

C. *Voting Shares or Ordinary Shares*

74. These are the most common shares issued by a company. Ordinary shares are also known as equity shares. Normally they carry full voting rights. Ordinary shares also confer the right to share in the profits of the company through the payment of dividends as declared by the general meeting of the shareholders. When the company is wound up, the ordinary shareholders also get to share in the surplus asset or profit of the company.

D. Non-voting Shares

75. Shares issued as non-voting do not confer on the shareholders any right to vote. One example of shares with no voting rights is the preference shares. Shares that are traded on the stock exchange are either ordinary shares or preference shares with limited or no voting rights.

E. Multiple Voting

76. Shares with multiple voting rights are commonly found in private companies and are sometimes referred to as 'shares with weighted votes'. This is because the former section 55, Companies Act 1965 expressly stated that all shares in a public company must have one vote per share, prohibiting public companies from issuing shares with multiple votes. However, the Companies Act 2016 does not contain this statutory provision. Listed companies are required by the BMLR to ensure that all voting shares in a public listed company must carry one vote per share. Shares with multiple voting rights cannot be traded on the stock exchange.

F. Preference Shares

77. These shares confer certain preferential rights on their holders over and above the rights conferred on the holders of ordinary shares. These shares do not entitle the holders the right to vote at a general meeting or to any right to participate beyond a specified amount in any distribution whether by way of dividend, on redemption, in a winding-up, or otherwise.[61] Preference shares may only be issued subject to the constitution and the rights are stated in the constitution. It is very important to ascertain what the rights of the preference shares as stated in the constitution or the terms of issue are[62] because courts have held that the rights of preference of shareholders are limited to only those that are stated in these documents.[63]

Preference shares do not confer any right to vote. However, the Act provides for certain situations when the preference shareholders will have a right to vote and these are:

(a) where there is any resolution which varies the rights attached to such shares; or
(b) upon any resolution for the winding-up of the company.

Preference shares may also confer cumulative or non-cumulative rights to dividends. If the preference shares have a cumulative dividend, it means that if the dividend is not paid in one year through a lack of profits in that year, the dividend accumulates until profits are sufficient. The accumulated dividends are to be paid in

61. Section 2.
62. *T.N.T. Australia Pty Ltd v. Normandy Resources N.L.* (1989) 7 *ACLC* 1,090.
63. *Scottish Insurance Corp Ltd v. Wilsons and Clyde Coal Co. Ltd* (1949) 1 *All ER 1068*.

priority to other shareholders. On the other hand, non-cumulative means that the lost dividend is not accumulated and is not made up in subsequent years.

It is possible to confer on preference shares the right to participate in surplus assets and/or profits upon the winding-up of a company.

G. Redeemable Preference Shares

78. Redeemable preference shares is a category of preference shares which is issued on the terms that these shares may be redeemed either at the company's options or on specified dates. They may only be issued if authorized by the constitution. Section 72(4) which is subjected to subsections (5) and (6) states the conditions that must be fulfilled before the redeemable preference shares may be redeemed. The company must ensure that it has available funds to redeem the preference shares and the funds must be from profits, the proceeds of fresh issue of shares issued for the purpose of using the consideration for the redemption of the redeemable preference shares or the capital of the company. The redeemable preference shares must also be fully paid up before they can be redeemed.

If the company uses the capital to redeem the redeemable preference shares, then an equivalent value of the preference shares so redeemed must be placed or transferred into the company's capital accounts.[64]

If the company fails to redeem the shares, the redeemable preference shares, when they are due for redemption, the court has held that this may amount to oppressive conduct and entitles the shareholder to the oppression remedy.[65] A company may also be able to apply for a winding-up order, although the court is likely to consider what are the terms of issue of the redeemable preference shares, especially in situations where the company argues that it has no available profits or funds to enable a redemption. In *Re Marra Developments Ltd* (No. 2),[66] the court was of the view that where the company failed to redeem but has available funds to do so, the holders of those shares could have the company wound up.

X. Variations of Class Rights

79. What is a variation? Where the company issues different types or classes of shares, the rights attached to the shares may be altered or varied by the company. The following are examples of variations of class rights:

(a) any changes, by way of either an alteration or an abrogation, of the existing rights attached to the shares;
(b) the issue of preference shares ranking in *pari passu* with the existing shares issued by the company is deemed to be a variation of the rights attaching to the

64. Section 72(5).
65. *Chloride Eastern Industries Pte Ltd v. Premium Vegetable Oils Sdn Bhd* (2002) *MSCLC* 92,518.
66. (1978) 3 *ACLR* 798.

existing preference shareholders: section 91(1) However, if the existing preference shares were issued on the terms that the company may in future issue new preference shares ranking in *pari passu* with the existing shares, the second issue is not a variation as this is in accordance with what is stated in the terms of issue of the existing preference share or in the company's constitution;

(c) any proposal that alters the provision in the constitution which relates to the procedure to alter class rights is also a variation: section 339(6)(a); and

(d) case law provides that a cancellation of preference shares is a variation if the preference shares have a right to share in surplus asset upon winding-up. If the preference shareholders have no right to participate in surplus profit/asset upon winding-up, the cancellation of the preference shares is not a variation and a separate class meeting need not be called.[67] It has also been held that the cancellation of the preference shares is a variation if the constitution or the terms of issue of the preference shares states that any cancellation is a variation.[68] Prior to 2018, the BMLR provides that there must be a provision in the constitution of all listed companies stating that the repayment or cancellation of preference shares (other than redeemable preference shares) is a variation.[69] This provision is no longer included in the BMLR.

80. However, there is no variation when a company subdivides its shares as the shareholder still enjoys the right to vote although the voting power has been diluted.[70] There is also no variation when the company issues new shares of the class already issued.[71] Note however that the issue of new preference shares is statutorily recognized as a variation. Where the company is issuing new ordinary shares, case law states that it is not a variation. Nonetheless, a company may provide in its constitution that the issue of new shares is a variation. An example can be found under the former Article 5 of Table A of the CA 1965.

81. Procedure. A company may alter the rights attached to existing shares by following the procedure as provided in the constitution. However, if the constitution does not contain a clause dealing with the method to vary class rights, section 91(1)(b), CA 2016 provides that the consent of the shareholders of that class must be obtained.

The consent may be obtained by way of a written consent from shareholders representing not less than 75% of the total voting rights of shareholders in that class. The company may also convene a meeting of shareholders of that class, i.e., a class meeting, where a special resolution must be passed by shareholders of that class. The quorum requirement for a variation of class rights meeting in respect of holders of a class of shares is:

---

67. *Scottish Insurance Corp v. Wilson & Clyde Coal Co.* [1949] *AC* 462.
68. *Re Northern Engineering Industries plc* (1994) 2 *BCLC* 704.
69. Paragraph 7.15 of the Listing Requirements of Bursa Securities Malaysia *Berhad.*
70. *Greenhalgh v. Arderne Cinemas Ltd* (1946) 1 *All ER* 512.
71. *White v. Bristol Aeroplane Co. Ltd.*

(a) for a meeting other than an adjourned meeting, two persons present holding at least one-third of the number of issued shares of such class, excluding any shares of that class held as treasury shares; and
(b) for an adjourned meeting, one person present holding shares of such class,

Since the general principle is that the provision in the constitution dealing with variation prevails over the statutory procedure, it is possible for the class right to be entrenched so that the variation cannot be carried out. The constitution may also provide for a higher voting percentage that is required by the constitution.

82. Challenging the variation. Section 93 allows holders of an aggregate of not less than 10% of total voting rights shares in the class concerned to apply to the court to have the variation or abrogation of their rights cancelled. The variation or abrogation will not be effective until the court has confirmed it. The application must be made within one month after the date on which the consent was given or the resolution for the variation or abrogation was passed. The fact that a shareholder has voted in favour of the variation does not preclude him from challenging the variation. The application to challenge the variation may be made personally by a shareholder or may be made by a shareholder who has been appointed in writing by other shareholders of that class.

83. The application to challenge the variation may be made personally by any shareholder or shareholders if they have not less than 10% of total voting rights in the class. The application may also be made, on behalf of these shareholders who represent 10% of the total voting rights by a shareholder who has been appointed in writing by all these other shareholders.

Apart from challenging the variation due to non-compliance with the statutory procedure, a member may also argue that voting on the proposal to vary class rights was conducted not in the best interests of the class as a whole. This could occur where the ones voting on the variation could have been influenced by the management's promise that those who support the variation would be given extra shares or voting shares.

XI. Transfer of Shares

A. Registered Shares and Share Registration Procedure

84. The CA 2016 relies on registration and inclusion in the register of members as evidence of a person's membership status. Although a person who acquires shares is a shareholder, he is not a member of a company until and unless the shares are registered in the person's name. A person becomes a member by either subscribing to the constitution of the company when the company was first registered or agreeing to become a member by having shares transferred to his name and having his name entered in the register of members of the company.[72] A person may also be a member if his name is registered as a member due to operation of law, i.e., due to him inheriting the shares.

The registration of the shares is done by entering the shareholder's name in the register of members. A person becomes a member only upon the entry of the person's name in the register of members. The register of members is prima facie proof of the shareholders' title to the shares as well as whether the shares have been fully paid up and the amount stated as fully paid up.[73]

A company must keep and maintain a register of members which must contain the following information:

(a) name and addresses of members and the identity card number of the members in the case of a company with share capital;
(b) in the case of a company having a share capital – a statement of shares held by each member. The shares must be distinguished by share numbers if any, or by the number of certificates and the amount paid on shares held by each member;
(c) date at which the name of each person was entered on the register as a member;
(d) date when any person who ceased to be a member during the previous seven years ceased to be a member a statement of shareholdings which; and
(e) the date of every allotment of shares to members and number of shares in each allotment.

It is possible that the information in the register of members may not be accurate or correct. In such cases, the court can make an order to rectify the register. Application for rectification may be made by the person aggrieved or by any member of the company.[74]

85. A shareholder is a member of a company if and when the shares are registered under the person's name in the register of members. If the existing shareholder intends to transfer the shares, the transfer must be done according to the transfer procedure stated in the Companies Act 2016. If the company is a public listed company whose shares are listed on the Stock Exchange, the rules of the stock exchange apply and shares are traded without any registration requirement. Since bearer shares are not recognized, it is not possible for a person to require the company to register the shares in his name merely by producing the bearer shares.

86. The process for transfer and registration of shares in a public company and a private company are the same. The existing shareholder who has agreed to sell his

---

72. *Ming Yueh Holdings Sdn Bhd v. Kong Ming Bank Bhd & Anor* (1990) 1 *MSCLC* 90,453 at p. 90,457; *Haidar J.* said that:

> The term 'shareholder' is often loosely used as a synonym for 'member'. The correct term to use in reference to any person having any shares in a company would appear to be member. Even the fact that a person owns shares does not make him a member of the company.

73. Section 100, CA 1965; *see Lim Poh Choo v. Absolute Ascend Sdn Bhd & Anor* [2008] 3 MLJ 740.
74. Section 49 & 602 CA 2016.

shares must submit a transfer form[75] and the share certificate to the company. The company will then make changes in the register of members in relation to the shares that have been transferred. The registration of the shares in the new owner's name in the register of members completes the transfer of the shares, and the new shareholder may be issued with a share certificate upon his request. The CA 2016 does not require that a share certificate be issued by a company unless the constitution so provides although a member may request that a share certificate be provided to him. Prior to 2016, the share certificate is prima facie evidence of title. This is no longer the case as evidence of title is the entry of a person's name in the register of members: section 101. However, evidence may be given to show otherwise: section 101.

87. A person may also become a member due to shares being transmitted to him. Any clause relating to restriction on transfer in the constitution is not applicable to a transmission of shares. Shares are transmitted when the change of ownership takes place due to the operation of law for example in the case of death or bankruptcy of the shareholder. The person to whom the shares are transmitted must notify the company in writing that the person wishes to be registered as a shareholder of the company in respect of the shares. The registration must be done within sixty days of receiving the notification. Where a member is deceased, the persons recognized as having any title to his interest in the shares or debentures shall be (a) the legal representative where the deceased was a sole holder or (b) the survivor, where the deceased was a joint holder. The company shall accept as evidence of the grant any document which is by law sufficient evidence of probate of the will or letters of administration of the estate of a deceased person. If the person entitled to have the shares transmitted to him elects to register another person as a member, this will be treated as a transfer of shares and all rules relating to transfer of shares shall be applied.

B. Stock Exchange

88. If the company's shares are listed, i.e., the company is a public listed company, the shares are traded 'scripless' where the sale and purchase of the shares are made through the Bursa Securities computerized share trading system known as 'System on Computerized Order Routing and Execution' (SCORE). There is no share certificate for these shares and there is no requirement for the submission of a transfer form to register or complete the transfer. A willing seller will instruct a stockbroker to find the buyer for an agreed price. A willing buyer will also give instruction to buy a company's shares at a price and the computerized share trading system will match the sale and purchase at the agreed price and with the agreement of both buyer and seller. Once this is concluded, the new shareholder's name will be included in the register of depositors in relation to the company. A person whose name appears on the register of depositors is a member of the company.[76]

75. Section 105 of the Companies Act 2016.
76. Section 107B of the Companies Act 1965 and the Securities Industry (Central Depositories) Act (M'sia).

C. Restriction on Transfer and Pre-emption Rights

89. Provisions restricting the transfer of shares are usually found in the constitution. Examples are provisions that state that the shares may be registered in the new shareholder's name subject to the directors' discretion or subject to a provision requiring that the existing shareholder must first offer the shares to other members of the company, i.e., a pre-emption rights clause. While the shares in a private company must be subject to some form of restriction of transfer, the shares of a listed company must be freely transferable and cannot be made subject to any restrictions. For a public company whose shares are not listed on the stock exchange, the law neither mandates nor prohibits restrictions on the transfer of shares.

90. The listing requirements require that all new issue of shares in a listed company is subject to a pre-emption rights clause that entitled the existing shareholders to be given the first offer of the shares to be issued but this pre-emption right clause is not the same as a pre-emption provision that restricts the right of an existing shareholder to transfer the shares.

D. Protection of Shareholders in Case of Tender Offer

91. This is explained in §7 Mergers and Takeovers.

E. Insider Trading

92. The conduct amounting to insider trading, its prohibition and the sanction are provided for under the CMSA. In general, insider trading occurs when a person trades in the securities of a company based on information he acquired which is price sensitive and not obtained from the public domain. Insider trading can also occur if a person tips or provides the information to others. Insider trading is an offence under the CMSA.

XII. Debentures

A. Debentures and Bonds: General

93. Debentures and bonds may be issued by the directors to raise capital. The statutory provisions relating to debentures are found in both the CA and the CMSA 2007.

Section 2 of the CA states that a 'debenture' includes debenture stock, bonds, notes and any other securities of a corporation whether constituting a charge on property of the corporation. However, section 4(1) of the *SCA 1993* further provides that the following instruments are not to be construed as 'debentures' and these are:

(a) any instrument acknowledging or creating indebtedness for, or for money borrowed to defray the consideration payable under, a contract for sale or supply of goods, property or services or any contract of hire in the ordinary course of business;
(b) a cheque, banker's draft or any other bill or exchange or a letter of credit;
(c) a banknote, an insurance policy or a guarantee;
(d) a statement, passbook or other document showing any balance in a current, deposit or savings account;
(e) any agreement for a loan where the lender and borrower are signatories to the agreement and where the lending of money is in the ordinary course of business of the lender, and any promissory note issued under the terms of such an agreement; or
(f) any instrument or product or class of instruments or products as the Minister may, on the recommendation of the Commission, prescribe by order published in the gazette.

94. A debenture holder or a bondholder is not a member of a company and thus has no voting rights. However, there are statutory provisions conferring on debenture holders the right to be informed on certain matters for example in relation to the amendment of the company's objects clause. The debenture holders may also bring an action for oppression under section 346.

A company may issue a debenture that is redeemable in some remote event or at some long-distant date: section 173 of the Act and section 285 of the CMSA. Section 174 of the Act and section 286 of the CMSA provide that a company may re-issue redeemed debentures provided there is nothing to the contrary (express or implied) in the constitution or in any contract it has entered into or provided the company has not bypassed a resolution to that effect or by some other act manifested its intention that the debentures are to be cancelled. A debenture may also be convertible into shares.

B. Convertible Bonds and Warrants

95. Bonds may be issued as convertible or non-convertible. Convertible bonds may be exchanged or converted to stock by the holder at certain specified dates without having to obtain the approval of the company. These are usually offered to existing shareholders on a rights basis to ensure that the shareholding in the company remains proportionate. The issue of convertible bonds has the potential of increasing the issued paid-up capital of the company.

A warrant gives the holder an option to subscribe to the number of ordinary shares at a predetermined rate within a specified time frame. The options attached to the warrants may be exercised by subscribing for ordinary shares in case, by exchanging them with loan stock/debenture or both. The SC has issued its guidelines for the Issue of Structured Warrants.

§5. Shareholders, Management and Control

I. Shareholder Control Mechanisms/Shareholders

A. *Relationship Between the General Meeting and Board of Directors*

96. Both the general meeting of shareholders and the board of directors have the authority to decide on what the company may do. Directors are accountable to the company, i.e., the shareholders collectively, but not to any individual shareholder.

The division of authority between these two organs of the company may be ascertained by considering whether there are any statutory provisions in the Companies Act of 2016 that expressly confers power on one organ.

Where the Companies Act of 2016 or the constitution confers authority on the board, the general meeting cannot impose its views on the board.[77] Similarly, when the Companies Act or the constitution states that a matter must be resolved by the company at a meeting, this requires the approval of the shareholders and the board's approval cannot replace the requirement for shareholders' meeting and approval. In most companies, the constitution usually will contain a provision stating that the directors shall manage the company's business and exercise all powers that the Companies Act or the constitution confers on the board. In this situation, the board has the power to make business decisions regarding the affairs of the company. Thus, in general, the general meeting has no power to interfere in the board's power to manage the company.[78]

However, section 195, Companies Act 2016 enables the general meeting to make recommendations, to propose and instruct the board on matters affecting the management of the company. Section 195 modifies the common law principle regarding the division of power between the board of directors and the general meeting.[79] Nevertheless, before the recommendations under section 195, Companies Act 2016 become binding on the Board, several conditions must be fulfilled. These are:

(a) For the recommendation to be binding, the general meeting must pass *a special resolution* to instruct the board to do or refrain from doing something and thus not all *shareholders' resolution* is binding on the board. Furthermore, for a resolution to be valid, it must comply with other rules relating to convening meetings and passing resolutions: *see* sections 309, 310 and 311, Companies Act.

---

77. In *Automatic Self-Cleansing Filter Syndicate Co. Ltd v. Cuninghame* (1906) 2 *Ch.* 34, the Court ruled that the directors were entitled to refuse to carry out an agreement for the sale of the company's assets notwithstanding that they had been directed to do so by a resolution passed by a majority of shareholders at a general meeting.

78. *John Shaw & Sons (Salford) Ltd v. Shaw* (1935) 2 *KB* 113; *Quin & Axtens Ltd v. Salmon* [1909] *AC* 442. But *see Marshall's Valve Gear Co. v. Manning Wardle & Co.* (1909) 1 *Ch.* 267.

79. *See* Aiman Nariman Mohd-Sulaiman & Shanty Rachagan, 'Shareholder primacy, controlling shareholders and Malaysia's Companies Act 2016' Vol 17(2017) Journal of Corporate Law Studies, 203–224.

(b) Section 195(3) of the Companies Act 2015 also provides that the recommendation shall not be binding on the Board *unless the recommendation is in the best interest of the company.*[80]
(c) Section 195 also has effect in relation to the member's right to requisition a meeting.

Under the common law, there are situations where the general meeting has residual power to act for the company. This may occur when the board is unable or unwilling to act, for example, where there is a deadlock on the board. In such a case, the general meeting will be able to exercise the power of the board for the purpose of breaking the deadlock.[81]

II. Shareholder Control Mechanisms: The Shareholders' Meeting

A. *Authority of Shareholders' Meetings*

97. The general meeting of shareholders has authority to carry out certain transactions that are required by the CA or the constitution to be effected with the shareholders' approval. The decision of the shareholders must be made at a meeting of shareholders since no individual shareholder has the authority to make decisions for the company. This collective decision making is arrived at through a meeting of shareholders where certain procedures and formalities must be observed.
Types of company meetings

1. The Annual General Meeting

98. The AGM must be held by a public company:

(i) within six months of the company's financial year-end; and
(ii) not more than fifteen months after the last preceding AGM: section 340, Companies Act 2016.

However, so long as the company holds its first AGM within eighteen months after its incorporation, the company need not hold the AGM in the year of incorporation or in the following year. A general meeting may be held at any time and the company may resolve that any meeting held or summoned to be held shall be the AGM of the company.

It is possible to get an extension of time if the company makes an application to the Registrar for an extension of time in which to hold the AGM. The Registrar may,

80. The consideration given to the company's interest is reiterated in s. 311(5)(d) of the Companies Act 2016 which requires that the resolution must not be one that if passed would not be in the best interest of the company. An earlier version of the new Companies Act at public consultation stage in July 2013 did not contain these wordings.
81. *Barron v. Potter* (1914) 1 *Ch.* 895.

if he thinks it is necessary to do so, extend the period and the extended period may go beyond the calendar year. An example of an extension was the Practice Directives issued to deal with the COVID-19 impact which allowed a ninety-day extension to hold AGMs for companies with financial year-end from 30 October 2020 to 31 January 2021. The ninety-day period starts from the last day their AGMs are supposed to be held.

The usual agenda or the ordinary business for an AGM is the retirement of the directors who are required to retire by rotation, and the re-election of any of them, the appointment of the company's auditor and the remuneration of auditors and any resolution or other business of which notice is given. The company may also include any other matters to be discussed or voted upon at the AGM. These other matters are categorized as special business and unlike ordinary business, the company must ensure that notice of the special business to be discussed at the AGM must be included in the notice calling the meeting.

Notice of an AGM must be given not less than twenty-one days before the date of the meeting or any longer period as stated in the constitution, to members, directors and auditors of the company: sections 316(2)(a) & 321, Companies Act 2016. The meeting can be convened with a shorter notice than is required by the Companies Act 2016 if all the members who are entitled to attend and vote at the meeting agree to the short notice: section 316(3) Companies Act 2016.

2. Extraordinary General Meeting

99. Any other meeting of the company is known as an extraordinary general meeting (EGM) and is often convened when appropriate if the shareholders' approval is required. All matters that are to be discussed at an EGM are a special business, and notice of the matters to be discussed at an EGM must be given to all persons who are entitled to attend and vote at the EGM.

3. Class Meetings

100. These are meetings which are attended by specific groups of shareholders, of a 'class' where the approval of the class is required, for example, in relation to variation of class rights.

B. Convening of a Shareholders' Meeting

101. These are persons who may convene a company's meetings:

(i) Directors. Section 310(a), Companies Act 2016 authorizes the board to convene a meeting of members. The constitution may also confer the power to convene a general meeting on a director whenever he sees fit.

(ii) Members convening a meeting. Any member who holds not less than 10% of the company's issued capital may call a meeting of the company. In companies not having a share capital, a meeting may be called by not less than 5% of the number of members: section 310(b). The constitution cannot exclude the application of this section and any provision to that effect is invalid.

(iii)Members' requisition of a meeting. Section 311 provides that the directors must convene a general meeting of the company on the requisition of certain members of a company. A member may requisition a meeting under section 311 by making the application in writing.

The board must convene a meeting when the board receives a request from:

(i) members representing at least 10% of the paid-up capital of the company which carries voting rights, excluding any shares held as treasury shares; or
(ii) for a company not having a share capital, members representing at least 5% of the total voting rights of all members entitled to vote at general meetings;[82]
(iii) members of a private company may also rely on section 311(4), Companies Act 2016 to request the board of directors to convene a meeting of members if twelve months have elapsed from the end of a meeting of members conducted as a result of requisition under this section. The member of a private company intending to rely on this section must represent at least 5% of the issued paid-up share capital of the company carrying the right to vote at a meeting of members.

The members' requisition must state the objectives of the meeting, and it must be signed by the requisitionists and deposited at the registered office of the company. If there are two or more requisitioning members and the requisition form consist of several documents in a similar form, each document must be signed by one or more requisitionists: section 311(2) The requisitionists must wait until there has been a default by the directors to convene the meeting before exercising their power to convene a meeting themselves. The directors are given fourteen days after the deposit of the requisition to convene the meeting. If the directors agree to convene the meeting as requisitioned by the members, the meeting must be held on a date not more than twenty-eight days after the date of the notice to convene the meeting. If the directors failed to convene the meeting within this time, the requisitionists, or any of them representing more than one-half of the total voting rights of all of them, may themselves convene a meeting: section 311. The meeting that is convened by the members under this section must be held within three months from the date when the original requisition was lodged with the company. When the members who requisition the meeting are able to convene the meeting due to the failure of the company to convene the meeting as requisitioned by the members, the cost of the meeting will be borne by the company.

82. Section 311(3).

1. Notice of the Meeting

102. Notice of a meeting is to be given to all members who are entitled to attend and vote at the meeting.[83] The right of a person to be given notice of a meeting and be allowed to attend depends first on whether the person is a member of the company. For a public listed company, this may be determined by going through the register of members and the register of depositors. Normally persons who own non-voting shares, for example, preference shareholders, are not entitled to attend and vote at a general meeting as the condition of ownership does not grant them any voting rights.

103. Section 317 requires that the notice of a general meeting must state the date, time and place of the meeting, and a general summary of the business to be transacted. The notice may also include the text of the resolution or any other information that the directors deem fit. The common law provides that the business to be transacted at an AGM which is general business, i.e., the consideration of accounts and the reports of the directors and auditors, the election of directors in the place of those retiring, or the appointment and fixing of the remuneration of the auditors need not be specifically mentioned. In general, a notice of all matters to be discussed at the meeting and resolutions to be approved by shareholders must be given. The purpose of the notice is to inform the members about the matters to be discussed at the meeting so that the members may decide whether or not to attend the meeting, whether to send their representative to vote on their behalf and whether to vote in support or against the proposal or resolution. If the business that is to be transacted is not stated in the notice convening the meeting, the meeting will not be able to deliberate on the issue unless all the members who are entitled to attend and vote at the meeting agree.

If the company proposes to pass a special resolution, not less than twenty-one days' written notice must be given: section 292. An ordinary resolution only requires not less than fourteen days' notice but the constitution may provide for a longer notice period. However, a shorter notice period may be agreed upon by a majority in number of the members entitled to attend and vote being a majority which holds not less than 95% of the shares, excluding any treasury shares: section 316(4) & (5).

For an AGM, the notice period is not less than twenty-one days and the constitution may provide for a longer period. For public listed companies, the BMLR requires not less than twenty-eight days' notice. For the AGM, a shorter notice is possible with the unanimous consent of all members entitled to attend and vote at the meeting. In reality, a shorter notice period is not easily obtained for a public company because of the large number of shareholders: section 316(3).

The Companies Act 2016 also provides that notice of meeting can be issued electronically to shareholders provided the company's constitution allows for it. Section 319 states that the notice of meeting may be given personally, by post or electronically or partly in hard copy and partly electronically. Section 319(2)(b) then provides that notices of meetings to shareholders may be sent electronically either to:

---

83. Section 321(1) & (2).

(i) the email address provided by a member for that purpose; or
(ii) published on a website.

In addition, section 612(1)(c), Companies Act 2016 allows a company to communicate with its shareholders on matters relating to meetings and resolution, supply of information or documents, by *other methods agreed between the company and the members*. This is reiterated by section 612(4), Companies Act 2016 which allows a company (subject to the constitution) to determine steps and procedures that will be applicable in using any method of communication.

104. Section 317 requires that the notice of a general meeting must state the place of the meeting. This has been accepted to mean that any meeting of a public company must be a physical meeting. However, on 18 April 2020, the SC issued the Guidelines on the conduct of general meetings due to COVID-19 where public companies may conduct a fully virtual meeting or a hybrid meeting. The initial guidelines stated that SC allows up to a maximum of eight individuals to gather, including the chairperson, Chief Executive Officer (CEO), Chief Financial Officer, company secretary, auditor and those providing audiovisual support. However, subsequent guidelines are more flexible where listed companies must ensure that there is a reliable infrastructure to enable effective participation and communication with members and attendees. A hybrid general meeting is where a company conducts its meeting at a physical meeting venue with shareholders physically present, with the same meeting broadcasted online.

105. Where there is a virtual meeting, the venue of the virtual meeting must be in Malaysia where the chairperson must be at the main venue, as required under Section 327 of the Companies Act 2016.

2. Quorum

106. A meeting can only commence when there is a quorum for the meeting. The quorum for a single-member company is one and for other companies, the quorum is two unless the constitution provides for a higher number. For the purposes of making up a quorum, one or more persons attending as a proxy or representing a corporate shareholder is deemed to be one.

The quorum must be present at the start of the meeting, i.e., when the meeting proceeds to business. For virtual or hybrid meetings, the quorum includes those participating online at the virtual or hybrid meeting. If there is no quorum after half an hour after the time stated for the meeting to start, the meeting is adjourned to the same day in the next week at the same time and place, or any other day, time and place as the directors may determine. If the meeting is convened at the requisition of members and there is no quorum, the meeting is ended, i.e., dissolved.

Sometimes, the quorum requirement cannot be fulfilled due to some reasons that make fulfilling the quorum requirement impractical. In such a case, an application may be made for an appropriate court order under section 314 to direct that a meeting of members be conducted according to such terms that the court thinks fit. This includes an order that one member present in person or by proxy shall be deemed to constitute a meeting.

3. Chairman's Role

107. The meeting must be conducted by a chairman who is responsible to keep and maintain the orderly conduct of a meeting. Normally, the constitution states that the chairman of the board shall be the chairman of the company's meetings: section 329. If there is no chairman or if the chairman is not present within fifteen minutes after the time appointed for the holding of the meeting or if the chairman is unwilling to act, the meeting may appoint any one of the members of the company to chair the meeting. A proxy may also be appointed to chair the meeting by a resolution passed at the meeting itself: section 336.

The chairman owes a duty to act in the best interest of the company in exercising his powers in chairing and conducting the meeting. This duty extends to deciding on whether the meeting may be adjourned, determining whether or not to accept a demand for a voting by poll, ascertaining the outcome of a voting on a resolution, to allowing members to speak and debate at the meeting. Where the adjournment of a meeting is concerned, the constitution normally provides that a meeting may be adjourned with the consent of the general meeting unless it is unreasonable to obtain the consent of the general meeting for an adjournment. A chairman of a meeting does not have the power to stop a meeting at his own will and pleasure and cannot adjourn the meeting without the consent of the meeting.[84] The chairman's exercise of his power to adjourn the meeting may be challenged in court.[85]

If a meeting is invalidly or wrongly adjourned, the remaining members of the company at that meeting may continue to hold the meeting and any decision arrived at is binding on the company. In *Dato Mak Kok & Ors v. See Keng Leong & Ors* (1990) 1 MSCLC 90,357, a general meeting was adjourned by the chairman on his own motion. The dissenting shareholders continued the meeting after appointing a new chairman. It was decided by the court that the chairman has no power over his own motion and will to adjourn a company's meeting without the consent of the shareholders. Since the meeting was improperly adjourned, the continuation of the meeting and appointment of a new chairman by the remaining shareholders were valid.

For public companies, the Listing Requirements state that a scrutineer must be appointed to validate the votes cast. Thus, even when the meeting is conducted virtually through remote participation and voting facilities, companies must make sure that a scrutineer is appointed. The scrutineer however is not required to be present at the physical meeting venue with the chairman and may log in virtually to ensure that the meeting and voting procedures are complied with.

---

84. *Tan Guan Eng @ Tan Guan Sooi v. B.H. Low Sdn Bhd & Ors* (1991) 1 *MSCLC* 90, 720.
85. *Dato Mak Kok & Ors v. See Keng Leong & Ors* (1990) 1 *MSCLC* 90, 357.

C. Voting by Members

108. Only members who hold voting shares are allowed to vote. This will preclude preference shareholders from voting. Section 293 states that every member of a company having a share capital is entitled to one vote per share, or one vote per unit/units of stock equivalent to one share held by him, when the resolution is to be passed by way of a written resolution, or by poll or by a show of hands at a convened meeting The constitution, however, may provide that a member may have more than one vote per share: section 293. The right to vote is given to a member only and not to a person who is a shareholder but not yet registered as a member. A member is entitled to exercise the vote in situations involving the member's own interest.

Voting is normally done first by a show of hands where each member gets one vote. If voting is by poll, each member's vote is based on the number of shares the person owns unless the constitution provides for additional votes to be ascribed to the share. Joint holders of shares shall be counted as one for the purpose of voting: section 295. If there is voting by poll, a person is not required to use all his votes or cast all his votes in the same way: section 332(1).

Section 330 provides that a resolution put to vote at a meeting shall be decided on a show of hands unless a poll is demanded before or on the declaration of the result of a show of hands. For public listed companies, the BMLR provides that voting must be done by poll. Section 330(1) provides that a poll may be demanded by the following persons:

(i) by the chairman;
(ii) by at least three members present in person or by proxy;
(iii) by any member present in person or by proxy and representing not less than 10% of the total voting rights of all the members having the right to vote at the meeting; or
(iv) by a member holding shares in the company conferring a right to vote at the meeting being shares on which an aggregate sum has been paid up equal to not less than 10% of the total paid-up shares conferring that right.

The constitution cannot restrict the right of these persons to demand a poll by providing for more restrictive conditions or requirements. Section 331 provides that any provision in a company's constitution is void to the extent that it has the effect of excluding or making ineffective the right to demand a poll at a general meeting by the following persons:

(i) at least five members having the right to vote;
(ii) by a member (or members) representing 10% of all the votes excluding treasury shares;
(iii) by members holding shares (conferring a right to vote) which, on the aggregate of the sums paid up, equal not less than 10% of the total sum paid up on all shares conferring a voting right.

The demand for a poll can also be made on all matters to be decided at a meeting. The constitution cannot restrict matters on which a demand for a poll may be made except in relation to the election of a chairman or the adjournment of the meeting. Any provision in a company's constitution is void to the extent that it has the effect of excluding the right to demand a poll at a general meeting on any question or matter other than the election of a chairman or the adjournment of the meeting: section 331(b). When a poll is demanded, it must be taken forthwith or after an interval or after an adjournment or otherwise as the chairman directs. However, where a poll is demanded on the election of a chairman or on a question of adjournment of the meeting, it must be taken forthwith: section 332(2).

Section 330(2) states that unless a poll is demanded, the declaration by the chairman that a resolution has on a show of hands been carried, or carried unanimously or by a particular majority (or lost), and an entry to that effect in the Minute Book should be conclusive evidence of the fact without proof of the number or proportion of the votes recorded in favour of or against the resolution. The minutes of the company's meetings must be signed by the chairperson of that meeting or the chairperson of the next meeting. Once signed, it is sufficient evidence of the proceedings of that meeting: section 343(3), Companies Act 2016. Unless the contrary is proved, the record of the proceedings of a meeting of members is also evidence that:

(i) the meeting has been duly convened;
(ii) all proceedings have been duly taken place; and
(iii) all appointments at the meeting are duly made: section 343(4), Companies Act 2016.

Every company must keep records comprising:

(i) all resolutions passed otherwise than at a meeting of members. This applies to the outcome of written resolutions;
(ii) minutes of all proceedings of members' meetings, including class meetings. Minutes of proceedings will include resolutions proposed and decisions on these resolutions;
(iii) details provided to the company in relation to a decision made by a sole member: section 341, Companies Act 2016.

In some cases, the constitution of a company provides that in the case of an equality of votes whether on a show of hands or on a poll, the chairman of the meeting shall be entitled to a second or casting vote. Without this clause, the chairman does not have a casting vote in common law.

D. Voting by Proxy and Eligibility to be Appointed as Proxy

109. Section 334 ensures that a member who is entitled to attend and vote at a meeting of the company or at a meeting of any class of members of the company, is able to appoint his representative or proxy to vote on his behalf and exercise all the rights of a member to attend, participate, speak and vote at a meeting of members. The former CA 1965 identified persons who may be appointed as proxy and unless the constitution allows, no other person may be appointed as proxy. Under the former CA 1965, the persons who may be appointed as proxies are:

(i) a member of the company;
(ii) an approved auditor; or
(iii) an advocate and solicitor.

The former CA 1965 is quite restrictive in relation to the persons who may be appointed as proxies. However, the CA 2016 has removed this restriction and a member is entitled to appoint any person as proxy: section 334. A member may appoint more than one person as a proxy provided the member determines the proportion of votes that may be exercised by each proxy. If more than one proxy is appointed and the resolution is to be voted on by a show of hands, the proxies are prohibited from voting. However, since a proxy may exercise the right to demand voting by poll as provided by section 337, this restriction from voting by show of hands can be circumvented by the proxies demanding a poll in accordance with section 331.

E. The Proxy Form

110. Section 335 requires that a statement of the right to appoint proxies must appear 'with reasonable prominence' on every notice convening a meeting of a company or of any class of members of a company and must state that a member entitled to attend and vote is entitled to appoint a proxy to attend and vote instead of the member. The Listing Requirement requires that proxy forms of listed companies must be a 'two-way' proxy form that clearly indicates whether the proxy may vote for or against a resolution. However, the member who appoints a proxy need not indicate whether the proxy is to vote for or against the resolution. Nonetheless, if there was an express instruction for the proxy to vote one way in the proxy appointment form and this instruction was not followed, the votes cast by the proxy are spoilt votes.[86]

Section 334(3) provides for the method of appointment. The proxy may be appointed by an instrument appointing a proxy, i.e., the proxy form.[87] A proxy may also be appointed by power of attorney or other authority. The proxy form or power of attorney or other authority must be signed or a notarially certified copy of the

86. *Tong Keng Meng v. Inno-Pacific Holdings Ltd & Anor* (2002) *MSCLC* 97,532.

87. Article 60 of Table A gives an example of the proxy appointment form '[*Name of company*] I/we, __________, of __________, being a member/members of the above-named company, hereby appoint __________ of __________ or, in his absence, __________ *annual general of __________ as my/our proxy to vote for me/us on my/our behalf at the __________ *extraordinary general meeting of the company to be held on the __________ day of __________ __________ and at any adjournment of that meeting. This form is to be used *in favour of The resolution. *against Signed this __________ day of ____________________. * *Strike out whichever is not desired.* [Unless otherwise instructed, the proxy may vote as he thinks fit.]'.

power of attorney or other authority must be deposited at the registered office of the company or at such other place within Malaysia that is specified in the notice of the meeting. Where attestation is required, the court has decided that a proxy holder cannot be the witness to his own proxy form.[88] The important criterion is that the proxy form must be complied with in substance. Thus, non-compliance with the form which is merely trivial or insignificant will not invalidate the form.[89]

A person who may be appointed as proxy may solicit an appointment from the members of the company. It is usual for directors to solicit for appointment as proxy and they may do so at the company's expense if this is done bona fide in the interests of the company. However, if proxies are solicited at the company's expense, the invitation must be sent to all persons entitled to be sent a notice of the meeting and to vote by proxy: section 335(2). This does not prevent the company from sending to individuals, upon their request, proxy appointment forms naming the proxy.

F. Invalid Proxy

111. The Chairman has the discretion to refuse to accept the proxy form on the basis that the proxy is invalid but the Chairman's decision may be challenged in court.[90] A proxy form may be rejected if it does not comply with the method of appointment stated under section 334(3). The proxy form may also be rejected if not submitted within time. Section 334(3) states that instruments appointing proxies must be deposited at the registered office (or some other specified place within Malaysia as stated in the notice of the meeting) not less than forty-eight hours before the time of the relevant meeting or adjourned meeting (in the case of a poll, not less than twenty-four hours before the time appointed for the taking of the poll). A proxy may also be invalid if the person appointed as a proxy could not have been validly appointed as proxy because of his own ineligibility or if the appointor/member is not eligible to vote. If the method of appointment or the time to deposit the instrument appointing the proxy is not complied with, the proxy is invalid: section 334(3).

The member may also revoke the appointment of a proxy but the company must be informed prior to the start of a meeting for which the proxy is appointed: section 338. If notice is not given prior to the start of the meeting, the termination of the authority of the person acting as proxy has no effect on the constitution of the quorum of the meeting. In addition, the person can also continue as chairperson and the exercise of powers as chairman is not affected by the termination of the authority. Furthermore, the termination of authority also has no effect on the validity of a poll demanded by the proxy or on the validity of the vote which he exercised. The Constitution may provide that the notice of termination can be sent to a person other

---

88. *Re Parrott*, Ex parte *Cullen* (1891) 2 *Q.B.* 151 *Re Parrott*, Ex parte *Cullen* (1891) 2 *Q.B.* 151.
89. In *ANZ Nominees Limited v. Allied Resources Corporation Limited & Ors* (1984) 2 *ACLC* 783, a proxy form which omitted the day of the month on which it was signed was found *not* to be invalid because such an omission was considered trivial, unimportant for any relevant purpose at the meeting and not sufficient to disenfranchise a member of the company.
90. *Tan Guan Eng @ Tan Guan Sooi v. B.H. Low Sdn Bhd & Ors* (1991) 1 *MSCLC* 90,720.

than the company. However, the constitution cannot require for the notice of termination to be received by the company earlier than forty-eight hours before the time of holding the meeting: section 338(4).

G. Grounds for Challenging the Decision of a General Meeting

112. The decision of the general meeting is binding if the decision relates to matters which are within the general meeting's authority and provided the procedure for convening and conducting the meeting has been complied with. While there is no specific statutory provision under the CA 2016 stating that the general meeting's decision may be challenged in court, the dissenting shareholders of a company may bring an action in court to obtain an injunction against the company from proceeding with a transaction that has been decided at a general meeting on the basis that the decision of the meeting was not validly made. The shareholders may apply to the court to declare that the decision of the general meeting is not binding due to its defective nature.

113. The challenge to the decision of the meeting is often brought by the dissenting shareholders or shareholders who have been affected by the defect in procedure, for example, where the shareholders have not been informed of the meeting. The petitioner must have a legitimate interest in the action.

114. Defect in procedure. There are procedures for convening and conducting a meeting as stated above and any defect or failure to comply with the procedure as stated in the CA or the constitution will make the meeting invalid and any decision made or resolution passed at the meeting is also invalid. However, the company may apply to the court under section 582 to decide that the defect should not affect the validity of the meeting. The court will only do so if the failure does not cause or result in any substantial injustice to any of the shareholders. The irregularity or non-compliance with the formal requirements of a meeting must not be deliberate. An example is if the company has unintentionally or accidentally omitted to inform some members of a meeting or where the company carries on a meeting when there is an insufficient quorum. In such cases, the members who have not been informed of the meeting may challenge the holding of the meeting and if the members do so, the meeting may be declared void unless the company or any interested parties or the court on its own motion makes an earlier application under section 582 to regularize the defect. Defect in procedure may also give rise to an action under section 346 where there is oppression.

115. Defect in authority. Where the general meeting or the class meeting does not have the authority to decide on a particular matter or resolution, the result of the meeting is not binding. This often involves situations where the matter that is discussed at the general meeting is outside the scope of authority of a general meeting, for example, in situations where the Companies Act of 2016 and the constitution confer authority to decide on these matters to the board of directors. Where the shareholders requisition a meeting, the directors need not comply with the request to convene a meeting if the requisition relates to a matter which the general meeting has no authority to decide. Defect in authority cannot be regularized under section 582 because this is not a mere irregularity. However, it is possible for the board to concede to the decision of the meeting and agree to be bound by the general meeting's decision.

116. Defect in the voting required to pass a resolution. Where the company passes a resolution but the necessary percentage of votes required to pass the resolution is not obtained, the meeting itself is valid (provided the formal procedures are complied with) although the resolution is not. This defect cannot be regularized under section 582.

H. Majority Rule: Legal and Statutory Protection of Minority and Majority

1. The Oppression Remedy

117. Interpretation of the section. Section 346 provides a statutory remedy against the conduct of the company or the directors of the company which is oppressive, unfairly prejudicial or unfairly discriminatory against the member or members or debenture holders.

Section 346(1)(a) provides that a member or a debenture holder of a company may apply to the court where the affairs of the company or the powers of its directors are being exercised in a manner oppressive to or in disregard of their interests.

Section 346(1)(b) provides that a member or a debenture holder may apply to the court where he believes that an act of the company or a resolution passed by a class of members is unfairly discriminatory or otherwise prejudicial.

While the wording of the first limb seems to suggest that there may be a need for the oppressive conduct to still continue at the time the application is made, this is not a true interpretation of the section. Discussing section 181 of the former CA 1965 which is in *pari materia* with section 346, CA 2016, in *Re Kong Thai Sawmill (Miri) Sdn Bhd*,[91] the Privy Council was of the view that the oppressive conduct must still be occurring when the application under section 181(1)(a) was made. Thus in this case, although the directors had utilized the company's funds for their own use, the oppression remedy was not granted as the money had been returned. However, this view has been found wanting in subsequent decisions of the Malaysian court. In *Owen Sim Liang Khui v. Piasau Jaya Sdn Bhd*,[92] the Malaysian court has confined the decision in *Re Kong Thai Sawmills*, by saying that the decision of Lord Wilberforce was merely a guideline. Thus, the prevailing view is that it does not matter whether the conduct complained about is still continuing so long as the

91. (1950–1985) *MSCLC* 14; (1978) 2 *MLJ* 227.
92. (1996) 1 *MLJ* 113.

effect of the oppressive conduct still persists at the time of presentation.[93] The section may also be relied on where the conduct has occurred or which is anticipated or proposed.

118. Section 346 is often referred to as the oppression remedy. 'Oppression', 'disregard of members' interest', 'unfairly prejudicial conduct' or 'unfairly discriminatory conduct' have been defined as conduct that is 'burdensome, harsh and wrongful' or displays a 'lack of probity and fair dealing'.[94]

In *Re Kong Thai Sawmill (Miri) Sdn Bhd*, Lord Wilberforce in this Privy Council decision said that:

> [T]here must be a visible departure from the standards of fair dealing and a violation of the conditions of fair play which a shareholder is entitled to expect before a case of oppression can be made … 'disregard' involves something more than a failure to take account of the minority's interest: there must be awareness of that interest and an evident decision to override it or brush it aside or to set at naught the proper company procedure … What is attacked by [the remedy] is not particular acts but the manner in which the affairs of the company are being conducted or the powers of the directors exercised. And these may be held to be 'oppressive' or 'in disregard' even though a particular objectionable act may have been remedied. A last minute correction by the majority may well leave open a finding that, as shown by its conduct over a period, a firm tendency or propensity still exists at the time of the proceedings to oppress the minority or to disregard its interests so calling for a remedy.

119. Remedy available to a member or a debenture holder. The minority shareholder must have suffered harm in his capacity as shareholder.[95] A petitioner must be a member and his name must appear on the register of members or register of depositors: section 345(a). Accordingly, relief will not be granted where a petition is presented by a member of the company's creditor or shareholder of a creditor.[96] A person who has sold his shares prior to bringing the action will not be allowed to bring the petition under section 346. However, it is arguable that a person who is no longer a shareholder due to alleged oppressive conduct, for example, if the shares have been wrongfully forfeited or fraudulently transferred, may be allowed to bring the action: 345(b).[97] Although the section allows a debenture holder to rely on the oppression remedy, there have been no reported judicial decisions on a debenture holder bringing an action under the oppression remedy. Generally, a debenture holder will rely on the rights given under the debenture to obtain relief and this is likely to involve the right to appoint a receiver and to sell the assets used as security for the debt.

---

93. In the Matter of Asahi Metal Pte Ltd; *see Soon Lee @ Kho Soon Lee v. Gan Cheong Or & Ors* (1995) 4 *MSCLC* 96,317.
94. *Scottish Co-operative Wholesale Society Ltd v. Meyer* (1959) *AC* 324.
95. *Re a Company* (1983) *Ch.* 178.
96. *Verghese Mathai v. Telok Plantations Sdn Bhd* (1988) 1 *MSCLC* 90,122.
97. *Owen Sim Liang Khui v. PiasauJaya Sdn Bhd* (1996) 1 *MLJ* 113.

120. Example of oppression: non-payment of dividends. Although there is no obligation on the directors of the company to recommend the distribution of dividends, the members can apply for the oppression remedy if the company has been making profits for several years but no dividends have been distributed or where dividends are not distributed but the directors have obtained excessive compensation or benefit.[98] The court will also grant the remedy if the company which is controlled by the directors do not pay dividends to maintain control of the company. In *Re SQ Wong Holdings*,[99] the directors who were the preference shareholders declared dividends but did not pay themselves the dividend. They held the majority of the issued shares. This was to ensure that they as preference shareholders have voting rights and as a result would be able to vote at the general meeting against the resolution to remove them as directors. This conduct prevented the ordinary shareholders from removing them and entrenched them on the board.

Example of oppression: Refusal of the right to vote or oppressive conduct in board or members' meetings. Since all members have the right to be informed of company meetings to attend and vote, any deliberate attempt to prevent members from exercising these rights amounts to oppression.[100] The fact that a member is outvoted at a general meeting does not mean that there is oppression. The oppression remedy cannot be used when there are differences of opinion in the way a company is managed.[101] Where the conduct of a meeting is concerned, the manner in which the meeting was conducted may amount to oppression, for example, if important and significant matters were not notified to members of the meeting or if the powers of a director in relation to the meeting have been exercised in an improper manner.[102]

Example of oppression: Directors' conduct not in the best interests of the company. Where directors have breached their duty or exercised their powers in breach of their duty, the members may make an application for the oppression remedy. Most of the application for a derivative action normally involves a breach of duty, for example, where there is a diversion of company business.[103] Section 346(1)(a) provides that the remedy is available where the directors act in disregard of the members' remedy.[104] The refusal by the company or directors to provide members access to financial records and documents of a company in relation to a particular transaction has been held to amount to oppression.[105]

121. Orders that the court may make. Section 346(2) specifies the types of orders that the court may make. These orders are discretionary and are as follows:

98. *Re Coliseum Stand Car Service Ltd* 9 (1972) 1 *MLJ* 109.
99. (1987) *MLJ* 298.
100. *Lim Hean Pin v. Thean Seng Co. Sdn Bhd* (1992) 2 *MLJ* 10.
101. *Dato Toh Kian Chuanv wee Construction & Transport Company (Malaya) Sdn Bhd* (1996) 1 *MLJ* 730.
102. *Khoo Choon Yam v. Gan Miew Chee* (2000) 3 *AMR* 3074.
103. *Scottish Co-operative Wholesale Society Ltd v. Meyer* (1959) *AC* 324, approved by *Owen Sim Liang Khui v. PiasauJaya Sdn Bhd* (1996) 1 *MLJ* 113; Re *Bright Pines Mills Pty Ltd* [1969] *VR* 1002.
104. *Edmund Charles Liebenberg v. ICB-Griffin Manufacturing Sdn Bhd & Ors* (2005) 3 *CLJ* 613.
105. *Chiew Size Sun v. Cast Iron Products Sdn Bhd* (1994) 1 *CLJ* 157; *Shum Yip Properties Development Ltd v. Chatswood Investment & Development Co. Pty Ltd & Ors* (2002) *NSWSC* 13.

(a) direct or prohibit any act or cancel or vary any transaction or resolution;
(b) regulate the company's affairs in the future;
(c) order the purchase of the shares by other members of the company or by the company itself;
(d) provide for a reduction of capital in the case of a purchase of shares by the company itself; and
(e) order that the company be wound up. If a winding-up order is made, the winding-up provisions of the Act apply as if the order had been made on the company's own petition.

Section 346(2)(a) and (b) are very wide in scope and enable the court to declare that a resolution which results in oppressive conduct be cancelled.[106] In *Re HR Harmer Ltd*,[107] the founder of a company managed the company without consulting the other members or the other directors and the court gave an order to restrain the founder from exercising any powers in the management of the company although he was allowed to remain as president of the company for life. In *Chiew Size Sun v. Cast Iron Products Sdn Bhd*,[108] there was mismanagement of company's affairs, delay in tabling the unaudited accounts, and no proper accounting records were kept by the company. There was also tax mismanagement due to the delay in the preparation of inadequate accounts which resulted in the company having to pay additional assessment rates and a tax penalty. The court held that there was oppression and the order for a company auditor to examine the records and prepare reports for shareholders was granted. The court allowed the application that an approved company auditor (other than the present auditor) be appointed to examine the accounts and records of the company from incorporation and to prepare proper accounts and a report for the shareholders for the purpose of evaluation of the company's assets. The costs for the examination and preparation of the company's accounts and records were to be borne by the company. Once this had been done the directors of the company were to purchase the shares of the petitioners in equal proportion.

122. Section 346(2)(c) dealing with an order to purchase the minority shareholding is the most sought-after remedy. Where the court makes an order for the purchase of the shares, the issue of evaluation becomes very important. The proper approach to evaluation is by considering what would have been the value of the shares at the commencement of the proceedings had it not been for the effect of the oppressive conduct of which the complaint was made.[109] It has been held in *Planeta Tullio v. Andrea G Maoro*[110] that the shares of an oppressed minority shareholder be repurchased at the price at which he first purchased them at the time of judgment, the company was inactive and the actual net value of the shares was much lower than the price at which the appellant first purchased them. The appellant, the minority shareholder, appealed for a variation in the order for the sale of the shares.

106. *Re Chi Liung & Sons; Tong Chong Fah v. Tong Lee Hwa & Ors* (1968) 1 *MLJ* 97.
107. (1958) 3 *All ER* 689.
108. (1994) 1 *CLJ* 157.
109. *Scottish Co-operative Wholesale Society Ltd v. Meyer* (1959) *AC* 324.
110. (1994) 4 *MSCLC* 96,093.

The trial judge had ordered that the shares be purchased from the appellant at their net value at the time of judgment. The Court of Appeal allowed the variation of the order. It held that the shares should be purchased at the same price at which the appellant first bought them. The court said that the value at which the shares ought to be repurchased should be fair to the particular case. Here, at the time of judgment, the company was inactive and the actual net value of the shares was much lower than the price at which the appellant first purchased them. The court also believed that there was evidence that after the appellant was excluded from the company, the respondent could have undermined the assets of the company by creating false trading. On the whole, valuing the shares at the date of judgment would not be fair to the appellant.

An order to wind up the company under section 346(2)(e) is a remedy of last resort and normally the court will not make this order if the company is a going concern and profitable.[111]

2. The Statutory Derivative Action

123. A derivative action is taken by a minority shareholder who wants to enforce the company's rights against the person who has committed a wrong against the company. In general, once a company is incorporated, the effect of incorporation is that a company has separate legal entity and can sue and be sued in its own name. This means that the company has the authority to decide whether or not to sue to enforce its rights. This is known as the 'proper plaintiff rule' as laid down in *Foss v. Harbottle*[112] which is that the proper plaintiff for a wrong done to the company is the company itself. If the actions of the directors of the company constitute a wrong to the company, it is the company that should take action against the directors and not the individual shareholder. This is a result of the company being a separate legal entity. However, the common law provides an exception to this rule under the derivative action. Under the common law, the derivative action allows a minority shareholder to bring an action to enforce the company's rights on behalf of the company. This exception is created by the courts because 'the company who has been wronged is unable to sue because the wrongdoers are themselves in control of its decision-making organs and will not, for that reason, permit an action to be brought in its name'.[113]

The minority shareholder has to fulfil the following criteria before he will be allowed to bring an action on behalf of the company against a wrongdoer under the common law:

(i) The wrongdoers must be in control of the company, and control was generally inferred from the fact that they held a majority of the votes.

111. *Hoy Pak Kwai v. Leong Kon Fah & Ors* (2005) 5 *CLJ* 179.
112. (1843) 2 *Hare* 461.
113. *Abdul Rahim b Akin v. Krubong Industrial Park (Melaka) Sdn Bhd* (1994) 4 *CLJ* 551.

However, in *Prudential Assurance Co. Ltd v. Newman Industries Ltd & Ors* (No. 2),[114] the court acknowledges that a person who is not a majority shareholder may have de facto control of the company. In this case, two directors of Newman deceitfully induced other members of the company to vote in favour of acquiring the assets of a company (Gladstone) in which they were personally interested in a gross overvaluation. The action was allowed to proceed even though the two directors did not possess a majority shareholding in Newman Industries. The fact that there is equality in the shareholding of a company does not prevent one shareholder from bringing a derivative action event.[115]

If the decision not to sue was made by the independent shareholders who are not under the control of the wrongdoer, the court will not allow individual/minority shareholders to bring a derivative action.[116]

(ii) The wrongdoer obtained benefit at the company's expense.

(iii) The wrongdoer prevents the company from enforcing its right. However, there is no requirement to show that there was a positive act by the wrongdoer to prevent the action. If the wrongdoer has control over the company, this element of control is sufficient to enable the court to allow the action as it is very likely that the wrongdoer will exercise his control to prevent the company from suing him.

Under the common law derivative action, judicial decisions have stated that the company must be joined in the action and is made a nominal defendant so that any decision will also bind the company.[117] Procedurally, the action is known as a representative action as the members who are making the application is acting as a representative of the company and other members.[118] Judgment is given in favour of the company. The company may be ordered to indemnify the shareholder acting on its behalf for his legal costs in the action if it is a reasonable and prudent course to take in the circumstances.[119]

124. The right of a member to sue on behalf of the company is also recognized by the Companies Act of 2016. Section 347 provides for the statutory derivative action. This was introduced by the Companies (Amendment) Act 2007 into the former CA 1965. The amendment enables a minority shareholder to rely on section 347 to bring an action on behalf of the company. The Companies Act 2016 also abrogates the right of a member to bring an action on behalf of the company under the common law. The Companies Act 2016 replaces the rule under the former CA 1965 which allows a minority shareholder to also rely on the common law to sue on behalf of the company in addition to the statutory derivative action.

---

114. (1980) 2 *All ER* 841.
115. *Ting Choong Maa v. Chow Sek Choon* (1989) 1 *MLJ* 477.
116. *Paidiah Genganaidu v. Lower Syndicate Sdn Bhd* (174) 1 *MLJ* 220.
117. *Abdul Rahim b Akin v. Krubong Industrial Park (Melaka) Sdn Bhd* (1994) 4 *CLJ* 551; *Chio Tan Seng & Ors v. Chong Chai Huat & Ors* (1997) 4 *CLJ* Supp 16.
118. O 15, r. 12 of the Rules of the High Court.
119. *Wallersteiner v. Moir* (No. 2) (1975) 1 *All ER* 849.

Section 346 of the CA 2016 allows a member of the company, a former member who ceases to be a member due to oppressive conduct, a director or the Registrar to apply to the court for leave to bring an action, intervene or defend an action on behalf of the company. The applicant must give thirty days' notice in writing to the company informing the company of the intention to apply for leave of the court. Once the leave has been granted under section 347, the petitioner must file the proceedings or the action, i.e., suing the wrongdoers, must be initiated in court within thirty days from the grant of the leave. This is done by lodging a statement of claim against the wrongdoer and serving the statement of claim to the wrongdoers. Section 347 is merely an application for leave to sue on behalf of the company. The actual legal action will be brought subsequent to the leave being given by the court. This means that when an application is made under section 347, there is no requirement to bring evidence or witnesses as these will be done at the full hearing of the case.

Where the action which has been initiated is to be discontinued, compromised or settled, the leave of the court must also be obtained. Proceedings brought under section 346 must be brought in the company's name.

In deciding whether or not to grant leave, the court must consider whether:

(i) the applicant is acting in good faith; and
(ii) it appears prima facie to be in the best interest of the company that the application for leave be granted.

The court also has the authority to make the following orders that it thinks appropriate such as:

(i) authorizing the applicant or any other person to control the conduct of the proceedings;
(ii) giving directions for the conduct of the proceedings;
(iii) for any person to provide assistance and information to the applicant, including to allow inspection of books;
(iv) requiring the company to pay reasonable legal fees incurred by the applicant; and
(v) an order as to costs.

3. Enforcing the Provisions in the Constitutional Documents

125. Once the company has been incorporated and if the company has a constitution, the constitution becomes a binding contract as between the members amongst themselves and between the members and the company.[120] The members and the company must comply with the contents of the constitution. A member is not entitled to argue that he is not bound by the terms in the constitution that were included in these documents before he became a member. The constitution has the

120. Sections 31(2) and 33.

effect of a valid binding document on all members and on the company as if these were signed by each member. Once a person becomes a member of a company, all the terms in the constitution will be enforceable and binding by and against him.[121] If there is any failure to comply with the terms of the constitution, the company or the members may enforce compliance by obtaining a mandatory or prohibitory injunction as a remedy.[122] Sometimes, the constitution may contain a provision that relates to an outsider. This fact does not confer on the outsider a remedy to obtain an injunction to enforce compliance with the constitution as the constitution is not a contractual document between the company or the members with the outsider.[123]

4. Conflict Resolution: Compulsory Sale or Acquisition of Shares

126. A shareholder may be able to obtain an order from the court for an order that the majority shareholders or the company acquires the petitioner's shares under section 346. This is not a stand-alone provision but can only be exercised when there are grounds for the court to decide that there was oppressive conduct. There is no statutory provision that enables a shareholder to request the company or a majority shareholder to acquire his shares except under section 346. However, the terms of the constitution may contain such a right, especially in relation to private companies. These exit rights must be expressly provided in the constitution.

I. Annual Account and Report; Profits and Dividends

1. Financial Statements

127. Under section 257, any members who are entitled to receive notice of general meetings of the company are also entitled to be sent a copy of the financial statements and the reports required under the Companies Act of 2016. The financial statements refer to the company's profit and loss accounts, the balance sheets, the Directors' report, the Auditors' report and any accompanying notes and statements to the accounts, including group accounts, if applicable.

128. These must also be circulated to:

(i) every person who is entitled to receive notice of general meetings;
(ii) every auditor of the company; and
(iii) every debenture holder of the company on a request being made to the company.

For newly incorporated companies, the circulation is within eighteen months from the date of a company's incorporation. Subsequently, for a public company, it

121. *Hickman v. Kent or Romney Masrh Sheepbreeders' Association* (1915) 1 *Ch.* 881.
122. *Salmon v. Quin & Axtens Ltd* (1909) 1 *Ch.* 311.
123. *Raffles Hotel Ltd v. Malayan Banking Berhad* (No. 2) (1965) 1 *MLJ* 262.

must be circulated at least twenty-one days before the date of its AGM: section 258(2), CA 2016.[124] However, the financial statements and reports may be circulated for a shorter period if it was agreed by all the members entitled to attend and vote at the AGM. The financial statements for a public company must be laid before an AGM under section 340, CA 2016.

Section 259, CA 2016 also requires a public company to lodge with the Registrar for each financial year the financial statements and reports within thirty days from its AGM. This applies to consolidated financial statements and reports in cases of holding companies. An extension of the period may be granted by the Registrar if an application is made before the expiry of the statutory period stated under section 259, CA 2016. A public listed company must also submit to the SC a copy of the audited annual accounts within two weeks from the date of its AGM.[125] The public listed company must also comply with the BMLR whereby it must issue its annual audited accounts within four months after its financial year-end.

To assist companies during the COVID-19 pandemic, CCM has issued a Practice Directive which is applicable on a temporary basis allowing a public company a one-month extension for circulation and lodgement of financial statements and reports.

129. The company accounts must present a true and fair view of the company's affairs to the shareholders. Where the company accounts do not show a true and fair view, the directors of the company are obliged to add to the accounts such information and explanations as will provide a true and fair view.

The financial statements of a public company to be laid before the general meeting must comply with section 244, CA 2016 which states that approved accounting standards are to be applied in relation to any financial statements of a company or to the consolidated financial statements of a holding company in Malaysia and of overseas subsidiaries and associated corporations where those accounts are to be incorporated in consolidated accounts in Malaysia. The approved accounting standard provides standards that a company must apply to measure and determine profit and loss and assets and liabilities of a company. Approved accounting standards mean new standards issued by the Malaysian Accounting Standards Board (MASB) and existing standards adopted by the MASB. In relation to foreign companies listed on a stock exchange in Malaysia, the financial statements must be prepared in accordance with acceptable internationally recognized accounting standards.

The financial statements must be accompanied by a statement by the directors in accordance with the resolution of the Board stating whether in their opinion the financial statements or, where applicable, the consolidated financial statements is or are drawn up, in accordance with the applicable accounting standards, to give a true and fair view of the financial position and financial performance of the company and of the group. This statement must be signed by at least two directors: section 251, CA 2016.

124. *See* the former s. 170(1), CA 1965 which stated that these must be sent at least fourteen days before the company annual general meeting.

125. Section 319(1)(a), CMSA 2007.

In some situations, following the approved accounting standards will not give a true and fair view of the business and the state of affairs of the company.

If the directors are of the opinion that following the approved accounting standards will not give a true and fair view of the business and the state of affairs of the company and of the companies dealt with in the consolidated financial statements, the directors must disclose by way of a note on the financial statements the reason for not making out the financial statements or consolidated financial statements in accordance with the approved accounting standards. The particulars in the note of the quantified financial effect on the financial statements or consolidated financial statements if the relevant approved accounting standards were complied with must also be given: section 244(4), CA 2016.

A director who attends a board meeting and votes in favour of the making of the directors' statement which is false or misleading in any way is deemed to have authorized the making of that statement and will be guilty of an offence. If an intention to deceive can be established, the director will also be guilty of furnishing a false and misleading statement to the shareholders: section 591.

130. Accounting records. Section 245 requires every company to keep accounting records which sufficiently explain the transactions and financial position of the company with accuracy. The accounting records must be kept in such a way as to enable:

(a) true and fair financial statements of the company to be prepared from time to time; and
(b) the financial statements to be conveniently and properly audited in accordance with the provisions of the Act.

The appropriate entries must be made in the accounting records within sixty days of the completion of the transactions to which they relate: section 245(2). The statutory period specified for a company to retain its accounting records is seven years after the completion of the transactions to which they relate: section 245(3). These records must be kept at the registered office and these must be made available to the directors for inspection. For operations outside Malaysia, the records may be kept outside Malaysia but these must be sent and kept in Malaysia and be made available to directors for their inspection at all times. The Court may order that these records be open for inspection by an approved auditor acting on behalf of a director subject to a written undertaking that the information acquired by the auditor is only for the use of the director: section 245(8).

131. System of internal control. The directors of a public company or a subsidiary of a public company must ensure that the company has a system of internal control. The company is required to report on the state of internal control in the annual report.[126] The statement should include sufficient and meaningful information as

126. Paragraph 15.26(b), BMLR and Bursa Malaysia Practice Note 9 and Guidance Note 11. Task Force on Internal Control 'Statement on Risk Management and Internal Control: Guidelines for Directors of Listed Issuers' (December 2012).

needed by shareholders to make an informed assessment of the main features and adequacy of the company's risk management and internal control system. A public listed company must ensure that the external auditors review a statement made by the board of directors regarding the state of internal control of the company and report the results to the board of directors.

132. If the company is a holding company, the directors are bound to have made out consolidated accounts dealing with:

(a) the profit or loss of the company and its subsidiaries for their respective last financial years; and
(b) the state of affairs of the company and its subsidiaries as at the end of their respective last financial years: section 249(2).

The accounting records and the consolidated accounts must be prepared in accordance with the approved accounting standards: section 166A. The directors of the company must ensure that the accounts/consolidated accounts laid before the company at its AGM comply with the applicable approved accounting standards: section 244.

For the purpose of the preparation of the consolidated accounts, the holding company shall have the power to request all relevant information from its subsidiaries to secure compliance with the Companies Act of 2016: section 250(4).

The CA 2016 states that any director who has failed to comply with the requirement to present the annual accounts to the general meeting may be liable for an offence. A company may also be fined for failing to file its annual return.

2. Registers

133. The CA 2016 specifies several registers that must be kept and maintained by each company and are available to shareholders for inspection. Shareholders also have access to company minutes and the minute book under section 342. Under this section, any member can inspect the books containing the minutes of proceedings of any general meeting at the company's registered office.

134. Other registers that must be kept and maintained by a company and are accessible by members are the register of directors, managers and secretaries, register of director's shareholdings and register of debenture holders and copies of trust deed.

3. Inspection Rights

135. The CA 2016 gives a general right of inspection of any 'register, minute book or document of a corporation' that is required to be kept under the Act. The former CA 1965 contained a clause, i.e., Article 97 of Table A which could still be found in a company's constitution. Article 97 of Table A stated that:

> The directors shall cause proper accounting and other records to be kept and shall distribute copies of the balance sheets and other documents as required by the Act and shall from time to time determine whether and to what extent and at what times and places and under what conditions or regulations the accounting and other records of the company or any of them shall be open to the inspection of members not being directors, and no member (not being a director) shall have any right of inspecting any account or book or paper of the company except as conferred by statute or authorized by the directors or by the company in a general meeting.

Where the company or the directors refuse to provide members access to financial records and documents of a company in relation to a particular transaction, this has been held to amount to oppression.[127]

III. Administration and Management of the Company

A. *The Board of Directors*

1. Appointment and Dismissal of the Director

136. Number of directors. Every public company is required to have at least two directors who are natural persons of full age.[128] These directors must have their principal or only place of residence within Malaysia. The constitution may specify the maximum number of directors for the company.

---

127. *See Shum Yip Properties Development Ltd v. Chatswood Investment & Development Co. Pty Ltd & Ors* (2002) *NSWSC* 13. The court identified the basis of the petitioner's right to corporate information:

    (a) In its capacity as a shareholder who is given right of inspection by statute to inspect registers that *Chatswood Investment & Development Co* (CIDC) was required to keep including the register of member (s. 173), minutes books for members' meetings (s. 251B) and to receive financial reports each year (s. 314).
    (b) However, the member has no right of access to detailed information about income and expenses beyond those stated in the company's financial statements and reports. Nonetheless, Shum Yip has the right to apply to the court under 247A for an order authorizing the inspection of any 'books' of the company, 'widely defined to include ledgers and documents of prime entry such as invoices and receipts' provided the court was satisfied that Shum Yip was acting in good faith and the inspection was for a proper purpose.
    (c) The right to inspect exercisable through Shum Yip's representative on the board of CIDC to have access to financial records and the company's books including minutes of directors' meetings.
    (d) The right under common law as a joint venturer to full information of the business and affairs of the company.

    The court then held that failure to provide information to a minority is capable of constituting a case of oppression of the minority.
128. Section 122(1).

137. Appointment. The persons who are named as the first directors of the company in the registration form must indicate their consent to the appointment. Section 205(3) provides that at the first AGM of a public company, all the directors must retire from office although they may be re-elected. Subsequent directors are appointed by the shareholders at a general meeting. Subsequent directors may also be appointed by the board if the constitution confers on the board the power to appoint additional directors or to fill in a casual vacancy arising out of the death or resignation or bankruptcy of an existing director. However, if the board appoints a director as a result of casual vacancy, the person appointed remains as a director until the next AGM for a public company and for a private company, in accordance with the term of appointment: section 208(4).

138. The resolutions on the appointment of directors of a public company must be voted on as separate resolutions; the appointment of two directors, for example, cannot be carried out by a single resolution. The CA 2016 provides that a single resolution can be utilized only when a motion that the voting be done by a single resolution has first been agreed to by the meeting without any vote being given against it. A resolution passed in accordance with the motion made in contravention of this rule shall be void, whether or not the resolution being moved was objected to at the time.

For public listed companies, the BMLR requires that a director must not hold more than 5 directorships in listed issuers: paragraph 15.06 Restriction on directorships in listed issuers. Every director of a public listed company must sign an undertaking letter to confirm full compliance with any requirement or restriction relating to the position as a director of a public listed company as required by Bursa Malaysia.

139. Removal. In a public company, the shareholders have the power to remove a director by passing a simple resolution notwithstanding anything in the constitution or in any agreement between the company and the director. However, the power of the shareholders under this section is subject to the proviso that if a director so removed was appointed to represent the interests of a particular class of shareholders or debenture holders, the removal resolution is not to take effect until his successor has been appointed: section 206(4). The director may be removed under section 206 if special notice of the resolution has been given to the company, i.e., not less than twenty-eight days' notice of the resolution to remove the director before the meeting is convened. This section does not restrict the method of removal of a director of a public company but merely provides that irrespective of any agreement or provision in the constitution relating to removal of a director of a public company, the general meeting of shareholders reserves the right to remove a director under this section.

Section 128(5) states that the vacancy resulting from the removal of a director by ordinary resolution, if not filled at the removal meeting, may be filled as a casual vacancy, i.e., the Board may appoint a new director. The term of any director appointed to fill that vacancy continues only until the term of the director he has replaced would have continued and the replacement director's term expires on the same day as the time in which the original director's term would have expired.

140. Retirement, resignation and maximum age. A director may resign from office before the expiration of the period of his appointment. Normally the constitution will indicate the method for resignation but section 208(2) provides that the director must submit the intention to resign in writing. Nonetheless, a director may not resign if this will cause the number of existing directors to fall below the minimum number required by the Companies Act 2016. A retirement occurs when the term of appointment expires and the director did not seek reappointment. The retirement of a director is provided under section 205 of the Companies Cat 2016. However, the constitution may provide for directors' retirement. The terms of appointment may also specify matters relating to retirement. The Companies Act 2016 does not specify a maximum age for a person to be able to serve as a director although the constitution may do so. Section 319 of the CMSA requires disclosure to be made to the SC whenever the chief executive or director of a listed company ceases to be the chief executive or director of the same company and of the names and particulars of any new chief executive or director of the listed company within two weeks of the occurrence of such event.

The office of a director is also vacated automatically in the following situations:

(a) resigns;
(b) after he retires and is not re-elected;
(c) is removed;
(d) due to disqualification under sections 198 or 199;
(e) unsoundness of mind;
(f) death;
(g) vacates his office in accordance with the constitution.

2. Composition of the Board

141. Although the Companies Act 2016 does not stipulate the composition of the board of directors other than requiring that there must be at least one director for a private company and two directors for a public company, public listed companies are required to comply with Chapter 15 of the BMLR. Thus, for public listed companies, there must be at least two directors who are independent directors or one-third of the board of directors, whichever is the higher, are independent directors. If the number of directors of the listed issuer is not three or a multiple of three, then the number nearest one-third must be used. In the event of any vacancy in the board of directors that results in non-compliance with the above rules, the company must fill the vacancy within three months. A public listed company is also required to establish a nominating committee and an audit committee.

A public listed company also must state an overview of the company's application of the recommendations in the Malaysian Code on Corporate Governance (MCCG) in its annual report and if there are any deviations to explain why and the alternative mechanism adopted by the particular company to achieve the Intended

Outcome of the principles laid down in the MCCG.[129] There is a requirement to have independent directors as well the method of appointment. The MCCG recommends that each public listed company must also have a nominating committee, an audit committee and a remuneration committee.

3. Independent Directors

142. The Companies Act of 2016 does not require a company to appoint an independent director. However, since a listed company is required by the Listing Requirements to state to what extent it has complied with the recommendations of the MCCG, the appointment of independent directors is the norm in a public listed company. The MCCG requires that independent directors make up at least one-third of the membership of the board of directors. The Listing Requirements of Bursa Malaysia (paragraph 3.14) also expressly deal with the need for independent directors on the board of a listed company as members of the audit committee where a majority of the audit committee members must be independent non-executive directors. Furthermore, the Listing Requirements of Bursa Malaysia also state that in order to form a quorum in respect of a meeting of an audit committee, the majority of members present must be independent directors.

143. An independent director is defined in paragraph 1.01 of the Listing Requirements of Bursa Malaysia as a director who is independent of management and free from any business or other relationship which could interfere with the exercise of independent judgment or the ability to act in the best interest of an applicant or a listed issuer.

The Listing Requirements identify an independent director as one who:

(a) is not an executive director of the company or any related corporation of the company;
(b) is not, and has not been within the last three years, an officer (except as an independent director) of the company. 'Officer' has the same meaning given in the Malaysian Companies Act of 2016;
(c) is not a major shareholder of the company;
(d) is not a relative of any executive director, officer or major shareholder of the company. For this purpose, 'relative' means the spouse, parent, brother, sister, child (including adopted or stepchild) and the spouse of such brother, sister or child;
(e) is not acting as a nominee or representative of any executive director or major shareholder of the company;
(f) has not been engaged as a professional adviser by the company under such circumstances as prescribed by the Exchange or is not presently a partner, director (except as an independent director) or major shareholder, as the case may be, of

129. Paragraph 15.25 of the Bursa Malaysia Listing Requirements.

a firm or corporation that provides professional advisory services to the company under such circumstances as prescribed by the Exchange; or

(g) has not engaged in any transaction with the company under such circumstances as prescribed by the Exchange or is not presently a partner, director or major shareholder, as the case may be, of a firm or corporation (other than subsidiaries of the applicant or listed issuer) that has engaged in any transaction with the company under such circumstances as prescribed by the Exchange.

If a person does not fall within paragraphs (a) to (g), it does not mean that the person is automatically qualified to be an independent director. The director and the board of directors must still apply the general test of independence, i.e., whether the said person is able to exercise independent judgment and act in the best interest of the company (Practice Note 13/2002).

In addition, the BMLR limits the tenure that a person can serve as an independent director for not more than a cumulative tenure of 12 years at which point the person will no longer be eligible as an independent non-executive director. This rule introduced in 2022 gives all long-serving independent directors until June 2023 to either resign or be redesignated as non-independent directors.

4. Remuneration of Directors

144. Approval of directors' remuneration. Section 230 of the Companies Act of 2016 requires that any fees and any benefits payable to the directors of public companies or a listed company and its subsidiaries (including public and private companies) must be approved at the respective companies' general meeting. This does not include the contractual salary of executive directors as these are payments made to an employee of a company which is paid based on the employee's contract of employment, as opposed to remuneration as *directors.*[130] The section enables both approval by way of 'ratification' where companies obtained shareholders' approval for the previous year's board's remuneration or 'prior approval' where companies obtain approval in advance for the coming financial year.[131] In relation to public listed companies, the BMLR also require shareholders to vote on any *increase* in remuneration and the award of stock option grants.

A company is also not allowed to make tax free payments to its directors and any provision contained in the constitution or in a board resolution or company resolution to that effect is void. The BMLR prohibits the payment of fees to non-executive directors by a commission on or percentage of profits or turnover while

130. There was some confusion regarding the term 'remuneration' adopted in earlier drafts of the new Companies Act and the term was changed to 'director's fees' to provide a distinction between fees paid to a director as a director and the salary paid to a director as an employee.

131. PriceWaterhouseCoopers *Board Remuneration & Practices in Relation to Board Effectiveness: An Update* (2004) (PWC: Kuala Lumpur). The respondents comprised 105 companies, representing 17% of Main Board Listed companies. Out of these 105 companies, 30 companies were top 100 companies on Bursa Malaysia based on market capitalization. Twenty-three (23) respondents had also participated in the 2001 survey.

salaries payable to executive directors may not include a commission on or percentage of turnover.[132] If there is an alternate director appointed by a director with the consent of the Board, the fees payable to the alternate director are to be paid from the original director's remuneration.[133]

Information on the remuneration of directors must be included in the accounts and as the accounts must be laid or tabled to shareholders at the general meeting, shareholders are informed of the remuneration paid to directors. Nonetheless, section 137 requires that the general meeting's approval must be obtained prior to any payment of any compensation that is to be paid to directors resulting from loss of office. In addition, the BMLR requires that general meeting approval be obtained prior to any increase in directors' remuneration.

145. The process to be followed to determine remuneration may be found in the Code on Corporate Governance which recommends that public companies should have a remuneration committee. Principle B of the MCCG states that:

(a) There must be a formal and transparent procedure for developing policy on executive remuneration and for fixing the remuneration packages of individual directors.
(b) The remuneration of executive directors should be linked to the companies and the individual's performance while for non-executive directors the level of remuneration should reflect the experience and level of responsibilities undertaken by the non-executive concerned.
(c) The details of the remuneration of individual directors must then be disclosed in the annual report.
(d) A company should have a remuneration committee[134] comprising wholly or mainly of non-executive directors. This remuneration committee recommends the remuneration of executive directors, and the executive directors are not to take part in decisions on their remuneration. However, the remuneration of non-executive directors is to be determined by the board as a whole.

146. Disclosure of directors' remuneration. Information relating to directors' remuneration must be included in the annual report. This is part of the information sent to members and laid before them at every AGM of a public company.[135] For publicly listed companies, the information relating to the remuneration of directors must be in the following:

---

132. Paragraph 7.23, BMLR.
133. Paragraph 7.31, BMLR.
134. A survey in 1998 found that most companies do not have a remuneration committee. However, a 2002 survey showed that at least 75% of listed companies have a remuneration committee. *See* Price Waterhouse Coopers and the KLSE, Malaysian survey on publicly listed companies, independent non-executive directors and institutional groups (2002). By 2005, at least 90% of the companies in Malaysia had a remuneration committee. *See* PriceWaterhouseCoopers, Board Remuneration & Practices in Relation to Board Effectiveness: An Update (2005). The 2005 survey showed that there has been an increase in the percentage of companies that establish remuneration committees, from 20% in 2001 to 90% in 2005.
135. *See* s. 249(4), 253 & the Fifth Schedule, Companies Act 2016.

(a) the aggregate remuneration of directors with categorization into appropriate components (e.g., directors' fees, salaries, percentages, bonuses, commissions, compensation for loss of office, benefits in kind based on an estimated money value) distinguishing between executive and non-executive directors; and
(b) the number of directors whose remuneration falls in each successive band of MYR 50,000 distinguishing between executive and non-executive directors. The remuneration of directors to be disclosed in the annual report shall consist only of the remuneration of directors of the listed company and not the directors of the subsidiaries who are not directors of the listed company. However, for the directors of the listed company, the remuneration to be disclosed should be for services rendered by such directors to the listed company as a group.[136]

The Companies Act 2016 requires *a public company* to keep and maintain a copy of each director service contract at the company's registered office and any variations of the contract which was entered into with the company or its subsidiaries. Members can inspect the service contract but must have:

(a) at least 5% of the total paid-up capital; or
(b) at least 10% of members in the case of a public company not having share capital: section 233, Companies Act 2016.

The company must also maintain a copy of the service contract to be made available for inspection for at least one year from the date of termination or expiry of the contract: sections 232(1)&(2).

Section 231 Companies Act 2016 explains that a director's service contract means a contract under which:

(a) a director of the company undertakes personally to perform services, as a director or otherwise for the public company or for a subsidiary of the public company; or
(b) services that a director of the public company undertakes personally to perform as a director or otherwise are made available by a third party to the public company, or to a subsidiary of the public company.
(2) The provisions of this Division relating to directors' service contracts shall –
    (a) be applicable to the terms of a person's appointment as a director of a public company; or
    (b) not be restricted to contracts for the performance of services outside the scope of the ordinary duties of a director.

136. Appendix C, Part A, para. 10. Questions and answers to Bursa Securities at www.bursamalaysia.com.my dated 1 Jun. 2001, para. 29.

B. Powers of Management and Representation

147. The board of directors is an organ of the company and has the authority to act for the company in matters within its area of authority as stated in the CA 2016 or the constitution. Decisions of the Board must be made collectively at a board meeting. Where the board meeting is concerned, the CA 2016 provides certain rules under section 212 and the Third Schedule that apply as default rules if the constitution of the company does not contain provisions specifying how a board meeting should be conducted.

A board meeting may be convened by any director or by the secretary is requested by a director to do so. A board meeting may be convened by giving notice of the meeting to all directors in Malaysia and must state the date, time, place and matters to be discussed. If there is any irregularity, it is waived if the director attends the meeting without any objection regarding the irregularity. Although there is no specific notice period, the court will consider what has been the practice of the company if the board meeting is challenged on the ground that there was insufficient notice given to members. The board meeting may also be conducted without the directors having to be physically present at one venue but merely by circulating the resolution of the board to all directors and obtaining their signature consenting to the resolution The quorum, if not fixed by the board, is a majority of the directors. The quorum must be present to transact any matters at the board meeting.

Each director has one vote and the chairperson shall have a casting vote. The chairperson is elected from the existing board members and the term of his office is determined by the directors. In his absence within fifteen minutes of the commencement of a board meeting, the directors may elect any one of their members to be the chairperson for that meeting. The minutes of each board meeting must be kept by the company. Any director present at a meeting of the board is presumed to agree to and to have voted in favour of a resolution of the board unless he expressly dissents from or votes to object against the resolution of the meeting.

148. The board of directors is also an organ of the company and may act for the company on matters which are within its authority as conferred by the Companies Act 2016 or the constitution. Nonetheless, the board of directors usually delegate its authority to the managing director or the CEO to manage the day-to-day operations of the company. The actual authority of the managing director or the CEO may be expressly laid down by the board's resolution. The managing director or the CEO also has implied authority to act in accordance with what the authority usually conferred on the managing director or the CEO. Thus, the managing director or the CEO has the authority to enter into contracts on behalf of the company and may not need to get the board or general meeting's approval for all the transactions entered into by him on behalf of the company unless the transaction involves transactions which the Companies Act requires shareholders' approval to be obtained.

C. Duties of Directors to the Company (Conflict of Interest) the Shareholders and Third Parties

149. Directors are accountable to and owe a duty to the company, i.e., the shareholders as a whole and do not owe any duty to any individual shareholder, for the management of the company's affairs and business. The directors may be sued by the company if any of the duties are breached. Some of the duty arises out of the common law, i.e., from case law and some are stated under the Companies Act of 2016 and other relevant securities legislation.

150. In common law, directors are required to act honestly and in the best interest of the company, avoid any conflicts of interest and exercise their management of the company with proper care, skill and diligence. These duties are also codified in the Companies Act of 2016 under section 213(1) which provides that a 'director shall at all times exercise his powers in accordance with the Companies Act 2016, for a proper purpose and in good faith in the best interest of the company'. Failure to do so amounts to a breach of his duty and would give rise to an action by the company for damages against him or for any profit made by him as a result of that breach both under the common law.[137]

In *Aberdeen Rly Co. v. Blaikie Brothers*,[138] it was held that:

> A corporate body can only act by agents, and it is, of course, the duty of those agents so to act as best to promote the interests of the corporation whose affairs they are conducting. Such agents have duties to discharge of a fiduciary nature towards their principal. And it is a rule of universal application that no one, having such duties to discharge, shall be allowed to enter into engagements in which he has, or can have, a personal interest conflicting, or which possibly may conflict, with the interests of those whom he is bound to protect. So strictly is this principle adhered to that no question is allowed to be raised as to the fairness or unfairness of a contract so entered into.

D. Duties and Liabilities

1. Disclosure of Interest

151. The directors are accountable to the company to avoid any conflict between their personal interests and the interest of the company. This means that directors may be liable to account for the profit that they have made as a result of any transaction between them and the company that is not disclosed to and approved by the general meeting of shareholders.[139]

Section 221 also requires a director who has an interest in a transaction with the company to disclose this interest to the board of directors as soon as he becomes

137. *Hytech Builders Pte Ltd v. Tan Eng Leong & Anor* (1995) 4 *MSCLC* 96,252.
138. (1854) 1 *Macq HL* 461; (1854) 23 *LT (OS)* 315.
139. *Regal (Hastings) Ltd v. Gulliver* (1942) 1 *All ER* 378.

aware of the interest. This disclosure is to be minuted by the company secretary at the board meeting. There are exceptions to this. If the director's interest consists only of his being a member or creditor of a corporation interested in a contract with his company, failure to disclose is not an offence against the subsection if the interest 'may properly be regarded as not being a material interest': section 221(2). The second exception is set out in section 221(3) where if the director's only interest is as guarantor of a loan to the company or as director of a related corporation with which the company has a contract, disclosure is not necessary.

A director who is interested in a contract entered into or proposed to be entered into by the company is also prohibited from participating in any discussion while the contract is being considered at the board meeting, although he may be counted to make the quorum for the meeting.[140] He is also prohibited from voting on the contract. The prohibition does not apply where:

(a) the company is a private company unless it is a subsidiary of a public company;
(b) where the private company is a wholly owned subsidiary of a public company and the contract is between the private company and the public company or with another wholly owned subsidiary of the same holding company;
(c) any contract of indemnity against any loss which any director may suffer by reason of becoming or being surety for a company;
(d) any contract entered into or to be entered into by a public company or a private company which is a subsidiary of a public company, with another company in which the interest of the director consists solely of:
   - in his being a director of the company and the holder of shares of not more than the number or value as is required to qualify him for the appointment as a director; or
   - in his having an interest in not more than 5% of its paid-up capital.

Where the director knowingly contravenes section 222, the director shall be guilty of an offence[141] but the contract is voidable at the option of the company.[142]

2. Duty to Avoid Conflict of Interest

152. Section 218 of the Companies Act 2016 states that a director or officer of a company shall not, without the consent or ratification of the general meeting, gain, directly or indirectly, a benefit for himself or any other person, or cause detriment to the company:

(a) use the property of the company;
(b) use any information acquired by virtue of his position as a director or officer of the company;
(c) use his position as such director or officer;

140. Section 221(1).
141. Section 221(4).
142. Section 221(3).

(d) use any opportunity of the company which he became aware of, in the performance of his functions as the director or officer of the company; or
(e) engage in business which is in competition with the company.

A director must not compete with the company to take away a business opportunity that belongs to the company. When a director diverts a business that has been awarded or secured by the company, this amounts to a breach of duty. In *Avel Consultants Sdn Bhd & Anor v. Mohammed Zain Yusof & Ors*,[143] the directors of the group of companies formed a firm which carried out the same business as the group of companies. The firm solicited the existing clients of the group of companies and, in a certain project, was even appointed to carry on work in place of the group of companies. The group of companies sued the directors for breach of fiduciary duties and sought damages. The Federal Court of Malaysia, upholding the decision of the trial judge, held that the respondents as directors of the group had committed a breach of their fiduciary duties.

However, the business opportunity must be something that the company is actively seeking or one that the company could be interested in view of the company's line of business. In *Industrial Equity Consultants v. Cooley*,[144] the third party with whom the director was negotiating on behalf of the company did not want to give the contract to the company and the director took it for himself without informing the company. The court held that he was in breach of his duty as the opportunity for the contract came to him while he was acting for the company. It does not matter that the company may not be able to obtain the contract.

A director who resigns from his directorship to enable him to take up the business opportunity for himself may be liable for breach of duty if the resignation was prompted by an intention to evade the duty and if the opportunity came to his attention while he was still a director.[145]

Where the board has rejected the opportunity, the director may take the opportunity for himself. However, the board's decision must not be influenced by the director concerned and the board must have acted in the best interest of the company in deciding not to accept or pursue the business opportunity.[146]

There is also a breach of duty if the director obtains a commission in relation to the business that he conducts on behalf of the company with a third party. Where the director had failed to declare to the Board of Directors that he was being paid commissions by the third party in relation to the purchases of goods from the plaintiff, he was obliged to make a full and frank disclosure, not only of the fact that he was being paid but also as to the amount.[147]

143. [1950–1985] MSCLC 145.
144. (1972) 2 *All ER* 162.
145. *Canadian Aero Services Ltd v. O'Malley* (1973) 40 *DLR* (3d) 371.
146. *Peso Silver Mines Ltd v. Cropper* (1966) 58 *DLR* (2d) 1; *Cooks v. Deeks* (1916) 1 *AC* 554.
147. *Magnifine Sdn Bhd v. Yap Mun Him* (2005) 6 *CLJ* 413.

3. Multiple Directorship and Conflict of Interest

153. While a person is not prohibited by law to hold more than one directorship, the BM Listing Requirements specify the maximum number of directorships that a director of a public listed company may hold. This does not mean that a person who holds multiple directorships is in breach of his duty towards the company, provided disclosure is made to the company as required by the common law. The duty to disclose multiple directorships is also found under the Companies Act 2016 where a director who holds any office or property which might lead to a conflict of interest must declare it to the board: section 221(6). In addition, although a person who is a director of several companies is not in breach of his duties towards any of the companies, his position is quite precarious as there is always a possibility that there could be disclosure of information belonging to one company to another company.[148]

4. Nominee Directors and Conflict Between Duty and Duty

154. A nominee director who is appointed to represent the interest of the appointer is still a director of the company and owes the same duty towards the company as is owed by any other directors of the company. If he acts in a way that is detrimental to the company but benefits the appointer, he is accountable to the company for any damage or loss suffered by the company as a result of his conduct.[149] This does not mean that he cannot act in the interest of a person other than the company. He may do so provided that his conduct is also in the best interest of the company.[150] Section 217 of the Companies Act of 2016 states that he cannot subordinate the interest of the company to that of his nominator.

5. Exercise of Powers for a Proper Purpose and in the Best Interest of the Company

155. Directors are given powers to manage the company's business and must ensure that the exercise of these powers is for the benefit of the company and not any other person.[151] Obviously, where the directors have profited personally or

148. *Kea Holdings Pte Ltd v. Gan Boon Hock* (2000) 3 *SLR* 129.
149. *Industrial Concrete Products Bhd v. Concrete Engineering Products Bhd* (2001) 2 *MLJ* 332; *Overseas–Chinese Banking Corp Ltd v. Justlogin Pte Ltd* (2004) 2 *SLR* 675.
150. *See also Charterbridge Corp Ltd v. Lloyds Bank Ltd* [1970] *Ch.* 64; *Equiticorp Finance Ltd (in liq.) v. Bank of New Zealand* (1993) 11 *ACLC* 952.
151. Section 213(1) of the Companies Act 1965. *See DM Divers Technics Pte Ltd v. Tee Chin Hock* (2004) 4 *SLR* 4 where the court ruled in the plaintiff's favour that the defendant should repay all monies owed to the plaintiff. The defendant had breached his fiduciary duties owed as a director to the shareholders of a company to act honestly and in good faith in the best interest of the company, not to exercise his power for an improper purpose and not to place himself in a position in which there was a conflict between his duties to the company and his personal interests or duties to others.

where the self-interest of directors is involved, the directors will not be allowed to assert that their action is bona fide in the best interests of the company.[152]

Where the board of directors is given the power to decide whether or not to register a transfer of shares in a private company and where there was no requirement in the constitution for the directors to give their reasons for the refusal, the court held that the decision must be made in good faith and in the best interest of the company. In this case, the directors were concerned that the transfer would be in breach of a statute and the court stated that it will not substitute the board's decision with its own in the absence of bad faith.[153]

6. Duty to Exercise Care, Skill and Diligence

156. Prior to the Companies (Amendment) Act 2007, the duty of care, skill and diligence was stated in section 132(1) of the former Companies Act of 1965. At the time, the Malaysian law on this point was influenced by the 1925 UK decision of *Re City Equitable Fire Insurance*[154] which has been subsequently repealed in the UK due to the low standard of care expected of directors. The case has also been rejected in Australia and Singapore as the decision no longer reflects the modern view regarding the role and responsibilities of a director. Subsequent to these developments, the Companies (Amendment) Act 2007 introduced section 132(1A) which embodied the modern duty of care, skill and diligence. Section 132(1A) of the Companies (Amendment) Act 2007 provides that a director shall exercise reasonable care, skill and diligence with the knowledge, skill and experience that may reasonably be expected of a director having the same responsibilities, and any additional knowledge, skill and experience that the director in fact has. This provision is restated as section 213(2) of the Companies Act of 2016. The duty of care, skill and diligence also requires directors to be actively involved in the management of a company. It is not a defence for the director to say that he should not be liable for any loss or damage suffered by the company due to his passivity or indifference to the company's affairs or financial situation. Although there is no positive duty for a director to attend all board meetings, non-attendance may be a breach of duty especially if it shows a lack of involvement in the company's management and affairs.

In *Daniels v. AWA Ltd*,[155] the following are the minimum standards of care, skill and diligence that must be demonstrated and exercised by directors:

(a) A director must acquire a basic understanding of the business of the company and must be familiar with the fundamentals of the company's business.
(b) Directors are under a continuing obligation to keep informed about the activities of the company.

---

152. *Lim Koei Ing v. Pan Asia Shipyard & Engineering Co. Pte Ltd* (1995) 1 *SLR* 49; *Howard Smith Ltd v. Ampol Petroleum Ltd* (1974) *AC* 821.
153. *Kwality Textiles (M) Sdn Bhd v. Arunachalam & Ors* (1990) 3 *MLJ* 361.
154. [1925] *Ch.* 407.
155. (1995) 13 *ACLC* 614.

(c) Detailed inspection of day-to-day activities is not required but there must be general monitoring of the company's affairs.
(d) Directors must maintain familiarity with the financial status of the company by a regular review of the financial statements.

In *Jurong Readymix Concrete Pte Ltd v. Kaki Bukit Industrial Park Pte Ltd (Chng Heng Tiu, Third Party)*,[156] the court held that the director's failure to obtain independent legal advice that resulted in the company giving a guarantee was in breach of the director's duty to exercise care and skill in the management of the company. The director had not obtained the board of directors' approval or views on the guarantee contract. The guarantee was not a routine matter and should have been discussed at the board meeting. The director concerned had failed to bring the matter to the attention of the board. He had committed the defendants to liability over a supply contract that he knew little of. The company was entitled to be indemnified by the third party for losses reasonably incurred under the guarantee.[157] In *Lim Weng Kee v. PP*,[158] Lim, who was the managing director of three companies involved in the pawnshop business, was found in breach of duty to exercise reasonable care in the management of the company and failing to ensure that the jewellery that was pawned to the company was only returned when the loan had been settled. The court held that no person of ordinary prudence would have authorized the release of the jewellery without first having the cheque given as full payment for the loan cleared and honoured.

157. While the directors may delegate any of their functions and powers, delegation does not justify total abdication of responsibilities. Instead, directors still retain the responsibility to supervise the exercise of powers by persons to whom powers have been delegated.[159] A director may also rely on information provided or made by the following:

(a) any officer of the company whom the director believes on reasonable grounds to be reliable and competent in relation to matters concerned;
(b) any other person retained by the company as to matters involving skills or expertise in relation to matters that the directors believe on reasonable grounds to be within the person's professional or expert competence;
(c) another director in relation to matters within the director's authority; or
(d) any committee to the board of directors on which the director did not serve in relation to matters within the committee's authority.[160]

---

156. (2001) 4 *SLR* 723.
157. *See also Lim Weng Kee v. PP* (2002) 4 *SLR* 327.
158. (2002) 4 *SLR* 327.
159. Section 215 and 216 of the Companies Act of 2016.
160. Section 215(2) of the Companies Act of 2016.

However, the reliance must be made in good faith and after making an independent assessment of the information, having regard to the directors' knowledge of the company and the complexity of the structure and operation of the company.[161]

7. Remedies Available to the Company

158. Where there is a breach of the director's duty, the company may obtain compensation or damages where the company has suffered loss due to the directors' breach of duty.[162] The company may also obtain an account of profit in situations where the directors have obtained a financial benefit but where the company did not suffer any loss.[163] This usually involves a breach of duty arising out of a conflict of interest or an improper exercise of power. Where a contract is entered into by the company and there is a breach of the director's duty, for example where the director did not disclose to the company that he has an interest in the contract, the company may rescind the contract.[164] A rescission means that the property will be returned to the original owner if the contract involves a transfer of assets. All the directors who are involved in the breach will be severally and jointly liable for the breach of duty.

159. For contracts entered into on behalf of the company, due to the separate legal entity doctrine, the directors would not be personally liable for any debts or obligations of the company except where the court has lifted the corporate veil. Directors will not be held personally liable even if they were the persons who acted on behalf of the company in relation to the third party.

8. Discharge and Expiation

160. Ratification. The general meeting of shareholders may decide to forgive any breach of duty after it has occurred. If this is decided, the ratification of any breach of duty means that the directors are no longer accountable to compensate the company. However, ratification is only valid and effective if it was made by independent shareholders, i.e., where the directors or their associates did not participate in the voting. Ratification is also not valid if this amounts to 'fraud on the minority' or 'oppression'. Where the duty is stated in the Companies Act of 2016, the view is that it is not possible for the general meeting to ratify the breach. This may not be a problem where the duty is only provided by the Companies Act (e.g., the duty to keep and maintain accounts).

161. Indemnification and insurance. A director who has been held liable for breach of duty cannot be indemnified by the company. Section 288 states that any indemnification for breach of duty of a director or an officer is invalid. This includes

161. Section 216(3) of the Companies Act of 2016.
162. *Lim Weng Kee v. PP* (2002) 4 *SLR* 327.
163. *Magnifine Sdn Bhd v. Yap Mun Him* (2005) 6 *CLJ* 413.
164. *Regal (Hastings) Ltd v. Gulliver* (1942) 1 *All ER* 378.

any insurance contract to indemnify the directors if the insurance is paid by the company. The company may nonetheless, indemnify the director only when the director has been successful in defending legal proceedings and the director or officer has incurred costs and expenses in the court action: section 289.

E. Company Secretary

162. A company is required to have a company secretary who must be a natural person, 18 years of age or above, a citizen or permanent resident of Malaysia and shall be ordinarily resident or has a principal place of residence in Malaysia: section 235. CA 2016. The appointment is to be made by the board of directors within thirty days of the company's incorporation. A company secretary must be either a person licensed by SSM or a member of any of the professional bodies prescribed by SSM. The company secretary must also be registered with SSM. There are also criteria to be disqualified from being appointed, for example, by being an undischarged bankrupt; where there has been conviction whether in or outside Malaysia of any offence under the Companies Act 2016 or related to bribe, fraud or dishonesty and if the person ceases to be a holder of a practising certificate issued by the Registrar. A company secretary may be removed by the board in accordance with the terms of appointment or the constitution. The company secretary may resign by giving notice to the board of directors but the office cannot be left vacant for more than thirty days at a time. A person is prohibited to act in a dual capacity as both a director and a secretary in a situation that requires or authorizes anything to be done by a director and a secretary.

F. Auditor

1. Requirement for Auditor

163. The Companies Act of 2016 makes audits mandatory for all public companies and thus, every public company is required to have its financial statement audited and to appoint an auditor or auditors. An auditor must be appointed for each financial year. The audit of a company may be carried out by an individual or by a firm of partners.

164. An auditor of a company must be a person who has been approved to act as an auditor by the Minister of Finance. Section 263, CA 2016 enables the Minister of Finance to approve a person to act as an auditor if he is satisfied that the person is of good character and competent. The approval may be made subject to such limitations or conditions as the Minister of Finance deems fit and may be revoked at any time by him by the service of a notice of revocation on the approved person. The approval and any renewal are for a duration of two years unless it is earlier revoked by the Minister of Finance.

Section 263(7), CA 2016 defines a 'person' as a chartered accountant as defined under the *Accountants Act 1967*. Thus, to be an approved auditor under the CA

2016, the person must be registered with the Malaysian Institute of Accountants (MIA) under the *Accountants Act 1967*. This person must meet certain criteria relating to professional training, expertise and experience and must demonstrate that he is capable of performing the duties of an auditor and of good character.[165]

165. The auditor of a public listed company must also comply with the *SCA 1993* that requires individual auditors and audit firms of public listed companies are fit and proper. Determination of fit and proper is assured through a registration process. The authority for this is the Public Companies Accounting Oversight Board (PAOB) which was established through the SC (Amendment) Bill 2009. Its functions are:

(a) To promote and develop an effective and robust audit oversight framework in Malaysia.
(b) To promote confidence in the quality and reliability of audited financial statements in Malaysia.
(c) To regulate auditors of public interest entities.

For auditors found not to be fit and proper, suspension, revocation or non-registration will be imposed.

166. Where an individual is appointed as the auditor, he must not be:

(a) An individual who owes more than MYR 2,500 to the company or a related body corporate of the company.
(b) An officer or the spouse of an officer of the company.
(c) A partner, employee or employer of an officer of the company.
(d) A partner or employee of an employer or an officer of the company.
(e) A shareholder or spouse of a shareholder of a corporation whose employee is an officer of the company.
(f) A person who is responsible for or if he is the partner, employer or employee of a person responsible for the keeping of the register of members or the register of holders of debentures of the company.
(g) an undischarged bankrupt within or outside Malaysia and has not obtained leave of court.
(h) A person who has been convicted of an offence involving fraud or dishonesty punishable with imprisonment for three months or more.

Where a firm of partners is appointed as auditors of a company, all the partners of the firm resident in Malaysia must be approved company auditors and no partner is disqualified from acting as the auditor of the company. All the partners of the firm must be qualified individually as an auditor. An LLP whether registered in Malaysia or a foreign LLP can be appointed as the auditor for a company. The appointment

165. Section 8, CA 1965.

is effective when the partners of the LLP are appointed as an auditor or when any employee of the LLP who is an approved auditor is appointed as auditor of the company.

2. Appointment

167. The first auditors of a public company are to be appointed by the board of directors at any time before the first AGM of the company: section 271(4). The auditors remain in office until the first AGM of the company where the shareholders decide whether to reappoint the existing auditors or make a new appointment.[166] Subsequently, a company must appoint an auditor at each AGM and this appointment period is until the next AGM.[167] Where there is a casual vacancy in the office of an auditor, the directors may appoint an approved company auditor to fill the casual vacancy. A casual vacancy occurs when there is a death, resignation or disqualification of a person who is acting as the company's auditor. If there is more than one auditor appointed and there is a casual vacancy, the surviving or continuing auditor or auditors (if any) may continue to act as auditors, and there is no obligation on the directors to appoint another auditor to fill the vacancy where there are other auditors acting for the company.[168] Where there is an outgoing auditor who is the sole auditor of a company, the new auditor does not take office until the previous auditor ceases to hold office.[169]

168. The resolution for the appointment of an auditor must be approved by an ordinary resolution of the members who are entitled to vote, voting either in person or by proxy.[170] To be appointed as an auditor, the person must be nominated by a member of the company and notice of his nomination must be given by the member to the company at least twenty-one days before the meeting.[171] Where the notice of the nomination is not sent to the company, the resolution to appoint the auditor cannot be passed and the meeting must be adjourned. The adjournment of the meeting may be to a date not earlier than twenty days, and not later than thirty days, after the proposed date of the original meeting.[172] The resolution to appoint the auditor at the adjourned meeting may be passed by a simple majority, i.e., by ordinary resolution. However, the notice of the nomination of a person or a firm for appointment as an auditor must be received by the company from a member of the company at least ten clear days before the date to which the meeting was adjourned[173] and the notice of nomination must also be sent to the proposed auditor before the resolution may be passed.[174]

166. Section 271(3)(a).
167. Section 273.
168. Section 271(2).
169. Section 273(a), CA 2016.
170. Section 271(4).
171. Section 172(11).
172. Section 172(7)(b).
173. *Ibid.*
174. Section 172(12).

The Registrar has the authority to appoint the company's auditor if the company or the directors fail to do so but there must be an application by the members for the registrar to exercise this power.

3. Removal or Resignation

169. The general meeting of shareholders may remove an auditor after a special notice of the removal has been given.[175] Special notice of the intention to move the resolution for removal must have been given to the company not less than twenty-eight days before the meeting at which the resolution is to be moved. Once the notice is received by the company, the company may convene a meeting to remove the auditor even if the meeting was called earlier than twenty-eight days. The company must inform the auditor and the Registrar of Companies once it receives notice of a resolution to remove an auditor and must send a copy of the notice to the auditor and lodge a copy of the notice with the Registrar.[176] This information enables the auditor to make a written representation in relation to his removal that must be made within seven days of the auditor receiving the copy of the notice and must be of a reasonable length. The auditor may request that a copy of the representations be sent at the company's expense to every member of the company to whom a notice of the meeting is sent, before the meeting at which the resolution is to be considered.[177] This procedure provides a measure of protection against the removal or dismissal of an auditor.

Where an auditor has been removed, the company may, at the same meeting, appoint a new auditor, to whom a copy of the notice of nomination must have been sent in accordance with section 280(2).

170. An auditor may resign by giving notice of resignation to the company. The resignation is effective twenty-one days after the notice is given to the company or from the date as may be specified in the notice: section 281, Companies Act of 2016.

171. Section 283, CA 2016 enables the auditor to give the notice of resignation together with a signed requisition calling on the directors of the company to immediately convene a general meeting of the company for the purposes of receiving and considering the explanation of the circumstances connected with his resignation as he may wish to place before the meeting.

172. The auditor may also request the company to circulate a statement in writing not exceeding a reasonable length of the circumstances connected with the auditor's resignation to its members (a) before the meeting convened on the auditor's requisition, or (b) before any general meeting at which the auditor's term of office would otherwise have expired or at which it is proposed to fill the vacancy caused by his resignation.

---

175. Section 276 & 277.
176. Section 277.
177. Section 277(3) & (4).

173. When the auditor resigns and he has made written representations regarding the circumstances connected to his resignation, he must submit a copy of his written representations to the Registrar. Where the company is a public listed company, the notice must also be forwarded by the company to the stock exchange including a copy of any written representations or written explanations of the resignation made by the auditors at the same time as copies of such representations or explanations are submitted to the ROC.[178] This must be submitted within seven days of the submission of his resignation to the company: section 284, CA 2016.

174. An auditor who has resigned has, notwithstanding his resignation, is required under section 285, CA 2016 to attend every AGM where the financial statements of the company for a financial year are to be laid, so as to respond according to his knowledge and ability to any question relevant to the audit of the financial statements.

4. Responsibilities and Liability of Auditors: Auditing for the Benefit of the Shareholders

175. An auditor of a company is obliged to report to the members of the company on the accounts which are to be laid before the company at the AGM. The auditor must also report to the members on the company's accounting records, and on other records relating to those accounts.[179] If the company is a holding company for which group accounts are required, the auditor must report to the members on the consolidated accounts.[180] The report must be attached to or endorsed on the accounts or consolidated accounts and must be read out before the company at the AGM if so required by a member. The report must be available and open for inspection by members at any reasonable time.[181]

176. The requirement that the audited accounts be laid before the general meeting ensures that the auditor reports directly to the shareholders and not to or through the directors. This is to ensure that the shareholders received 'independent and reliable information respecting the true financial position of the company at the time the audit was concluded'.[182] *Caparo Industries plc v. Dickman & Ors*[183] has ruled that any duty of care owed by auditors towards shareholders is owed to the shareholders as a body and not to individual shareholders. The auditor's report is provided to shareholders as information to enable them to better exercise their respective proprietary rights. As an auditor owes a duty to the company that he is

178. Paragraph 15.22, BMLR.
179. Section 266.
180. *Ibid.*
181. Section 266(7).
182. Per Lord Justice *Lindley* in the case of *In Re London and General Bank* (No. 2) (1895) 2 *Ch.* 673.
183. [1990] *BCC* 164.

auditing, the company may sue him for negligent audit. He does not, however, owe a duty to a person, nor a shareholder, who is contemplating the purchase of shares in the company.

While a contract entered into by the auditor and the company he is auditing to exempt him from or to exclude liability is void, the company may indemnify its auditor against liability incurred by the auditor where the liability is incurred in defending any proceedings whether civil or criminal in which judgment is given in his favour, in which he is connected; or in connection with any application in which relief is granted to him by the court under the Act.[184]

177. Although an auditor is also required to report breaches or non-observance of the provisions of the Companies Act 2016 to the Registrar, this is a qualified duty as an auditor and he is only bound to inform the Registrar of any breach if he feels that the matter will not be adequately dealt with by comment in his report on the accounts or by notifying the company directors of the matter.[185] All breaches whether relating to the accounts, accounting records or other aspects of the Act will have to be reported if the auditor feels that the breaches will not be adequately dealt with in his report.

178. To enable the auditor to perform his auditing responsibilities effectively, the company's own auditor has a right of access at all reasonable times to the records of the company.[186] In the case of consolidated accounts, the auditor of the holding company has a right of access to the records of any subsidiary. The auditor is also able to require from any officer of the company and of the subsidiary including its auditors such information and explanations as he desires for audit purposes.[187]

179. The auditor is also given a qualified privilege and will not be liable for any defamation action for any oral or written statement which he makes in the course of his duties as auditor. This qualified privilege is intended to enable him to report his findings freely and without fear of reprisals through the courts in defamation actions. The auditor is only protected where there is an absence of malice on his part. Where malice can be proved, an action for defamation may succeed.[188] This protection also extends to publishers of audit reports or documents prepared by an auditor who also enjoys a qualified privilege, if the documents are prepared by the auditor in the course of his duties as an auditor and the documents are required to be lodged with the Registrar of Companies.[189] An auditor shall not be liable to be sued in any court or be subject to any criminal or disciplinary proceedings for any report to the members on the financial statements and on the company's accounting and other records relating to those financial statements submitted by the auditor in good faith and in the intended performance of any duty imposed on the auditor under the CA 2016.

184. Section 288–290.
185. Section 266(1).
186. Section 266(40.
187. Section 266(5).
188. Section 286.
189. Section 286.

5. Remuneration

180. Where the members appoint the auditor, the auditor's remuneration which includes sums paid for expenses and payments otherwise than in cash is fixed by the member in a general meeting by ordinary resolution. Where directors appoint the auditor, the remuneration is fixed by the directors and if not, may be fixed by the company.[190] If the auditor is appointed by the Registrar of Companies, his fees will be fixed by the Registrar. If the directors or the Registrar failed to fix the auditor's fees, the fees may be determined by the members in a general meeting as if the auditor had been appointed by the company.[191]

The details of the auditor's fees are available to the shareholders if notice requiring particulars of all the emoluments paid to the auditor in respect of services apart from auditing services is served to the company by:

(a) at least five of the members of the company; or
(b) the holders of at least five of the company's issued share capital.[192]

When a company receives such notice from its members, it is obliged to immediately carry out the following tasks:

(a) to prepare a statement showing particulars of all the emoluments paid to the auditor and of the services for which the payments were made during the financial year immediately preceding the service of the notice;[193]
(b) to forward a copy of the statement to all persons entitled to receive notice of the company's general meetings;[194] and
(c) to lay the statement before the company in a general meeting.[195]

While there is no statutory requirement for mandatory rotation of auditors/auditor firms, the MIA by-laws require that there must be a mandatory rotation of audit partners.

190. Section 274(1)(a) & (b).
191. Section 274(1)(c).
192. Section 275(1).
193. Section 275(1)(a).
194. Section 275(1)(b).
195. 275(1)(c).

§6. LIQUIDATION

I. Grounds for Winding-Up

A. *Members' Voluntary Winding-Up*

181. The members of a company may resolve to wind up the company under section 439. If the company was incorporated for a fixed period either due to a specific time or the occurrence of certain events, and the term has expired, the members may pass an ordinary resolution to wind up the company.[196] In any event, the members may always resolve to wind up the company by passing a special resolution.[197]

A members' voluntary winding-up occurs when a declaration of solvency has been made by the board that the company is able to pay its debts, i.e., is solvent, followed by an ordinary resolution of members. Thus a members' voluntary winding-up occurs in a liquidation of a solvent company.

In a members' voluntary winding-up, the process starts with the board of directors, who must resolve that the company is solvent. The solvency declaration must be made in writing by a director, or if there is more than one director, then by a majority of them, that they have made an enquiry into the affairs of the company, and that at a meeting of directors they have formed the opinion that the company will be able to pay its debts in full within a period not exceeding twelve months after the commencement of the winding-up, which is the date the members pass the resolution (either an ordinary or special resolution) to wind up the company.[198]

182. The solvency declaration must be made at a directors' meeting and lodged with the Registrar and must be made before the notice to call a members' meeting to pass the winding-up resolution is sent to members. The declaration will have no effect unless it was made within five weeks before the passing of the resolution. The directors are guilty of an offence if they make the declaration of solvency without having reasonable grounds for the opinion that the company will be able to pay its debts within the twelve-month period: section 443(5). The directors would rely on the company's accounts to enable the directors to make a declaration of solvency. However, if a company does not pay or provide for its debts in full within this twelve-month period, it shall be presumed that any director, who made the declaration of solvency, did not have reasonable grounds for his opinion and the onus is on him to show the contrary: section 443(6). At the members' meeting, the members must also appoint a liquidator.

---

196. Section 439(1)(a).
197. Section 4394(1)(b).
198. Section 443(1).

B. Creditors' Voluntary Winding-Up

183. The creditors' voluntary winding-up occurs when the directors are not willing or cannot make a declaration of solvency. In such a situation, the company must convene a members' meeting to pass a resolution to wind up the company and must also convene a creditors' meeting immediately after the holding of the members' meeting. A company may not resolve to wind up voluntarily when there is already a petition to wind up the company by an order of the court.

In some cases, a winding-up may start off as a members' voluntary winding-up but after the appointment of the liquidator, the liquidator finds that the company is not able to pay its debts, i.e., the company is insolvent. The liquidator must immediately convene a creditors' meeting.[199] Notices of the meeting of creditors must be sent by post simultaneously with the sending of the notices of the meeting of the company.[200]

184. At the meeting, the liquidator must lay before it a statement of the company's assets and liabilities. The creditors have the right to appoint some other liquidator other than the liquidator appointed by the company.[201] However, if creditors do not appoint a liquidator at the convened meeting, the liquidator appointed by the members continues to act as the company's liquidator, except that the winding-up is deemed to be a creditors' voluntary winding-up. The liquidator must lodge a notice in the prescribed form with the Registrar and the Official Receiver within seven days after the meeting of creditors has been held.[202] The court may appoint a liquidator if there is no liquidator acting in a voluntary winding-up. The court also has the power to remove a liquidator and appoint a new liquidator: section 453.

The liquidator may exercise all the powers and duties specified under the Eleventh Schedule of the Companies Act of 2016.

C. Winding-Up by the Court/Compulsory Winding-Up

185. A winding-up by court order occurs when there is a petition to wind up the company under certain grounds laid down in section 465 where the application is to be made by persons having *locus standi* as stated under section 464. The grounds for petitioning to court to wind up a company are stated below.

A winding-up by order of the court may occur when the company itself may resolve that the winding-up is made by an order of the court: section 465(1)(a). However, unlike a voluntary winding-up where the general meeting passes a resolution to wind up, a petition to the court usually involves situations where the company board is not able to make a declaration of solvency under a voluntary winding-up or where shareholders are unwilling to do so or cannot be contacted to obtain the resolution. In this situation, the board of directors will present the petition and they

199. Section 447.
200. Section 449(2).
201. Section 450 (1) & (2).
202. Section 447(4).

must act in the best interest of the company. A petition to the court under this provision could also be made where the company might want to bring legal actions against certain officers and wishes the court to be more involved in the process.

Once a public company with a share capital is incorporated, there are certain restrictions imposed on a public company before it may commence its business. This is specified under section 190. The company is required to lodge a statutory declaration by the secretary or one of its directors verifying that the conditions imposed on the company before it may commence business have been fulfilled. Failure to do is a ground for the company to be wound up, normally via a petition from SSM.[203]

A winding-up order may also be made against a dormant or non-active company if a company does not commence business within a year from its incorporation or suspends its business for a whole year. This ground under section 465(1)(c) enables members of a company to get back the capital that they have invested in the company.

Under the former Companies Act 1965, the minimum number of members is two. Thus, except in the case of a company that is the wholly owned subsidiary of a company, a company may be wound up if the number of members is reduced to below two. However, under section 465(1)(d), Companies Act 2016, a company may be wound up if there is no member.

A company may be wound up by the court where creditors make an application where the company is unable to pay its debts: section 465(1)(e). Once a petition is made under this ground, the company may not resolve to wind up voluntarily without the leave of the court. Section 466 provides several scenarios where a company is deemed to be unable to pay its debts:

(a) First, if the company has been served with a statutory demand to pay its debts and has not been able to do so within twenty-one days. The amount of debts is as prescribed by the Registrar under the CA 2016 was MYR 10,000 (EUR 2900).[204] As a temporary and short-term measure to address the impact of COVID-19 on the ability of businesses to continue operating, section 465(1) was modified through the Company Order (Exemption) 2020 where the company is given a period of up to six months and the amount of debt is increased to MYR 50,000 (EUR 10,500). As of 1 April 2021, the Company Order (Exemption) 2021 (GN No. 4159 of 2021) increased the value of indebtedness to MYR 50,000. However, the time given reverts back to within twenty-one days.

    A creditor who wants to rely on this ground must comply with the requirement to send a statutory demand.[205] If the company fails to comply with the statutory demand or if the debts failed to be settled or to be secured, the company is deemed to be unable to pay its debts and a petition to wind up the company may

203. Sections 190 and 465(1)(b).
204. The former CA 1965 puts the amount as exceeding MYR 500 (EUR 105).
205. *Yap Kim Kee & Sons Sdn Bhd* (1990) 1 *MSCLC* 90,499.

be made to the court. However, this presumption can be rebutted by the company and the court will make an order if the debt is disputed or if the company can prove that the failure to pay its debts is not due to it being an insolvent company.

(b) Second, a company is deemed to be unable to pay its debts if there is an execution or other process issued on a judgment, decree or order of any court in favour of a creditor of the company which is returned unsatisfied in whole or in part;
(c) Third, a company is deemed to be unable to pay its debts where it is proved to the satisfaction of the court that the company is unable to pay its debts; and in determining whether a company is unable to pay its debts the court shall take into account the contingent and prospective liabilities of the company.

A winding-up order may be made where the directors have acted in affairs of the company in their own interests, rather than in the interests of the members as a whole, or in any other manner whatsoever that appears to be unfair or unjust to other members. This ground indicates that the board of directors' conduct may be a ground petition to the court.

A petition to wind up the company may also be made if an inspector who is appointed to investigate the affairs of a company is of the opinion:

(a) that the company cannot pay its debts and should be wound up; or
(b) that it is in the interests of the public, of the shareholders or of the creditors that the company should be wound up.

A company is sometimes incorporated for a fixed period or until the occurrence of certain events. Under section 465(1)(g), if the period which has been fixed for the duration of the company by the Memorandum or Articles expires or the event, if any, occurs on the occurrence of which the Memorandum or Articles provide that the company is to be dissolved.

A company may be wound up under the 'just and equitable ground' under section 465(1)(h). This ground is only available for a private company and is explained in Part I, Chapter 2 below.

Section 465(1) j) provides that a winding-up order may be made against a company which has held a license under the Financial Services Act 2013 or the Islamic Financial Services Act 2013 and that license has been revoked or has expired and has not been renewed. A company which carries on banking business in contravention of the Financial Services Act 2013 or the Islamic Financial Services Act 2013 may also be wound up by the court.

A company may also be wound up if it was used for any unlawful purpose or any purpose prejudicial to or incompatible with peace, welfare, security, public interest, public order, good order or morality in Malaysia.

A company may also be wound up if it is a company declared to be a company under investigation by the Minister.

II. Effects of Winding-Up

186. Once the winding-up commences, the directors cease to have any powers of management except powers conferred by the liquidator. The commencement of winding-up also affects any action or proceedings that are to be taken against the company since any such proceedings can only be instituted by leave of court. Any disposition of the company's assets is also invalid unless the court's approval or validation order has been obtained. Any action to be taken by the company shall only be instituted with the consent of the liquidator.

187. Under section 528, any transfer, mortgage, delivery of goods, payment, execution or other act relating to property made or done by or against a company which was made with the intention of preferring one creditor over the other and made within a specified time frame that, had it been made or done by or against the individual, would in his bankruptcy under the law of bankruptcy be void or voidable shall in the event of the company being wound up be void or voidable in a like manner.

188. Section 529 provides that any floating charge on a company's undertaking or property created within six months of the presentation of the petition to wind up the company by the Court or the passing of the resolution for a voluntary winding-up shall be invalid unless it can be shown that the company was solvent immediately after granting the charge. If the charge was given in consideration of the payment of an amount of cash at the time of or subsequent to such charge being given, the charge is not invalid but the charge is limited to:

(a) the amount of money actually paid to the company at the time of the creation of the charge; and
(b) interest of 5% in respect of that sum.

A. The Liquidators and Their Powers

189. Appointment. The liquidation process is handled by a liquidator. Where the company is wound up voluntarily, the liquidator is appointed by the shareholders at the general meeting. Where the winding-up is a creditors' voluntarily winding-up, the liquidator appointed by the creditors will be in charge of the liquidation process if they did not appoint the same liquidator as was appointed by the members.

In a winding-up by the court, section 476 also allows the appointment of an interim liquidator at any time after the presentation of a petition and before the winding-up order is made (in which case the appointment may be regarded as an interlocutory step in the winding-up proceedings) and the provisional liquidators are required to notify the Registrar of his or her appointment and address.[206] Section 440, requires the directors to immediately appoint an interim liquidator where the

206. Section 476.

directors have made a statutory declaration that the company cannot carry on its business by reason of its liabilities and after summoning the meeting of creditors for a date within thirty days of the date of the declaration.

Where the winding-up is by an order of the court, i.e., compulsory winding-up, the court will appoint the liquidator for the company. The liquidator appointed by the court must be either the Official Receiver or an approved liquidator.

190. Powers. Section 476 provides that an interim liquidator has and may exercise such functions and powers of a liquidator subject to such limitations as may be prescribed by the rules or as the court may specify (for the exercise of the powers of the liquidator). An interim liquidator is appointed for the purpose of preserving the assets and undertaking of a company which is alleged to be insolvent. The main function of such an appointee is to get in and control all the assets of the company to preserve the status quo pending the making of a winding-up order.[207]

In the case of a liquidator, some of the liquidator's powers may only be exercised with the approval of the committee of inspection or the court: sections 456 Eleventh Schedule & 457. Some powers which are conferred on a liquidator in a winding-up by the Court may also be exercised by a liquidator in a voluntary winding-up. These include powers to:

(a) carry on the business of the company so far as is necessary for the beneficial disposal or winding-up of that business;
(b) pay any class of creditors in full (subject to the priority provisions contained in section 527;
(c) make any compromise or arrangement with creditors;
(d) compromise any calls and liabilities to calls, debts and liabilities capable of resulting in debts and any claims (present or future, certain or contingent, ascertained or sounding only in damages) subsisting or supposed to subsist between the company and a contributory or other debtor or person apprehending liability to the company; and
(e) appoint a solicitor to assist him in his duties.

191. The powers which may be exercised by the liquidator without authorization are contained in section 472, Part 1 Twelfth Schedule where the liquidator may:

(a) bring or defend any legal proceeding in the name and on behalf of the company;
(b) compromise any debt due to the company other than calls and liabilities for calls and other than a debt where the amount claimed by the company to be due to it exceeds MYR 1,500;
(c) sell the immovable and movable property and things in action of the company by public auction, public tender or private contract with power to transfer the whole thereof to any person or company or to sell them in parcels;

---

207. *Re Dry Docks Corp of London* (1888) 39 *Ch.D* 306; *Re Carapark Industries Pty Ltd* (in liq.) (1967) 1 *N.S.W.R.* 337; *Re Chateau Hotels Ltd* (1977) 1 *N.Z.L.R.* 381; *Re M.L. Industries Pty Ltd* (1981) *CLC* paras 40–736; *Re Clearwater Pty Ltd* (1982) 1 *ACLC* 129.

(d) do all acts and execute in the name and on behalf of the company all deeds, receipts and other documents and for that purpose use when necessary the company's seal;
(e) prove, rank and claim in the bankruptcy of any contributory or debtor for any balance against his estate, and receive dividends in the bankruptcy in respect of that balance as a separate debt due from the bankrupt and rateably with the other separate creditors of the company or under any deed executed under that Act;
(f) draw, accept, make and endorse any bill of exchange or promissory note in the name and on behalf of the company with the same effect with respect to the liability of the company as if the bill or note had been drawn, accepted, made or endorsed by or on behalf of the company in the course of its business;
(g) raise on the security of the assets of the company any money required;
(h) take out letters of administration of the estate of a deceased contributory or debtor, and do any other act necessary for obtaining payment of any money due from a contributory or debtor, or his estate, that cannot be conveniently done in the name of the company (in all such cases, the money due shall be deemed to be due to the liquidator himself); and
(i) make all payments necessary for a company to carry on its business;
(j) appoint any agent to do business which the liquidator is unable to do;
(k) appoint a lawyer to assist him in his duties; and
(l) do all such other things as are necessary for winding up the affairs of the company and distributing its assets.

These powers do not prevent a liquidator from making an application to the court for directions in performing the functions of the liquidator.[208] Certain other powers may only be exercised with approval of the Court or the committee of inspection: section 486, Part II, Twelfth Schedule.

192. The liquidator must give due regard to directions given by:[209]

(a) resolutions of the creditors or contributories at any general meeting; or
(b) the committee of inspection.

In cases of conflict, directions given by the creditors or contributories override those of the committee. The liquidator may convene general meetings of the creditors or contributories for the purpose of ascertaining their wishes. But, he must convene meetings at such times as the creditors or contributories:

(a) by resolution direct; or
(b) if requested to do so by not less than one-tenth in value of the creditors or contributories.

208. Section 486.
209. Section 237.

193. A committee of inspection must be constituted when there is a request from either a creditor or contributory to convene separate meetings of creditors and contributories for the purpose of determining:

(a) whether a committee of inspection should be appointed; and
(b) where a committee of inspection is to be appointed the persons who will be members of the committee.[210]

B. Treatment of Creditors

194. The liquidator's main function is to recoup any of the company's assets and realize these to enable the payment of the company's debts at the request of either a creditor or contributory to convene separate meetings of creditors and contributories for the purpose of determining:

(a) whether a committee of inspection should be appointed; and
(b) where a committee of inspection is to be appointed the persons who will be members of the committee.

Creditors of the company must be identified and must participate in 'proof of debts' to enable the liquidator to distribute the company's assets. The creditors whose debts are secured, provided that they have the security registered under section 352, in general, will be given priority and the assets subject to the security will be realized to pay off the debts owed to the secured creditor. Amongst the secured creditor, there are priority rules that must be observed. The unsecured creditors however must be treated equally amongst themselves. There are nonetheless, preferential creditors under section 527 who are actually unsecured creditors but who will be paid out of the assets subject to the floating charge if the general assets to be used to pay unsecured creditors are insufficient. The preferential creditors include employees of the company.

C. The Liquidator and the Shareholders

195. The liquidation process may take more than a year. If this happens section 458 requires the liquidator to call a general meeting of the company (in the case of a members' voluntary winding-up) or call a general meeting of the company and a meeting of the creditors (in the case of a creditors' voluntary winding-up), at the end of the first year from the commencement of the winding-up and the end of each succeeding year, or not more than three months thereafter, and lay before the meeting or each meeting an account of his acts and dealings and of the conduct of the winding-up during the preceding year.

210. Section 241.

However, where a members' voluntary winding-up becomes a creditors' voluntary winding-up,[211] the liquidator does not have to convene an annual meeting of creditors at the end of the first year from the commencement of the winding-up if the meeting held in accordance with section 449(1) was held less than three months before the end of that year: section 447(5).

196. In a voluntary winding-up, where the company's affairs are fully settled, the liquidator must:

(a) make up an account showing how the winding-up has been conducted and the property of the company disposed of; and
(b) call a general meeting of the company (in the case of a creditors' voluntary winding-up, a meeting of the creditors and members of the company) for the purpose of laying the account before it and giving any necessary explanations.[212]

Notice of the meeting must be advertised in an advertisement published in a newspaper circulating generally throughout the country and this must be done at least one month before the meeting and the advertisement must specify the date, time, place and object of the meeting: section 459(2).

The liquidator must, within seven days after the meeting, lodge with the Registrar and the Official Receiver a return of the holding of the meeting and of its date with a copy of the account attached to the return: section 459(3). But, if a quorum was not present at the relevant meeting, the liquidator must lodge with the Registrar and the Official Receiver, a return (with account attached) stating that the meeting was duly summoned but no quorum was present.

197. Stay and termination of the winding-up order. Winding-up proceedings may be stayed under section 243. The section empowered the court to stay the winding-up proceedings for a limited period of time or altogether, i.e., permanently. In the case of the latter, the winding-up proceedings are terminated, allowing the revival of the wound-up company to life. From this point onwards, the company can resume its business and operations as if no winding-up order existed: section 493. The company ceases to be in liquidation and the liquidator ceases to hold office and will be released from all liability in respect of any act done or default made by the liquidator in the administration of the affairs of the company, with effect from making of the order or on such date as may be specified in the order.

D. Dissolution of a Company

198. A company ceases to exist only upon dissolution. This usually follows after the company has been wound up and there is a final settlement of the company's

211. Section 448.
212. Section 459.

debts and obligations. In some cases, the dissolution of a company may also be terminated by the court.[213] Where the company's affairs have been fully settled, a company is dissolved three months after the return of the holding of the final meeting under section 272 is lodged with the Registrar and the Official Receiver.[214] However, the court may, on the application of the liquidator or of any other party who appears to the court to be interested, defer the date at which the dissolution is to take effect.[215] Nonetheless, the application must be made within three months after the lodging of the return with the Registrar and the Official Receiver. This is considered as deregistration following winding-up.

When the court orders for the liquidator to be released and the wound-up company to be dissolved pursuant, the company shall from the date of the said order, be dissolved accordingly[216] The Dissolution Order shall discharge the liquidator from all liability in respect of any act done or default made in the course of administering the affairs of the company. Notwithstanding this, section 535, Companies Act of 2016 confers on the court the power to declare, on terms that it thinks fit, the dissolution of the company void and allows for proceedings which could have been initiated if the company had not been dissolved to be commenced. However, this power can only be invoked if an application to that effect is made to the court within two years after the date of dissolution.[217]

The Registrar also has the power to deregister a defunct company off the register if the Registrar has reasonable cause to believe that the company is not carrying on business or not in operation.[218] The power to deregister also exists in the following situations:

(a) where the liquidator is no longer acting;
(b) the company has been fully wound up and the return of the final meeting that the liquidator should have lodged is at least six months late; and
(c) the company has been fully wound up in insolvency and it has no property or not enough property to cover the costs of obtaining a court order for deregistration.[219]

§7. Mergers and Takeovers

I. Historical Background

199. The principal statute that governs takeovers and mergers in Malaysia is the CMSA. The CMSA has imported Division 2 of Part IV of the SCA of 1993

213. Section 307.
214. Section 272(5).
215. The court may defer the time for the dissolution of the company where it is not satisfied with the conduct of the winding-up, where the liquidator has failed to take steps to recover a debt due to the company: *Re G.K. Pty Ltd* (in liq.); Ex parte *D.F.C. of T.* (1983) 1 *ACLC* 848.
216. Section 491(1), CA 2016.
217. Section 535(1).
218. Section 308(1).
219. Section 308(3)(c).

(CMSA). Prior to the introduction of the CMSA, mergers and takeovers of companies were governed by the Take-Overs and Mergers Code of 1987 which heavily resembles the London City Code. The Code of 1987, which has no statutory backing, was administered by the then Take-Over Panel.

200. Upon the establishment of the SC in 1993, the Take-Over Panel was abolished and its powers were absorbed by the SC. In 1995, the SCA was amended to improve the provisions on mergers and takeovers. The 1995 Amendment has brought significant changes to the SCA, which are now embodied in Division 2 of the CMSA. The new division in the SCA recasts the Malaysian Code on Take-overs and Mergers of 1998 (the Code) as a subsidiary legislation backed by criminal sanctions for breach of its provisions.[220] A new Division 2 of Part IV entitled 'Take-overs Mergers and Compulsory Acquisitions' was introduced, comprising ten sections: section 33–33E and section 34–34C. Division 2 of the CMSA refines the law on compulsory acquisition of shares of the dissenting shareholders in the target company. The amendments have also vested a wide range of power to the SC to enable it to regulate mergers and takeovers of companies.[221] Apart from regulating the Code, the Commission is also given the power to exempt certain parties from the obligation to undertake mandatory general offers.[222] The SC also issues a number of Practice Notes that set out the manner in which it would exercise its discretion and interpret the Code.

The 1998 Code was subsequently replaced by the Code on Take-overs and Mergers 2010 which came into effect on 15 December 2010. Along with the Code, the Commission published *Practice Notes* and *Guidelines on Contents of Application relating to Take-overs and Mergers* which also came into force on 15 December 2010. The revision of the Code was prompted by developments in the capital market in the last twelve years. The Code addressed a number of concerns relating to takeovers and mergers and enhanced greater protection for shareholders and a wider group of investors. Further amendments were made in 2016, with the introduction of the Malaysian Code on Take-overs and Mergers 2016 which took effect on 15 August 2016. The 2010 Code was repealed. Along with the 2016 Code, the SC also introduced a rule book, *The Rules on take-overs, Mergers and Compulsory Acquisitions*, issued by the SC pursuant to section 377 of the CMSA. The Take-over Rules must be read together with the 2016 Code. Due to the coming into force of the Companies Act 2016, some amendments were made to the *Rules on take-overs, Mergers and Compulsory Acquisitions* in 2017.

---

220. Section 218 of the CMSA provides that non-compliance with the Code will make a person guilty of an offence of fine not exceeding MYR 1 million or ten years imprisonment or both. The Code on Takeovers and Merger 1998 came into force on 1 Jan. 1999.
221. Section 15(1)(d) of the SCA 1993.
222. The Exemptions are provided in Practice Notes 15–24 to the Malaysian Code on Takeovers and Mergers.

II. Principles of the Code

201. The principal stated objective of the Code is to ensure fair and equal treatment of shareholders in relation to takeovers and mergers. Although the Code refers to all shareholders, in practice the SC's primary focus of concern is usually the shareholders of the target company.

202. Companies listed on the stock exchange are also governed by Chapter 11 of the BMLR which sets out the disclosure requirements that must be complied with in relation to the takeover of a listed company.

203. The 2016 Code contains principles and rules governing the conduct of all persons or parties involved in a takeover offer, merger or compulsory acquisition. The 2016 Code seeks to ensure that the takeover framework is reflective of commercial reality while conferring protection on shareholders where required. The Code also seeks to keep up with the capital market developments and evolutions in corporate control mechanisms. Generally, takeovers in Malaysia are made either through voluntary offers or mandatory offers. Although the Code applies to mergers and takeovers, merger is not defined in the Code. The disclosure requirements and procedures in the Code apply equally to mergers and takeovers. Generally, a merger is an arrangement whereby the assets of two companies become vested in one company or are put under the control of one company that has as its shareholders all, or substantially all, of the shareholders of the two companies. A merger is normally effected either by the shareholders of one company or by the shareholders in both of the merging companies exchanging their shares for shares in a third company. In Malaysia, despite the term 'merger' being used, most 'mergers', especially those involving the banking sector, are in the technical sense, takeovers.

The 2016 Code considers that a takeover offer includes a scheme of arrangement, compromise, amalgamation or selective capital reduction that enables a person to obtain control or consolidate his control in a company. The Code also allows for acquisition of control in a company through the making of a reverse takeover. Although the Code applies to mergers and takeovers, merger is not defined in the Code. The disclosure requirements and procedures in the Code apply equally to mergers and takeovers. Generally, a merger is an arrangement whereby the assets of two companies become vested in one company or are put under the control of one company that has as its shareholders all, or substantially all, of the shareholders of the two companies. A merger is normally effected either by the shareholders of one company or by the shareholders in both of the merging companies exchanging their shares for shares in a third company. In Malaysia, despite the term 'merger' being used, most 'mergers', especially those involving the banking sector, are in the technical sense, take-overs. Where a takeover offer is effected by way of a scheme of arrangement, compromise, amalgamation or selective capital reduction the law requires the following conditions: first, the scheme is approved by at least 50% in number and 75% in value to the votes attached to the disinterested shares that are cast either in person or by proxy at a duly convened meeting of the holders of the disinterested shares. Second, the number of votes cast against the resolution to approve the scheme at such meeting is not more than 10% of the votes attached to all disinterested shares of the total voting shares of the target.

The 2016 Code provides for twelve general principles to be observed by all persons engaged in any take-over or merger transaction. Some of the general principles reiterate the foundation of the law laid down in the CMSA. The Code requires all shareholders of the same class in the target company to be treated equally. Both the bidder and the board of directors of the target company are required to act in good faith and that all shareholders must not be oppressed or disadvantaged by their treatment or conduct.[223] The board of directors of the target company must act in the interests of the shareholders as a whole and cannot deny the shareholders the opportunity to decide on the take-over offer.[224] In the case of a partial offer, the bidder must accept such voting shares or voting rights in the same proportion from each shareholder of a target company in order to achieve the specified percentage of shareholding.

III. Types of Takeover Offers

A. *Mandatory Offer*

204. A mandatory offer is an offer for all the remaining voting shares that are not already held by the bidder in the target company. Mandatory offer emanates from a person who already has control in the target company either through market purchase or private agreement with one or more of the shareholders in the target company.

205. The Take-over Rules identify two situations when a mandatory general offer is triggered unless exempted by the SC. In the first, a mandatory offer is triggered when control is acquired by the bidder in a company. Under Malaysian law, control is presumed when a person or a corporate body holds more than 33% of shares in a company regardless of whether there is a de facto control in the company. Thus, 33% depicts the threshold for triggering the mandatory offer. When the shareholding threshold is over 50%, the mandatory offer ceases to be conditional. This means that the offeror must proceed with the offer and is obliged to purchase the shares in the target company which was tendered in acceptance of the offer. If the 50% shareholding is not obtained before the closing date of the offer, the offer lapses and shareholders who have tendered their shares in acceptance of the offer will have their shares returned to them. The only condition that can exist in the mandatory takeover offer is the condition that the offeror has received acceptances which would result in the offeror and persons acting in concert holding in aggregate more than 50% of the voting shares or voting rights of the offeree.

In the second, a mandatory offer is triggered in a situation involving a creeping takeover. The term refers to an incident where there is a purchase of the shares in small numbers in several transactions. This occurs when there is an acquisition of

223. Principle 2, 2016 Code.
224. Principle 12, 2016 Code.

more than 2% of the voting shares or voting rights of a company in any period of six months by an acquirer holding over 33% but not more than 50% of the voting shares or voting rights of the company. The 2016 rules recognize a netting-off position in relation to a creeping acquisition where a person or persons acting in concert are free to acquire and dispose of further voting shares within the 2% band without triggering a mandatory general offer. Thus, if a person who holds more than 33% voting shares in a company acquires a further 1.5% shares and subsequently disposes of 0.5%. He is considered to have only acquired 1% voting shares in the company and is has not triggered a mandatory general offer requirement.

The obligation of making a mandatory general offer applies to the bidder and the 'parties acting in concert'.[225] The concept of 'parties acting in concert' is used to define the sphere of persons to which it applies.[226] The need for this is simply to prevent the provisions of the Code from being avoided by a number of persons acting together so that the specific threshold for the application of this provision is not met. Consequently, the effectiveness of a significant part of the Code relies upon its ability to identify and govern the concert parties.

The CMSA provides a list of persons who are presumed to be parties acting in concert with the bidder.[227] The Act simplifies the definition of 'parties in concert' to cover a company, its directors and its shareholders where there is an arrangement between them that restricts the director or shareholder from offering or accepting a takeover offer for the voting shares of the company or from changing his shareholdings in the company. Those people who fall under the presumption of parties acting in concert will have to rebut the presumption if they contend otherwise. The Take-over Rules list down a number of factors which the parties in concert may rely upon in rebutting such presumption.[228]

Despite the fact control is achieved in the target company, The Take-over Rules prohibit the bidder/acquirer from appointing new directors to the board of the target or exercising the voting rights attached to their shares in the target company before the offer document is sent to the shareholders of the target company even though the bidder may have achieved control in the target company. The Take-over Rules also prohibit a director in a target company from resigning from the board of directors until the first closing date of the takeover offer or prior to the offer becoming or being declared unconditional.

The consideration to be offered to the target shareholders for their shares must be in form of cash. However, where there is more than one consideration offered, at least one consideration must be a cash consideration. Although the requirement of cash consideration seems onerous upon the bidder, it ensures that the shareholders in the target company are allowed to exit the company.

The Take-over Rules provide for certain exemptions from mandatory offer obligations in certain circumstances as enumerated in Practice Notes to the Code on

225. *Chin Yew Loy Holdings Sdn Bhd v. AU Metalvest (M) Sdn Bhd.*
226. Rule 4.03, Takeover Rules.
227. Section 216 (3) of the CMSA.
228. Rule 4.05; Notes to para. 4.05.

Take-overs and Mergers.[229] The SC's power to give exemptions is conferred by the CMSA. The application for a waiver from having to make a mandatory general offer must be made to the SC.[230]

The most popular exemption is based on the 'whitewash' policy. The whitewash policy envisages approval by the SC, as a regulatory body, to exempt the making of the mandatory general offer, subject to independent shareholders' approval to waive their right to the mandatory general offer being made. The policy behind it is to give shareholders who are independent of the party that will gain control a chance to weigh up the commercial merits of the proposal, in light of the proposed acquisition of control by the party. Hence, independent shareholders may resolve to waive their rights to receive a mandatory takeover from the offeror shareholder (and the parties acting in concert) who intends to control the company.[231]

Generally, the exemptions apply where there is an issue of new shares in the following situations:

(a) the offeror is issued new voting shares or voting rights as consideration for the sale or disposal of assets and/or interests by him;
(b) the offeror subscribes for new voting shares or voting rights in cash;
(c) the offeror exercises any conversion or subscription rights or options into new voting shares or voting rights;
(d) where as an underwriter, the offeror receives new voting shares or voting rights as a result of his underwriting obligation (*see* note below); and
(e) the offeror:
  (i) acquires new voting shares or voting rights for the purpose of restoring his holding to the level prior to the issuance of new voting shares or voting rights; and
  (ii) the acquisition of new voting shares or voting rights is from persons who will be allotted the voting shares or voting rights as consideration for the sale or disposal of assets and/or interests by them.

The whitewash procedure applies in the above situations. The SC may exempt the making of the mandatory general offer if an offeror and persons acting in concert have satisfied the two conditions:

(1) there is no acquisition of shares or instruments convertible into shares and options in respect of shares (other than subscriptions for new shares or new instruments convertible into or options in respect of new shares which have been disclosed in the whitewash circular) by the offeror and persons acting in

229. Practice Note 23.
230. The exemptions which are provided in the Take-over Rules resemble the same grounds of exemptions as contained in the London City Code.
231. Khan, Mushera Ambaras (2018). 'The Regulation of Takeovers and Mergers in Malaysia'. In Wan, Wai Yee; Varottil, Umakanth (eds.). *Comparative Takeover Regulation: Global and Asian Perspectives*. Cambridge, England and New York: Cambridge University Press. p. 464.

concert with him, *in the six months prior to the announcement of the proposals* but subsequent to negotiations, discussions or the reaching of understandings or agreements with the directors of the company in relation to the proposed issue of new securities until completion of the subscription; and

(2) approval has been obtained from independent holders of voting shares or voting rights of the offeree at a meeting of the holders of the relevant class of voting shares or voting rights to waive their rights to receive the mandatory offer from the offeror and persons acting in concert.

Another situation where exemption can be made by the SC involves a rescue scheme. Where a company finds itself in a severe financial situation, the SC may grant an exemption when the only way to save the company is via the urgent issue of new shares or the acquisition of the existing shares by a rescuer.[232]

An exemption may also be granted where there is foreclosure of voting shares.[233]

An exemption is also possible arising out of a share buy-back exercise, but subject to certain conditions:[234]

(a) there is no acquisition/purchase of voting shares or voting rights in the company (save for subscriptions for new shares which have been fully disclosed in the whitewash circular) by the offeror and persons acting in concert with him, before the date on which the authority of the share buy-back expires, if such acquisitions, taken together with the share buy-back would cause them to incur a mandatory offer obligation; and
(b) approval has been obtained from independent holders of voting shares or voting rights of the offeree at a meeting of the holders of the relevant class of voting shares or voting rights to waive their rights to receive the mandatory offer from the offeror and persons acting in concert.

An exemption may be applied for from the SC where there is acquisition of additional voting shares or voting rights by members of a group acting in concert in the following situations:[235]

(a) a group of persons acting in concert holding over 33% but not more than 50% of the voting shares or voting rights of an offeree, and as a result of an acquisition of voting shares or voting rights from one or more members of the group, a member of the group will control the offeree;
(b) a group of persons acting in concert holding over 33% but not more than 50% of the voting shares or voting rights of the offeree and one member of the group who holds over 33% but not more than 50% of the voting shares or voting rights, acquires more than 2% voting shares or voting rights of the offeree in any six-month period from one or more members of the group;

---

232. *See* para. 4.09 of the Code.
233. *See* para. 4.10 of the Code.
234. *See* para. 4.15 of the Code.
235. *See* para. 4.13 of the Code.

(c) a group of persons acting in concert having statutory control of an offeree and as a result of acquisition of voting shares or voting rights either from members of the group or non-members, a member of the group will control the offeree; or

(d) a group of persons acting in concert having statutory control of an offeree, and one member of the group who holds over 33% but not more than 50% of the voting shares or voting rights, acquires more than 2% voting shares or voting rights of the offeree in any six-month period either from members of the group or non-members.

A bidder may also apply for an exemption if the acquisition causes him to incur a mandatory offer obligation that has been approved based on national policy. The SC may grant an exemption upon this ground if the bidder has obtained the necessary approval from the respective sector regulators.[236]

An exemption is also possible in relation to a placement of voting shares or voting rights arising out of a restructuring exercise or issuance of new voting shares or voting rights as consideration. SC may give the exemption where an offeror who obtains control in an offeree makes a prior arrangement or gives a written undertaking to the SC to reduce his holding in the voting shares or voting rights of the offeree to 33% or less. The private placement, however, cannot be used as a ruse to circumvent direct control and thus such placement must not be made to parties who are acting in concert with the offeror, and there must be an underwriting arrangement for the placement.[237]

An automatic exemption is also given in relation to Islamic Securities Selling and Buying-Negotiated Transactions.[238] In an Islamic securities selling and buying-negotiated transaction, if the buyer sells back similar or equivalent voting shares or voting rights to the seller who sold him the securities earlier, the seller would be exempted from a mandatory offer obligation in the following circumstances:

(a) If the seller holds more than 33% but not more than 50% of the voting shares or voting rights of a company at the point of selling the securities to the buyer, and the seller's holding drops to 33% or less or reduces by more than 2% of the voting shares or the voting rights of the company in any six-month period as a result of selling of the securities:
    (i) the purchase of the securities (without the seller initiating the transaction) would, but for the exemption referred to above, trigger a mandatory offer obligation; and
    (ii) the purchase of the securities (without the seller initiating the transaction) will not increase the seller's holding (including subsequent acquisition, if any) to more than 50% of the voting shares or voting rights of the company; or

236. *See* para. 4.14 of the Code.
237. *See* para. 4.11 of the Code.
238. Summary of Amendments made to the Rules on Take-overs, Mergers and Compulsory Acquisitions (Issued: 5 Dec. 2017).

(b) If the seller holds more than 50% of the voting shares or voting rights of a company at the point of selling the securities to the buyer, and the seller's holding drops to 50% or less as a result of selling of the securities, his holding (including subsequent acquisitions which do not trigger a mandatory offer obligation) together with the purchase of the securities from the buyer would, but for the exemption referred to above cause the seller to trigger a mandatory offer obligation.

The seller to which the exemption applies under this paragraph is required to:

(a) inform the SC of the likelihood of him being subjected to a mandatory offer obligation when the seller purchases the securities from the buyer; and
(b) provide a declaration, within three days upon the purchase of the voting shares or voting rights, that the seller has complied with either sub paragraph (a) or (b) above.

B. *Voluntary Offer*

A voluntary offer can be either a full offer or a partial offer:

(a) A full or general offer refers to an offer for the entire issued share capital of the target company. It emanates from a person who intends to acquire control by using the technique of the takeover bid.
(b) A partial offer, refers to an offer to buy a selected number or percentage of shareholding, instead of acquiring 100% of the shares of a company. Subject to the approval by the Commission, a partial offer may be made for any number of shares in the target company that would result in the bidder holding less than 100% of the voting shares in the target company.[239] In ensuring that the equality principle is adhered to, the Take-over Rules provide that the bidder shall accept the same proportion from each target shareholder up to the percentage of voting shares proposed to be acquired by the bidder. During the period of the offer, the offeror and the persons acting in concert shall not acquire any voting shares or voting rights to which the partial offer relates other than through acceptances of the offer.

A takeover offer is a voluntary offer if there are no triggering events as found in the mandatory general offer. The terms of a voluntary general offer are normally left for the parties involved in the takeover to decide. But one important condition is that the offeror should have received acceptances which would result in the offeror holding in aggregate more than 50% of the voting shares or voting rights of the offeree. Other conditions can be included before the obligation arises on the offeror to make the purchase.

239. Section 10 of the Code.

The Take-over Rules, however, require that all shareholders of the same class of the target company be treated equally. Thus, the procedure and the disclosure requirements in the Take-over Rules apply to a voluntary general offer. It is worth noting that in cases where the bidder or its/his concert party has acquired 15% or more of shares in the target company six months prior to the making of the offer and the consideration was paid in cash, the Code imposes a minimum price for the consideration of the voluntary general offer. The Code requires that the bidder must offer a cash sum or, where there is more than one consideration, that one consideration shall consist solely of a cash sum not less than the highest price paid for the voting shares purchased during the offer period or within six months prior to the beginning of the offer period.[240] Currently, the law allows a bidder, in a voluntary offer, to state a higher level of acceptances subject to the bidder having satisfied the Commission that he is acting in good faith in imposing such high level of acceptances.[241] The move to allow a higher threshold is aimed at providing certainty to the bidder on the outcome of a successful take-over. The CMSA 2007 allows a bidder to compulsory acquire the shares of dissenting shareholders in the target if the bidder has obtained 90% acceptance from the target shareholders.

In the case of a partial offer where the offeror and the persons acting in concert would have an aggregated holding of over 33% but not more than 50% of the voting shares or voting rights of the offeree, the offeror shall state in the offer document:

(a) the precise percentage of voting shares or voting rights proposed to be acquired;
(b) the partial offer will only be declared unconditional as to acceptances when the percentage as stated in (a) is achieved; and
(c) the partial offer is conditional upon obtaining approval from independent shareholders holding more than 50% of voting shares or voting rights of the offeree not held by the offeror and the persons acting in concert, signified by means of a separate box in the form of acceptance. However, the SC may exempt compliance with this requirement if an independent shareholder holding more than 50% of such voting shares or voting rights has indicated his approval.

Any person who intends to make a partial offer for the same offeree within twelve months from the date of the close of a previous partial offer must seek the SC's prior approval. The SC will not normally grant approval unless the subsequent partial offer is recommended by the offeree board.

C. Reverse Takeover

206. In a reverse takeover, the bidder makes a takeover offer for the voting shares of the target company by means of an exchange of shares that will result in

240. Section 18 of the Code.
241. Section 17(5) of the Code.

the shareholders of the target controlling the bidder. The BMLR requires a summary of the key audited financial data of the assets of the business of interests to be acquired for the past five financial years or since the date of incorporation as additional information in relation to reverse takeovers. In addition, the acquirer must also provide an accountant's report on the unlisted company to be acquired and a pro forma balance sheet of the group as reorganized.

In Malaysia, reverse takeovers have been used as a vehicle to obtain an exchange listing without engaging in an initial public offering (IPO). Typically, the management of the previously private company acquires control of the public acquirer and indirectly obtains the benefits of public status without the corresponding financial and temporal costs associated with an IPO.

IV. Regulation

A. Procedure

207. The procedure for voluntary offers and mandatory offers is similar. The only difference between the procedures for the two is that the voluntary offer commences with negotiations between the board of directors of the target company and the bidder. On the other hand, a mandatory offer is normally made known to the board of the target company only after control has passed to the bidder.

The Take-over Rules require the announcement of a take-over offer by press notice, followed by a written notice to the board of directors of the target company, the SC and the Stock Exchange.[242] The main consequence is that 'an offer period' will commence. The 'offer period' continues until the first closing date of an offer or, if later, the date when the offer becomes or is declared unconditional as to acceptances or lapses. The minimum time frame required by the Code is twenty-one days from the date the offer document is first posted. A potential bidder or target company is also required to make an announcement on possible offers where there were unusual movements in the price of shares of the target. Should the potential bidder deny making an offer, it would be prohibited from making a takeover offer for the same target company for a period of six months.

The written notice requires the disclosure of information relating to the identity of the bidder, its percentage of holding in the target company and the terms of the offer. More detailed disclosure will be provided in the offer document that will enable the shareholders in the target company to decide on the merits of the offer.[243] The board of directors of the target company is under obligation to post notification to all shareholders within seven days of receipt of the takeover notice and to circulate its comments on the takeover offer within ten days of the receipt of the offer document.[244] In giving its comment, the board of directors of the target company will have to evaluate the offer to see whether it is in the best interest of the company to recommend such an offer. Failure to act in the best interest of the company

242. Part V of the Code.
243. Section 12 of the Code.
244. Section 14 of the Code.

will induce a breach of duties of the directors to the company. The board of directors of the target company is also required to appoint an independent advisor in relation to the takeover offer and send the circular within ten days from the date the offer document was posted after obtaining approval from the SC.[245]

The Take-over Code and the Stock Exchange Rules require absolute secrecy during discussion stage and before a formal bid is announced in order to prevent the creation of a false market in the securities of the target company and insider trading.[246] The Code also requires the parties to ensure that their conduct does not lead to the creation of a false market in the securities of the target. The parties must take every possible precaution to ensure confidentiality. The due diligence exercises must be conducted discreetly to avoid rumour and speculation.

After a successful takeover, the bidder and its concert party are not allowed to acquire further voting shares or voting rights in the target on more favourable terms than the previous takeover, within six months immediately after the close of the takeover offer.

B. Scope of Application

208. The application of the Take-over Code is limited to public companies whether listed or unlisted and private companies which have shareholders' funds or paid-up capital of MYR 10 million or more and where the purchase consideration over a period of twelve months is MYR 20 million or more. The purpose of making the Code applicable to this type of private company is to ensure that the shareholders in those private companies get protection from any unfair dealing.

The Code applies equally to acquisition of control through the making of takeover offers as well as through mergers. A takeover offer means an offer made to acquire all or part of the voting shares, or any class or classes of voting shares. A merger, on the other hand, refers to an arrangement whereby the assets of two companies become vested in, or under the control of, one company. A merger is effected either by the shareholders of one company or the shareholders in both of the merging companies exchanging their shares for shares in a third company.

A takeover offer means an offer made to acquire all or part of the voting shares, or any class or classes of voting shares. A merger, on the other hand, refers to an arrangement whereby the assets of two companies become vested in, or under the control of, one company. A merger is effected either by the shareholders of one company or the shareholders in both of the merging companies exchanging their shares for shares in a third company.

245. Section 14(1) of the Code.
246. Paragraph 11.03, Part C, Ch. 11 BMLR.

C. Summary of Duties of Directors and Independent Advisers During a Takeover, Merger and Compulsory Acquisition

209. Generally, a director has to monitor changes on the share register during the pre-bid period as directors need to know the identity of potential bidders. In relation to a takeover, the board of the target company is not only responsible to the shareholders with voting rights; the responsibility of directors also extends to the holders of convertible securities of the target company.[247] The board of the target must provide a firm recommendation on whether the takeover offer should be accepted or rejected. Where the member of the board of the target has a diverging view, the director must disclose his diverging view in the board's circular.

The board of the target must refrain from taking any action which will result in the frustration of the offer unless a prior approval is obtained from the shareholders at a general meeting. The Take-over Code lists down a number of situations which will result in the frustration of the offer. The Take-over Code identifies the list of actions that may lead to frustration of the offer. These include the selling of treasury shares into the market, the disposal of assets or liabilities that is the condition to the offer and any action which may cause the target or its subsidiary or associate to purchase or redeem shares in the target or provide any financial assistance for such purpose.

The Code imposes an obligation upon the board of directors of the target to appoint an independent advisor as soon as possible after it becomes aware of the possibility that a takeover offer may be made.[248] The law also requires the appointment of an independent adviser by the board of the bidder where a reverse takeover occurs or where the board of directors of the bidder is faced with a conflict of interest situation. The adviser is required to prepare an independent advice circular for the shareholders of the company. The duties of the adviser are to provide objective and appropriate advice that would enable the shareholders concerned to make informed decisions regarding the offer. Advisers are encouraged to consult the Commission at an early stage in takeover related matters. The Code further requires that the substance of the advice must be made known to the holders of the class of the voting shares to which the offer relates. The circular can only be sent to the shareholders with the consent of the SC. The circular is meant to assist the shareholders of the target in making their decisions as to whether to accept or reject the offer. In carrying out their tasks, advisers are required to observe a high standard, the failure of which will subject the advisers to liability. In addition, an adviser who fails to comply with the standard imposed by the law has future implications; the Commission may refuse to accept or consider any future submission relating to a takeover from the same adviser.[249]

The adviser when recommending the acceptance of the offer should ascertain that the take-over offer is 'fair' and reasonable. The Commission proposed a review of the content of the independent advice circular in order to enhance the quality of information provided in the independent advice circular. The Commission proposed

247. Section 14(10).

248. Section 15 of the Code.

249. Practice Note 7.

to decouple the phrase 'fair and reasonable' when evaluating a takeover offer. The phrase 'fair and reasonable' has not been previously defined in Malaysia.

V. Protective Measures[250]

210. The CMSA and the Take-over Code and Rules provide certain measures to protect the right of minority shareholders in the target company. The most obvious is the corresponding right of minority shareholders locked up in the target company to force the bidder to purchase their shares on the same terms of the takeover offer even after the takeover offer comes to an end.[251] The minority shareholders are also allowed by section 224 to apply to the court for an order preventing the compulsory acquisition from proceeding or specifying terms of acquisition that are different from the terms of the takeover offer so long as they can convince the court that the price offered earlier does not represent the fair value of their shares.[252]

To effect the compulsory acquisition, the offeror must, within two months after the takeover offer has been accepted, give notice to any dissenting shareholders that he desires to acquire the outstanding shares held by the dissenting minority shareholders together with a statutory declaration.[253] The CMSA clearly states that the bidder can exercise the power to compulsorily acquire the shares only if first, it had made a 'takeover offer' for all of the shares in the target company, and second, it must have received acceptance in respect of at least 90% in nominal value of those shares. The CMSA also requires that the 90% threshold figure must be reached within four months after the making of the offer. In calculating the 90% threshold, the CMSA excludes those shares held by an associate of the bidder, its nominee or its subsidiary, as they must be excluded in calculating the statutory minimum percentage required for exercising the power of compulsory acquisition. Where the bidder does not obtain the 90% acceptances required entitling it to issue the compulsory acquisition notice, the bidder may nevertheless apply for a court order authorizing it to give such notice. However, as a measure to protect the right of minority shareholders in the target company, the court may only allow the bidder to send out the notice if the court is convinced that the price offered is fair and reasonable and the bidder has made reasonable enquiries to trace the non-accepting shareholders and they have not been located.

211. Apart from the above right conferred upon minority shareholders, the mandatory bid rule is adopted with the assumption that the substantial shareholder will seek to maximize the price at which it sells its shares and thus allowing the minority shareholders to benefit from the follow-up offer.

250. *See* Mushera Ambaras Khan, 'An Insight into the latest developments on Takeovers and Mergers law in Malaysia' (2011) CSLJ at 125.
251. Section 223(1)(b) of CMSA 2007.
252. The term 'fair value' is not defined.
253. Section 222(1) of CMSA 2007.

A. Brief Survey of Defensive Measure[254]

212. Section 217 of the CMSA imposed a duty on the SC to ensure that the directors of both the acquiring and target companies act in good faith when responding to, or making recommendations with respect to a take-over offer. It is clearly important that the directors of the target company should ensure that, consistent with their fiduciary duties, the shareholders have an adequate opportunity to appraise the offer made for their shares and to consider any alternative or better one. The most important issue in a take-over context that is likely to be considered by the shareholders of the target company is the value placed on the company by the bidder. Directors are well aware of this fact and the practice has been that defensive tactics engaged in by many companies are specifically designed to maximize the share price for the benefit of shareholders.

Thus, as a general rule, the board of directors of the target company may adopt certain strategies or tactics as defensive measures although these should not amount to measures that will frustrate the bid. Difficulties often arise in the context of defensive tactics and strategies designed to prevent hostile takeovers. The suitability of a particular tactic or strategy for a company will depend on the circumstances surrounding the company, including whether the measure can be justified as promoting the interests of shareholders and whether shareholder approval is required in order to adopt such a strategy. It is worth noting that in Malaysia, there is cultural adversity to hostile takeovers.

The most common defensive measures that have been adopted in Malaysia include 'white knight' or issuing a significant number of shares to a person who is perceived as friendly, 'golden parachute' or a contract between a company and an executive that provides for a significant termination payment on the event of losing their position to a successful bidder, Employee Stock Ownership Scheme (ESOS) and share buy-back. It is important to note that from the moment the board of directors of the target has reason to believe that a bona fide take-over offer might be imminent, the board shall not take any steps to frustrate the bid without getting approval from the shareholders in the target company. The board of the target company is also prohibited from taking any steps to frustrate or thwart the bid during the course of a takeover offer.[255]

Although the phrase 'defensive measures' is not mentioned in the Code, the Code lists down certain actions that could amount to frustration of the bid. Examples are the issuing of any authorized but unissued shares of the target company or creating new shares and issuing them in an attempt to dilute the shareholding of the bidder in the target company. The disposition and selling of a 'crown jewel' or assets of the target company of a material amount are also prohibited unless approval from the shareholders in the target is obtained. In general, the following actions are considered as actions that could frustrate a bid and include:

– issue any authorized but unissued shares of the target company;
– issue or grant options in respect of any unissued shares of the target company;

254. Mushera Ambaras Khan, *Defensive Tactics and Strategies in Take-overs,* 4 MLJ liii (2005).
255. Section 35 of the Code.

- create or issue or permit the creation or subscription of any shares of the target company;
- sell, dispose of or acquire or agree to sell, dispose of or acquire assets of the target company of a material amount; or
- enter into or allow contracts for or on behalf of the target company to be entered into otherwise than in the ordinary course of business of the target company.

The above restrictions do not apply if they are carried out:

> pursuant to a prior bona fide contract, which is not designed to frustrate a takeover or change the activity of the target company; or pursuant to some other obligation or other special circumstances which the SC may approve in writing.

213. Any attempts of any action or any decision (other than in the ordinary course of business) by the board must not be carried out without obtaining the approval of shareholders at a general meeting if the action or decisions could effectively result in any bona fide takeover offer being frustrated or the shareholders being denied an opportunity to decide on the merits of a takeover offer.

§8. Holding Companies and Subsidiaries

214. The Companies Act 2016 categories a company as a subsidiary of another company where the other company:

- Controls the composition of the board of the subsidiary. There is control of the composition of the board when the other company can appoint or remove all or majority of the directors of the subsidiary, when the directors cannot be appointed except with the consent of the other company or where the directors of the subsidiary are appointed due to the employment or directorship in the other company.
- The other company has control over more than half of the voting shares in the subsidiary.
- The other company holds more than half of the shares in the subsidiary.

A subsidiary may also be a wholly owned subsidiary where all its shares are held by another company.

Holding and subsidiary companies are legally separate entities and the courts are guided by the common law principle relating to 'lifting the veil' (i.e., exception to the separate legal entity) before a holding company would be held liable for its subsidiaries' legal obligations. In relation to financial recording obligations, companies within the same group must prepare the financial accounts on a consolidated basis.

A subsidiary company is prohibited from providing financial assistance to any person for the purpose of or in connection with the acquisition of shares in its holding company.

§9. Taxation of Corporations and Shareholders

215. Companies are taxed separately from their shareholders. The tax payable by a company is provided under the Income Tax Act 1967 based on the corporate income tax bracket on income accruing in or derived from Malaysia. There are tax deductions available as provided by the Income Tax Act. The tax on a company's profits is a final tax and dividends paid, credited or distributed to members are tax exempt.

216. The Director-General of Income Tax is empowered to make adjustments on controlled transactions of goods, services or financial assistance entered into on an arm's-length basis or disregard a structure which is commercially irrational. Control is determined by:

(a) common shareholding of 20% or more; and
(b) the operations of the affiliate depend on the proprietary rights of the 20% shareholder or its affiliate; or
(c) the shareholder/ affiliate is able to influence decisions relating to the business activities of the company, including the receipt of services and the pricing of the acquisition of such services; or
(d) one or more of the directors or members of the board are appointed by the shareholder/ affiliate.

Chapter 2. Closed Corporation: Private Company – Limited Liability Company

§1. Distinctive Features

217. In general, a private limited company shares many of the characteristics of a public company. A private limited company is also a legal person once all the incorporation procedures have been complied with. There is no difference between a public and a private company in respect of the consequence of a separate legal personality and exceptions to the separate legal entity.

218. The Companies Act of 2016 imposes more onerous obligations on a public company than on a private company and in some situations enables private companies to carry out certain transactions that are prohibited for public companies. On the other hand, there are certain transactions that are not allowed for private companies, such as buying back their issued shares, which are only available to public companies.

219. The Companies Act of 2016 categorizes a private company according to the following criteria:[256]

(a) The number of members in a private company must not be more than fifty.
(b) A private company shall restrict the transfer of its share.
(c) A private company is prohibited from raising capital from the public.
(d) A private company is prohibited from inviting the public to lend money to the company: section 43.

220. While there are private companies that are similar to incorporated associations or partnerships because of the very small number of members and the involvement of all members in the company's day-to-day business, there are also private companies that are large in terms of economic size and operations.

I. Formation of the Company

221. While the general requirement for the formation of a private company is similar to that of a public company, the name of the private company must contain the words 'Sendirian Berhad' or the abbreviations 'Sdn Bhd'.[257] The minimum number of subscribers is one and the maximum number of members is fifty. Some private companies are categorized as 'exempt private companies'. These are private companies whose members do not exceed twenty where all of the members are not body corporate.[258]

---

256. Section 42.
257. Sections 25(1)(a).
258. Section 2.

II. Annual Accounts and Audit Requirements

222. All companies are required to keep and maintain their accounts and these accounts must be audited. However, an exempt private company is not required to lodge its audited accounts with the Registrar of Companies. Section 258(1) of the CA 2016 provides that a private company must circulate its financial statements and reports to its shareholders within six months of the end of its financial year and submit its financial statements and reports to SSM within thirty days from the date its financial statements and reports are circulated. The company may apply to the Registrar for an extension of time.

III. No Prospectus Requirement

223. Since a prospectus is required to be issued by a public company and since a private company is prohibited from raising capital from the public, the prospectus requirement does not apply to a private company. A private company is prohibited from raising its capital from the public

§2. Different Legal Treatment Compared to Public Company

I. Capital and Shares

224. Shares and other securities. The capital of a private company may be divided into different types of shares with different rights attached to the shares. Similar to public companies, private companies may issue ordinary shares, preference shares and founders or deferred shares while bearer shares are not recognized. Shares with multiple votes are also often found in private companies. While the CA 2016 does not prohibit the issue of shares with multiple votes, the former CA 1965 only prohibits this type of shares in public companies. However, the issue of multiple voting shares must be expressly stated in the constitution of the private company.

225. Ability to carry out share buy-back, reduction of capital and provide financial assistance. There is one major difference between a private and a public listed company in relation to the share buy-back where section 127, CA 2016 allows a public listed company to buy back its shares. A private company cannot buy back its shares. A private company is also prohibited from giving financial assistance in connection with or for the purpose of the acquisition of its shares or shares in its holding company unless this is done in compliance with shareholders' approval in accordance with section 126. This section requires a special resolution of the general meeting, a directors' solvency statement and is limited to not more than 10% of the shareholders' funds. The rules relating to the reduction of capital and payment of dividends also apply to a private company.

226. Transfer of shares and share certificates. Membership in a private company is determined by the fact that a person/shareholder's name appears on the register of members and a private company must also keep and maintain a register of members. The transfer procedure requires that the share certificate be submitted with the transfer form to the company. The share certificate will be cancelled when a member submits it to the company for the purpose of any transfer of shares. Unlike a listed company where the register of depositors and the register of members are records of ownership and title to shares, the only record of ownership that can be relied on for a private company is the register of members. A share certificate is no longer evidence of title under the CA 2016 unlike under the former CA 1965 where the share certificate is evidence of title and must be delivered to the company to enable them to transfer their shares. Under the CA 2016, a company is not required to issue a share certificate unless this is requested by a member.

227. Restriction on transfer. A very important characteristic of a private company is the legal requirement that its constitution must contain a provision that restricts the right of the member to transfer shares. However, a total restriction of transfer is also not valid.[259]

Examples of restrictions on transfer provisions are:

(a) that the shares may be transferred to or registered in the new shareholder's name subject to the directors' discretion; and
(b) a provision requiring that the existing shareholder must first offer the shares to other members of the company, i.e., a pre-emption rights clause, who may take the shares at fair value.

228. In cases where the directors are given the discretion to refuse to register the transfer, this discretion must be exercised bona fide in the best interests of the company. Directors are under a duty to exercise any of their powers for a proper purpose and in the best interests of the company. If the refusal to register the transfer is due to *mala fide*, the directors' discretion may be challenged in court.

229. Section 106 provides a time frame for the company to inform the shareholder whether or not the application to transfer the shares and registration of the shares in the new shareholder's name has been approved. The company is given thirty days from the receipt of the instrument of transfer to do so and if the company failed to give the information within the time frame, the company is deemed to have waived its discretion or to have approved the transfer of the shares.[260] The court, however, has waived compliance with this provision where the delay is due

259. *Kwality Textiles (M'sia) Sdn Bhd v. Arunachalam & Ors* (1990) 3 *MLJ* 361.
260. *See Royal Trust Nominees Ltd v. Sri Hartamas Development Sdn Bhd* (1989) 2 *CLJ* 1069 where it was held that if the right to veto was not exercised within one month, the board will cease to have any right to refuse to register the transfer of the shares; *Long Ah Leong & Ors v. Lo Mu Sen & Sons Sdn Bhd & Anor* (1995) 5 *CLJ* Supp 510.

to circumstances beyond the company's control for example where the company has to obtain approval from governmental agencies.[261]

230. A sale for the transfer of shares which contravenes the restriction on transfer provision is not invalid. However, since the shares will not be registered in the new shareholder's name but are still registered in the seller's name, the seller is a member of the company and the company is entitled to communicate only with the seller as the registered owner of the shares. The transfer of the shares confers on the buyer the equitable title to the shares and the buyer who has sold the shares but in whose names the shares are still registered must act in accordance with the instruction of the buyer.[262]

231. A person may also become a member due to shares being transmitted to him. Any clause relating to restriction on transfer in the constitution is not applicable to a transmission of shares. Shares are transmitted when the change of ownership takes place due to the operation of law for example in the case of death or bankruptcy of the shareholder. The person to whom the shares are transmitted must notify the company in writing that the person wishes to be registered as a shareholder of the company in respect of the shares. The registration must be done within sixty days of receiving the notification. Where a member is deceased, the persons recognized as having any title to his interest in the shares or debentures shall be (a) the legal representative where the deceased was a sole holder or (b) the survivor, where the deceased was a joint holder. The company shall accept as evidence of the grant any document which is by law sufficient evidence of probate of the will or letters of administration of the estate of a deceased person. If the person entitled to have the shares transmitted to him elects to register another person as a member, this will be treated as a transfer of shares and all rules relating to transfer of shares shall be applied.

II. Meetings Procedures

232. The use of written resolution. A private company may pass resolutions without having to hold a physical meeting by relying on the written resolution procedure. The CA 2016 permits members of a private company to pass a resolution or make a decision without having to hold a physical meeting. Instead of a meeting, members may use the written resolution procedure to pass a resolution. The resolution is circulated, i.e., sent to all eligible members of a company and they signify their consent to or their rejection of the proposal or resolution. Due to this flexibility, private companies do not face problems making decisions during the COVID-19 pandemic, unlike public companies. However, a private company cannot utilize the written resolution procedure to pass a resolution:

(a) for the removal of a director; or

---

261. *David Hey v. New Kok Ann Realty Sdn Bhd* (1984) 1 *MLJ* 167.
262. *Liu, Ren-Shuenn v. Lee* (1999) 2 *CLJ* 35.

(b) removal of an auditor: section 297(2), Companies Act 2016.

In these two situations, a private company should follow the SC's guidelines regarding the conduct of general meetings for public companies which clarifies the method of conducting a virtual members' meeting.

Where the written resolution is to be relied upon by a private company, the resolution may be proposed to be passed by way of a written resolution by:

(a) the Board. The Board must send a copy of the written resolution to all eligible members of the company. Accompanying a copy of the written resolution, there must be a statement informing a member as to:
   - the procedure for signifying agreement or otherwise to the resolution; and
   - the date by which the resolution shall lapse if it is not passed. This date is twenty-eight days after the circulation date unless the constitution provides otherwise: section 307.

(b) any member of a private company who has a total of 5% or any lower percentage specified in the constitution of the total voting right so of all eligible members. Eligible members are members who would have been entitled to vote on the resolution on the circulation date of the resolution. The member must make a request to the company to circulate the resolution. The request must be signed or authenticated by the member making the request. Section 302(2), CA 2016 2016 also requires that the resolution to be passed by way of the written resolution procedure must be one that can be properly moved by members. The expenses incurred by the company in complying with the members' request shall be borne by the members making the request unless the company resolves that it is to be borne by the company. Unless the company resolves otherwise, it is also not bound to comply unless there is deposited with or tendered with it, a sum reasonably sufficient to meet its expenses in doing so. If the director fails to circulate a written resolution, any member who has made the request for the circulation of the written resolution may circulate the resolution. In this situation, any reasonable expenses incurred by the members circulating the resolution themselves shall be reimbursed by the company: section 303(7).

233. Shareholders' meeting. Unlike a public company, a private company is not required to hold a statutory meeting. A private company is also not required to hold an AGM unless requested to do so by any members who hold not less than 10% of the issued shares or any higher percentage as stated in the constitution or if the company does not have a share capital, by at least 5% in the number of members. Where these members request that an AGM be held, the private company should follow the SC's guidelines regarding the conduct of general meetings for public companies.

234. A private company may also convene an EGM or a class meeting whenever it is appropriate to do so. Members of a private company may also require directors to convene a meeting of members, similar to the rights of members in a public company and relying on similar procedures: section 311, 312 and 313, CA 2016.

235. Voting. In a private company, it is possible to confer on certain shareholders weighted voting rights. It is possible for the constitution of a private company to state that certain shareholders have more than one vote per share in certain situations.

236. Shorter notice period. The CA 2016 requires not less than fourteen days' notice for the passing of an ordinary resolution and not less than twenty-one days' notice for the passing of a special resolution. However, a shorter notice period is allowed if agreed upon by a 95% majority, i.e., a majority in number of the members having the right to attend and vote at the meeting being a majority which holds not less than 90% of the shares, or a higher percentage that the Constitution may specify but not exceeding 95%, excluding any treasury shares.

Since a private company has a smaller number of shareholders, the agreement on the required percentage is easier to obtain.

237. Removal of the directors. Section 206, CA 2016 states that the removal of a director in a private company is by way of an ordinary resolution but subject to the constitution. This enables the constitution to confer power to remove to any person if so stipulated in the constitution or to provide for a higher voting percentage than an ordinary resolution. There are court decisions recognizing the use of shares with multiple voting rights or shares with veto power in relation to the removal of a private company's director. Shareholders of a private company have more freedom in relation to the removal of the directors and are not constrained by the CA 2016 unlike in the case of a public company. Where the constitution provides for the removal method, the special notice required for the removal of a director under section 206, CA 2016 also does not apply.

III. Management of Companies

238. A private company is required to have a minimum of one director. Where the private company has a sole director, the director cannot resign until a meeting of members has been called to receive notice of resignation and appoint a new director. In situations where the sole director vacates office due to disqualification, unsoundness of mind, death or vacates his office in accordance with the constitution, the company secretary must convene a meeting of members or the next of kin or the personal representatives. Subsequently, if a director cannot be appointed, the Registrar may make an order that the company be struck off the register.

239. It is usual to find in a private company that the directors are also the shareholders. In some private companies with a very small number of shareholders, it is not unusual that all the members are also directors. In such cases, the line distinguishing the board from the general meeting of shareholders is often blurred. In some cases where all the members are also the directors, a board of directors meeting may also be considered as the general meeting of shareholders and vice versa.

240. Because some private companies have a small number of shareholders and are owner-managed, most of the formal decision-making processes in terms of a formal meeting, notice period, for example, are often not strictly adhered to. This does not necessarily mean that the private company and its officers and members are in contravention of the Companies Act 2016. The Companies Act 2016 provides a shorter notice period or doing away with a physical meeting, provided a very substantial number of shareholders agree for a shorter period or if there is unanimous consent of the shareholders not to have a physical meeting.

241. Duties owed by the directors. In general, there is no difference between the duties owed by the directors of a public company and a private company. Although directors of a private company owe the same duties that are owed by directors of public companies towards their respective companies, there are some transactions which are conflict of interest transactions which are not prohibited if carried out by a private company. An example is in relation to an exempt private company which is not prohibited from giving any loan or securing any loans given to its directors, the directors of its subsidiary company or persons connected to its directors or directors of its subsidiary.

242. Where there is a transfer of a company's assets to a director or acquisition of an asset by a director from a private company under section 228, the interested parties, i.e., the director who is also a shareholder or other shareholder connected to the director is not prohibited from voting on the transaction. The restriction on certain persons from voting on the transaction is imposed by the BSLR and as such is not applicable to a private company.

243. A director who is interested in a contract entered into or proposed to be entered into by the company is required to disclose that interest to a general meeting and the board of directors.[263] However, unlike a director of a public company, there is no prohibition on a director of a private company from voting and participating in any discussion while the contract is being considered at the board meeting unless the constitution states so. This is because section 222, which states that interested directors cannot participate or vote in any discussion while the contract is being considered at the board meeting, does not apply where:

(a) the company is a private company unless it is a subsidiary of a public company;
(b) where the private company is a wholly owned subsidiary of a public company and the contract is between the private company and the public company or with another wholly owned subsidiary of the same holding company;
(c) any contract of indemnity against any loss that any director may suffer by reason of becoming or being surety for a company;
(d) any contract entered into or to be entered into by a public company or a private company that is a subsidiary of a public company, with another company in which the interest of the director consists solely of:

263. Section 131 of the Companies Act 1965.

(i) in him being a director of the company and the holder of shares of not more than the number or value as is required to qualify him for the appointment as a director; or
(ii) in him having an interest in not more than 5% of its paid-up capital.

244. Remuneration of directors. For a private company including one which is not a subsidiary of a listed company, any fees, any benefits payable including any compensation for loss of employment may be approved by the Board, subject to the constitution: section 230(2), Companies Act 2016. The constitution may specify that the remuneration shall be approved from time to time by the general meeting. An example of a provision in the constitution relating to remuneration is Article 70 in Table A of the former Companies Act 1965:

> The remuneration of the directors shall from time to time be determined by the company in general meeting. That remuneration shall be deemed to accrue from day to day. The directors may also be paid all travelling, hotel, and other expenses properly incurred by them in attending and returning from meetings of the directors or any committee of the directors or general meetings of the company or in connection with the business of the company.

In this situation, the director's entitlement to the remuneration does not accrue until and unless a resolution has been passed by the general meeting,[264] However, in the absence of such a provision in the constitution, section 230(3) Companies Act 2016 states that any approval made by the board must be recorded in the minutes of the board meetings and the board must notify the shareholders of the approval within fourteen days from the date it was given. The board's decision to approve the remuneration may be challenged by any members holding at least 10% of the total voting rights and who consider the payment as not fair to the company. The member may apply within thirty days after he has received the knowledge of the payment to require that the general meeting approve the payment either by way of a written resolution or at a general meeting: section 230(4), Companies Act 2016.

Where the resolution is not passed, the fees payable is not approved to be made by the company and any payment made is a debt due from the director to the company: section 230(5), Companies Act 2016.

245. The oppression remedy. It is easier for the members of a private company to bring a claim under the oppression remedy specified under section 346 CA 2016, on the basis that the members' legitimate expectation has not been respected and fulfilled. Due to the nature of the relationship of the members in a private company, members have a legitimate expectation that the company's management and business should be conducted in a certain way as agreed to by them, even though the constitution does not provide so. Thus, in a private company, the failure to comply or give effect to the legitimate expectation of the members enables the member to bring an action under oppression. An example of a legitimate expectation is the

---

264. *Nagateck Sdn Bhd v. Chong Lou Chan @ Cheong Lou Chan*[2015] MLJU 770.

understanding that all members or certain members shall be involved in the management and cannot be removed from the board of directors. This type of legitimate expectation is not recognized in a public company.[265]

IV. Winding-Up under the Just and Equitable Ground

246. The same statutory provisions that are applicable to wind up a public company also apply to a private company. A private company may be wound up voluntarily by its members or be wound up by an order of the court. However, one of the grounds to wind up the company compulsorily is if the court is of the view that it is just and equitable to do so: section 465(1)(h). This section has been used by private companies only. This section is also one of the remedies available to minority shareholders of a private company.

Winding-up under section 465(1)(h) is available for a private company that is managed as an incorporated association, i.e., a private company in form but is actually a partnership.

247. In *Ebrahimi v. Westbourne Galleries Ltd*,[266] Lord Wilberforce identified three elements in the presence of any one of which might, in the case of a particular company, enable the company to be wound up under the just and equitable ground:

(a) an association formed or continued on the basis of a personal relationship, involving mutual confidence – this element will often be found where a pre-existing partnership has been converted into a limited company;
(b) an agreement, or understanding, that all, or some (for there may be 'sleeping' members) of the shareholders shall participate in the conduct of the business; and
(c) restriction on the transfer of the members' interest in the company – so that if confidence is lost, or one member is removed from management, he cannot take out his stake and go elsewhere.

248. An order for winding-up will be made on the just and equitable ground where there is fraud, misconduct or oppression by the directors or majority shareholders.[267]

249. A private company may be wound up under the just and equitable ground where there is a failure of the objects of the company or failure of the substratum. The objects of the company are stated in the Memorandum but in the case of an incorporated association, there may be an agreement amongst the members on what the company should be involved in. In *Re German Date Coffee Company*,[268] the main object of the company was to exploit a German patent for making coffee from

265. *Tuan haji Ishak b Ismail v. Leong Hup Holdings Bhd & Ors* (1996) 1 *MLJ* 661.
266. (1972) 2 *All ER* 492.
267. *Loch v. John Blackwood Ltd* (1924) *AC* 783.
268. (1882) 20 *Ch.D* 169.

dates and the patent was never obtained. The court held that the company's substratum had failed. It was impossible to carry out the objects for which the company was formed and it was just and equitable that the company should be wound up.

250. A private company may also be wound up under the just and equitable ground where it can be shown that there is a breakdown in mutual trust and confidence amongst the members. The basis of the trust could be certain terms that all members agree to abide by, for example, that all members are to be involved in the management or that there should be equal shareholding. In *Tay Bok Choon v. Tahansan Sdn Bhd*,[269] the company was a private company with four shareholders holding equal numbers of shares. They were all directors and no single shareholder could transfer his shares without the consent of at least two others. One shareholder had acquired his 25% holding after agreeing with the then directors that he would be appointed a director and chairman of the board. As chairman he introduced a finance company to refinance the company; he took up new shares for cash, loaned money to two other director shareholders to do so, and guaranteed the company's liabilities to the finance company. A year and a half later, when for the first time the company looked set to make substantial profits, he was removed as director and chairman. He presented a petition to wind up the company on a just and equitable ground. The Privy Council held that it was just and equitable to wind up the company. The petitioner had discharged the burden of proving that the other shareholders were not entitled to use their voting powers in the company to oust him without cause, and were under an obligation to continue his appointment as a director. The petitioner was led to believe that even though there was no express assurance, he would participate in the management and would, in any event, be entitled to a seat on the board so long as he held his shares.

251. Deadlock in management has also been allowed as a reason for the winding-up of a private company under section 465(1)(h). In *Perak Integrated Network Services Sdn Bhd v Urban Domain Sdn Bhd & Anor*[2018] 4 MLJ 1, there is a deadlock in management where the board of a company is equally split between directors with opposing views. There is also a deadlock where the shareholding of a company is equally split between shareholders taking opposing stances.

252. In *Re Yenidje Tobacco Co. Ltd*,[270] two businesses were amalgamated into one company and the two owners became the sole shareholders and directors of the company, with equal voting rights with no casting vote. Disagreements in major areas of the business developed. As these two directors will not speak to each other, no business of the company can be carried on despite the company's business being profitable.

269. (1987) 3 *BCC* 132.
270. (1916) 2 *Ch.* 426.

V. Auditor of a Private Company

Appointment and removal

253. A private company must have an auditor appointed for each financial year of the company. However, exemption may be given by the Registrar according to the conditions as determined by the Registrar.

The appointment of the auditor of a private company may be made by:

- the Board. If the company is a newly incorporated company, the board must appoint an auditor at least thirty days before the end of the period for the submission of the first financial statements to the Registrar. The board also have the power to appoint an auditor to fill a casual vacancy in the office of the auditor.
- the members by ordinary resolution. The appointment is to be made for subsequent years following the submission of its first financial statements within the period for appointing auditors. The period for appointing auditors means the period of thirty days (a) before the end of the period allowed for the lodgement of the previous year's financial statements with the Registrar; or (b) if the previous year's financial statements were lodged earlier, before the day on which financial statements were lodged with the Registrar. The members may also appoint the auditor if the Board fails to appoint an auditor

  The private company may utilize a written resolution procedure to appoint a person as an auditor in place of an outgoing auditor. For the written resolution, the company shall send a copy of the proposed resolution to the person proposed to be appointed as an auditor and to the outgoing auditor. The outgoing auditor may make a statement in writing explaining the circumstances connected with his resignation not exceeding a reasonable length to the company within fourteen days from receiving the proposed resolution referred to in subsection (1) and may request a copy of the statement to be sent to every member of the company. The company shall send a copy of the statement to every member of the company to whom resolution under this section has been circulated prior to the period for agreeing to written resolution.

A special notice is required of such a resolution if the period for appointing an auditor has ended since the outgoing auditor ceased to hold office due to his resignation or removal, or such a period has ended and an auditor should have been appointed but is not appointed.

- the Registrar. If a private company fails to appoint an auditor, the Registrar may appoint one or more auditors upon application in writing from any member of the company.

Term of office of auditors of private company

254. Section 269, CA 2016 provides that the auditor of a private company shall hold office in accordance with the terms of his appointment. However, the auditor does not take office until the previous auditor ceases to hold office. The auditor ceases to hold office thirty days from the circulation of the financial statements to the members unless he is reappointed. Where the office of an auditor becomes vacant and no auditor has been appointed by members of the company, the auditor who holds office immediately before the vacancy shall be deemed to be reappointed, unless:

(a) he was appointed by the Board;
(b) the constitution requires actual reappointment;
(c) the deemed reappointment is prevented by the members under section 270; or
(d) the members have resolved that he should not be reappointed.

Nevertheless, an auditor of a private company shall not be deemed to be reappointed if the company has received notice under this section from members representing at least 5% of the total voting rights of all members who would be entitled to vote on a resolution that the auditor should not be reappointed.

Rights and duties.

255. The auditor has certain rights and duties irrespective of whether the company to whom audit services are provided is a public or private company, as discussed earlier. However, there are some differences.

In the case of a private company, if due notice is given to an auditor of the intention to move a resolution requiring the presence of the auditor at a general meeting of the company where financial statements of the company for any financial year are to be laid, the auditor shall attend that meeting so as to respond according to his knowledge and ability to any question relevant to the audit of the financial statements.

Part II. Partnerships

Chapter 1. Overview of the Difference Between General and Limited Partnerships

256. There are several types of partnership legally recognized in Malaysia, namely the general partnership, the LLP and the LP structure. In Malaysia, the LP structure is currently available in Malaysia in the Federal Territory of Labuan under the LP and LLPA 2010. Both the general and LPs possess no legal personality. Only the LLP is recognized as having a separate legal personality from the partners.

In a general partnership, the law states that there must be an agreement between two or more persons to carry on business in common with a view of profit.[271] A general partnership is established, once all these elements are present, even though the business arrangement is not registered or no formal business name is used. For an LP, the same elements are required to establish an LP.

The Labuan LP and LLPA provides that the rules of the PA and those of equity and common law are applicable to LP so far as it is consistent with the LPA.[272] In fact, 'firm', 'firm name' and 'business' of an LP have the same meaning as in the PA. Hence, it can be concluded that in order to establish an LP, the same required elements, namely agreement between two or more persons to carry on business in common with a view of profit are necessary. However, the name of a limited partner or a body corporate shall not appear in the name of the LP unless it is also the name of one of the general partners or the LP has been carried on under that name before the admission of that partner or corporate partner as a limited partner.[273]

257. One of the main differences between a general partnership and an LP is the registration requirement. For general partnerships, formal registration is not a requirement for the establishment of a partnership relation. As long as all the elements prescribed by the PA are fulfilled, a partnership can validly exist despite non-registration. Although businesses must be registered under the RBA, this is to enable enforcement of legal rights by the firm against third parties. Registration under the RBA may be evidence of a partnership relation but a firm is not established merely by registering under the RBA and non-registration does not affect the enforcement of partners' rights amongst themselves or the right of a third party to sue the firm. However, for LP, formal registration is very important. Under the LLP

271. PA (Malaysia) 1961; s. 3(1).
272. *See also* Labuan Limited Partnerships Act 1997; s. 7.
273. LLP and LLPA 2010; s. 7(3) and (4) p. 10.

and LLPA 2010, an LP must be formally registered with LFSA.[274] The LP requires that the firm must be formed in the manner provided by the Act and registration of the firm is a condition for the limited partners to get the advantages of limited liability. Failure to register the LP will render the firm as a general partnership and all partners are deemed as general partners, with unlimited joint and several liabilities for the firm's debts. For this reason, a contract to form a LP will normally specify that the firm is not to come into existence or commence trade until it is duly registered.

258. Another difference between LP and general partnerships is the management rights. In general partnerships, all partners have the right to decide for the business. In matters concerning the nature of the firm, consent of all partners must be obtained while in ordinary matters concerning the business, decision of the majority is sufficient. On the other hand, in LP, the management rights are only vested in general partners while limited partners are not entitled to take part in the management of the firm. A limited partner who refused to adhere to the restriction by taking part in the management will be lifted from the protection of limited liability and will have unlimited liability similar to general partners.

259. There are also differences between LP and general partnerships in terms of partners' liability. In general partnerships, partners have unlimited liability towards debts of the firm. In the case where the firm's assets are not sufficient to pay the debts of the firm, a partner's personal property can be seized. In addition, as the firm is a collective of all partners, debts of the firm are actually debts of all partners. In LP, some of the partners referred to as limited partners, are allowed to limit their liability in the firm. However, the structure of an LP does not allow all partners to have limited liability. The law requires that there must be a composition of both general and limited partners in an LP.

In an LP, there are general and limited partners. The limited partners are not liable for debts and obligations of the firm and they cannot participate in the management of the firm. If they do so, the limited partners will lose their status as limited partners and become general partners.

In a general partnership, the partners may not limit their liability as far as their obligation to outsiders is concerned. However, there are many instances where the partners in a general partnership agree amongst themselves on their management participation rights where there are partners who are considered as 'sleeping partners'. Nonetheless, this is an internal arrangement and insofar as the 'sleeping partner' is known as a partner, he will be liable along with the other partners for the partnership's obligations.

274. LLP and LLPA 2010; s. 5(1).

Chapter 2. Characteristics of a General Partnership

§1. Identification of Individual Partners with the Firm

260. Partners and the firm are not distinct from each other. Section 6(1) of the PA provides that:

> Persons who have entered into partnership with one another are, for the purposes of this Act, called collectively a firm, and the name under which their business is carried on is called the firm name.

In commercial and legal terms, partners are collectively referred to as 'a firm'. From the commercial perspective, the firm is treated very similar to a company, whereby the firm is regarded as a separate entity distinct from the partners. This view is strongly reflected in the account records of the firm. For example, in the partnership's accounts, monies due to or from a partner are shown as owed to or by the firm and not from other partners. The firm also has its own separate account opened under its own name and not the partners. The consequence of this attitude is the tendency to regard the firm's rights and obligations as unaffected despite any change in the composition of the partners. Partners are seen and regarded merely as agents of the firm and the partnership liabilities are deemed to be the partners' liabilities but only to that extent and not more.

The commercial view is actually encouraged by certain features which characterize most partnerships, for example, in general, the firm's name is normally distinctive and does not represent the partners or coincide with the partners' name. Similar to the ways of a private individual, the firm can trade under any name it pleases, provided that it does not mislead the public or implicate any other person, particularly regarding liability to creditors.[275] A change of partners often has no visible effect on the continuity of the partnership as the partners will usually agree that any change in the identity of the partners will not terminate the partnership; thus, partners come and go but the firm usually stays on as it was originally set up.

261. The legal view of a firm is very different from the commercial view. The court generally does not recognize the firm to be distinct from its partners. J. Farwell, in *Sadler v. Whiteman*,[276] took the view that:

> In English law, the firm as such has no existence; partners carry on business both as principals and agents for each other within the scope of the partnership business; the firm's name is a mere expression, not a legal entity.

275. *See Burchell v. Wilde* (1900) 1 *Ch.* 551 (CA).
276. (1910) 1 *KB* at p. 889. *See also Meyer & Co. v. Faber* (No. 2) (1923) 2 *Ch.* 421, *Hoare v. Oriental Bank Corp* (1877) 2 *App Cas* 589, *Ex p Corbett* (1880) 14 *Ch. D* 122, *R v. Holden* (1912) 1 *KB* 483.

In a Malaysian Federal Court case, *Keow Seng & Company v. Trustees of Leong San Tong Kho Kongsi (Penang) Registered*, L.P. Raja Azlan (as he then was) clearly stated:[277]

> We start with the premise that a partnership is not a legal entity in law (*see Alagappa Chettiar v. Colliseum Café*)[278] and as such cannot hold a tenancy. ... The firm name is not in itself the name of any person other than the partners.

Hence, from the legal perspective, the partners are deemed to be the firm and vice versa,[279] and the firm's debts and liabilities are the partners' debts and liabilities.[280] The law also emphasizes that a partner may become the debtor or creditor of his co-partners but he cannot become the debtor or creditor of his firm.[281] Furthermore, a partner cannot be employed by the firm in which he is a member as he 'could not employ himself'.[282] In short, from the legal view, the firm has no legal entity separate from the partners.

262. Despite the statutory provisions and theory on identification of partners with a firm, in practice, the entity of partnership is not actually clear and absolute. The question that often recurs is whether the firm and the partners as a group are an 'aggregate', or is the firm distinct and has its own entity, separate from the partners. Generally, a partnership is identified with the partners to the extent that the partnership entity is dissolved upon dissociation of the partners,[283] but in circumstances such as bankruptcy proceedings, partners are treated as distinct from the firm. It is observed that from the practical aspect, the commercial view is more realistic than the legal view. For example, in assessing income tax, a partnership is regarded as a separate entity and each partner's assessment is calculated according to each partner's individual tax position.

I. Formalities and Registration

263. Under the partnership law, a firm can exist without being registered and there is no obligation for the firm to file documents at any central registry.[284]

277. (1983) 2 *MLJ* 103 at pp. 104–105. Followed in *Shahinuddin bin Shariff v. Mohd Amin bin Hasbollah* [1998] 3 MLJ 693, *Mohamed Abu Bakar s/o Yusuf v. PA Syed Aboo Tahir s/o P Ahmed* [1990] 1 MLJ 26.
278. [1962] *MLJ* 111.
279. Section of the PA 1961.
280. Section 11 of the PA 1961.
281. *Green v. Hertzog* (1954) 1 *WLR* 1309, *Richardson v. The Bank of England* (1838) 4 *My. & Cr.* I65; *Lee v. Neuchatel Asphalte Co.* (1886) 41 *Ch. D* 361; *Rye v. Rye* (1961) 1 *WLR* 209.
282. *Ellis v. Joseph Ellis & Co.* (1905) 1 *KB* 324, *MacKinlay v. Arthur Young McClelland Moores & Co.* (1989) 3 *WLR* 371.
283. Section 35 of the PA 1961.
284. David Milman & Terence Flanagan, *Modern Partnership Law* 104 (Croom Helm 1983).

In *Adams v. Newbigging*[285] and *Weiner v. Harris*,[286] the court came to the same conclusion and held that the fact that the term partnership had not been used was not enough to disregard the existence of a partnership. Once the court is satisfied that the elements of partnership exist in the agreement between the parties, the fact that it does not undergo formalities and is not registered as a partnership is immaterial. This principle is derived from the acceptance of law that the existence of a partnership is mainly based on the agreement and contractual relationship which exist between the parties. The agreement itself is not required to be in writing; for example, in *Gray v. Smith*[287] and *Munro v. Stein*,[288] the court concluded that it was possible to have a partnership created orally. As long as the parties could prove that there was an agreement to carry on a business in common with a view of profit, a partnership could validly be established. In the case of *Dr Rajan Sinha v. Dr P.C. Harman*, J. Peh Swee Chin took the view that:[289]

> I find that a partnership agreement in writing was not a condition precedent to the formation of the partnership, but having regard to all the circumstances, a mere form which all parties had decided to adopt.

264. The partnership agreement is also not intended to exclude the rights and obligations of partners which are implied by the PA or by the general law. In *Smith v. Jeyes*, Lord Langdale held that:[290]

> The transactions of partners with each other cannot be considered merely with reference to the express contract between them. The duties and obligations arising from the relation between the parties are regulated by the express contracts between them, so far as the express contract extends and continues in force, does not reach to all those duties and obligations, they are implied and enforced by the law.

265. Section 3(1) of the PA 1961 defines a partnership as the 'relation which subsists between persons carrying on business in common with a view of profit'.
There are three essential elements of a partnership, namely:

(a) a relationship between persons carrying on a business;
(b) carrying on of a business in common; and
(c) with a view of profit.

285. (1888) 13 *App Cas* 308. *See* the observations of the Lord Chancellor at p. 315.
286. (1910) 1 *KB* 285. *See* the judgment of Master of the Rolls at p. 209.
287. (1889) 43 *Ch.D* 208.
288. [1961] *SC* 362.
289. (1988) 1 *CLJ* 37 at p. 39.
290. (1841) 4 *Beav* 503 at p. 505.

As regards formalities, a general partnership does not really emphasize procedural matters. Once all the required elements are established, the fact that the organization has not been registered as a partnership is irrelevant.[291]

A. Relationship Between Persons Carrying on a Business

266. Section 2 of the PA 1961 defines business as 'every trade, occupation, or profession'. In *Smith v. Anderson*,[292] the court held that a single act or undertaking could not amount to 'carrying on a business'. J. Brett, in this case, took the view[293] that:

> The expression of 'carrying on' implies a repetition of acts and excludes the case of an association formed for doing one particular act which is never to be repeated. That series of acts is to be a series of acts which constitute a business.

However, case law has held that a single adventure and an activity of a commercial nature can also amount to business within the meaning of the provision. For example, in *Reid v. Hollinshead*,[294] *Re Abenheim*,[295] *Mann v. D'Arcy*[296] and *Windsor v. Schroeder*,[297] the courts held that one commercial adventure undertaken by the parties would be considered a business and that the parties were partners. In *Soh Hood Beng v. Khoo Chye Neo*,[298] the court applied J. Brett's decision in *Smith v. Anderson*[299] and held that in order for the activities to amount to 'business', there must be a repetition of acts and cannot be confined to one transaction only.

267. In order to amount to 'business', the adventure or undertaking taken by the parties must be of a commercial adventure whether selling goods or services for reward. In *Customs and Excise Comrs v. Lord Fisher*,[300] the defendant was a person who invited friends and relatives to shoot pheasants on a paying basis. The court held that no business was carried on, despite the fact that there were financial contributions involved, as the shoot did not amount to 'business' since it was not undertaken with the intensity usually associated with a 'commercial shoot'. Furthermore, the activity was only open to friends and relatives. If the shoot had been operated

291. *Ratna Amal & Anor v. Tan Chow Soo* (1964) 30 *MLJ* 399 at p. 400.
292. (1879) 15 *Ch.D* 247.
293. *Ibid.* at 277.
294. (1825) 4 *B & C* 867.
295. (1913) 109 *LT* 219.
296. (1968) 2 *All ER* 172.
297. (1979) 129 *New Law Journal* at p. 1266.
298. (1897) 4 *S.S.L.R.* 115.
299. (1879) 15 *Ch.D* 247.
300. (1981) 2 *All ER* 147. The court listed down six factors which were relevant to determine whether an activity involving remuneration for services amounted to an economic activity. In *Longridge on the Thames v Revenue and Customs Commissioners* [2016] *EWCA Civ* 930, the court highlighted that these factors were 'useful tools' but the list was not exhaustive.

more intensively and advertised to the general public, it could amount to a 'business' and subject to the VAT claimed by the plaintiff.

268. The date of commencement of the business is also important in determining the existence of a partnership since the Act requires the 'carrying on' of the business. A partnership cannot exist before the business is commenced. Persons who are contemplating a future partnership or enter into an agreement to become partners at some future time cannot be considered partners prior to the commencement date of the business.[301] The element and test required for a partnership is the carrying on of a business and not an agreement to carry it on. In *Keith Spicer Ltd v. Mansell*,[302] the defendant and Mr Bishop agreed to go into business together and to form a limited company. The latter ordered from the plaintiff some goods to be used by the company after it had been formed. The price of the goods was not paid and the plaintiff sued the defendant on the ground that there was a partnership between the latter and Mr Bishop. The Court of Appeal rejected the claim and held that there was no evidence that the defendant and Mr Bishop were partners within the meaning of section 1(1) of the PA 1890. The evidence merely showed that they were preparing to carry on a business as soon as they could.

Nevertheless, if two or more persons who have agreed to go into business with a view of profit choose to ignore the agreed commencement date and start to carry on business prematurely, they will become partners.[303] On the other hand, if only one person from the group acted prior to the commencement of the agreed business, no immediate partnership will be created.[304] 'Relation which subsists' in section 3(1) of PA 1961 infers that the partnership relation must actually exist and not a mere description of such relation.[305]

269. Under the PA, for a partnership to be created there must be two or more persons carrying on the business.[306] Nonetheless, there is a maximum limit on the number of persons who may form a partnership. In Malaysia, the law provides that there must not be more than twenty persons in a partnership except for professional firms, which have no maximum limit on the number of partners.[307] In *Tan Teck Hee v. Cheng Tian Peng*,[308] the partnership consisted of twenty-five partners and the court held that the partnership was not valid and had no right to take legal proceedings.

---

301. *See* judgment of Parke, J. in: *Dickinson v. Valpy* (1829) 10 *B & C* 128 at pp. 141–142.
302. (1970) 1 *All ER* 462.
303. R.C. Banks, *Lindley & Banks on Partnership* (16th ed., Sweet & Maxwell 1990) highlighted the importance of the element carrying on businesses in distinguishing actual and contemplated partnerships.
304. *Ibid.*
305. *Malaysian International Trading Corp(Japan) Sdn Bhd v Bentini SPA & Ors* [2014] 11 *MLJ* 255 at 268.
306. Section 3 of the PA 1961.
307. Section 47(2) of the PA 1961; s. 14(3) of the Companies Act 1965.
308. (1915) 2 *F.M.S.L.R.* 161. *See also Tan Ching Cheang v. Estate & Trust Agencies Ltd* (1932) *F.M.S.L.R.* 129.

Apart from the limitation on the maximum number of partners, the word 'persons' under the PAs is also read conjunctively with the Interpretation Acts,[309] which define 'person' as inclusive of 'a body of persons corporate or un-incorporate'.[310] Hence, a partnership can exist between an individual and a limited company, individuals with individuals or between two or more companies.

B. Carrying on a Business in Common

270. Corresponding to the requirement of 'persons', the law provides that not only must there be two or more persons cooperating commercially, they must also be acting 'in common' in relation to a single business so that the business is jointly constituted. In *Chooi Siew Cheong v. Lucky Height Development Sdn Bhd*,[311] the Federal Court held that no partnership resulted from a joint venture agreement between a landowner and a housing developer because each party to the agreement intended a wholly separate business and that there was no business in common with a view of profit. This was distinguished in *Malaysian International Trading Corp (Japan) Sdn Bhd v. Bentini SPA & Ors,*[312]where it was held that the elements for the existence of a partnership in the joint venture were satisfied. The parties, in this case, had a business in common (namely the project) with a view of profit.

The notion 'in common' also refers to the participation of partners in the partnership business. For a partnership to exist, it is not essential for all partners to take an active part in the management of the business. What is necessary is that the business must be carried on either by or on behalf of all partners. Whether a business is being carried on by or on behalf of the partners is a question of facts, which varies according to the facts and circumstances of the case.[313] In *Lang v. James Morrison & Co. Ltd*, C.J. Griffith[314] applied the test 'does the person who, in fact, carries on the business do so as agent for the person alleged to be partners?' in determining the element of 'carrying on in common'. Nonetheless, establishing liability to third parties from the acts of persons who conducted the partnership's business cannot of itself constitute carrying on business in common. A further requirement is required to establish mutuality of rights and obligations between the persons on whose behalf the business is carried on. Such mutuality can only arise if the parties have the legal duty to perform their obligations.[315] In *Smith v. Anderson*, L.J. Smith stated that:[316]

---

309. Section 3 of the Interpretation Act 1967.
310. *See also* s. 4(4) of the Limited Partnerships Act (UK) 1907; s. 3(6) & (7) of the Limited Partnerships Act (Labuan).
311. [1995] 1 *MLJ* 513.
312. [2014] 11 *MLJ* 255.
313. *Osman v. Chang Kang Swee* (1924) 4 *F.M.S.L.R.* 292; *Sivagami Achiv Ramanathan Chettiar* (1959) 25 *MLJ* 221.
314. (1911) 13 *CLR* 1 at p. 11.
315. Keith L. Fletcher, *The Law of Partnership In Australia and New Zealand* 31 (LBC Information Services 1996).
316. (1879) 15 *Ch.D* 247 at p. 275. *See also Re Ruddock* (1879) 5 *VLR (IP & M)* 51 and *R v. Willis*; Ex parte Martin (1879) 5 *VLR (L)* 149.

> Persons who have no mutual rights and obligations do not, according to my view, constitute an association because they happen to have no common interest or several interests in what is to be divided between them.

271. The element of carrying on in common also emphasizes participation in the business. It follows that if there is no participation, even if there is an intention to draw up a partnership agreement, the court will not declare a partnership. In *Saywell v. Pope*,[317] the court held that the partnership agreement could only be applied from the date it was signed and even though it contained a statement that the partnership had actually begun earlier, that in itself could not make them partners. There was no evidence that during the relevant time, the parties did anything to integrate themselves into the partnership. Hence, no partnership existed at the earlier date.[318]

On the other hand, where there is participation in a business, those involved can become partners prior to the drawing up of a formal partnership agreement. In *Ratna Amal & Anor v. Tan Chow Soo*, C.J. Wylie took the view that:[319]

> Notwithstanding the avoidance of any reference in the agreement to a partnership and the use throughout of the word 'syndicate', I consider that the arrangement arrived at is in fact a partnership … they have agreed to carry on this business 'in common with a view of profit'.

The Federal Court in *Chooi Siew Cheong*[320] had considered the intention of the parties in determining the existence of partnership and this was later referred by the Court of Appeal in *Sinnathamby a/l Klondakoudan & Ors v Brijkishore a/l Shuparshad.*[321] The Court of Appeal quoted *The Law of Partnership in Australia and New Zealand*[322] which emphasized that 'The intention is not to be determined by an examination of the private intention of each party but is to be ascertained by inference from their conduct and actions, throughout the whole course of their dealings with each other.'[323]

C. Business Is Set up with a View of Profit

272. Another vital element in determining a business is profit-making. Even though there are commercial activities which are non-profit making and which the

317. (1979) 53 *TC* 40.
318. For further discussion, *see* Geoffrey Morse, *Partnership Law* 10 (Blackstone Press Ltd 1995).
319. [1964] *MLJ* 399 at p. 400. *See also Kriziac v. Ravinder Rohini Pty Ltd* (1990) 102 *FLR 8*.
320. [1995] 1 *MLJ* 513. According to the Federal Court 'the intention of the parties as appearing from the whole facts of the case and the contract they had made'.
321. [1998] 1 *MLJ* 31. In this case the Court of Appeal held that there was no element of any joint intention on the part of the parties to constitute a joint venture partnership. Refer also *Malaysian International Trading Corp(Japan) Sdn Bhd v Bentini SPA & Ors* [2014] 11 *MLJ* 255 at 270.
322. Keith L. Fletcher, *The Law of Partnership in Australia and New Zealand* 31 (LBC Information Services 1996).
323. *Ibid.*, at 90.

court holds as 'business',[324] such activities cannot form the basis of partnership which mainly requires the party's intent on gaining and sharing profits. In *Smith v. Anderson*,[325] the court held that trustees of a unit trust were not partners, although they were paid on a proper commercial basis for the activities they undertook since they were not carrying on a business. L.J. James stated[326] that:

> [N]othing that is done under this deed by the trustees comes within the ordinary meaning of 'business', any more than what is done by the trustees of a marriage settlement who have large properties vested in them, and who have very extensive powers of disposing of the investment, charging the investments, and selling them and re-investing in other investments according to their discretion and judgment, with or without the consent of their *cestuis que trust*. That is not a business.

Accordingly, from the profit-making element, it was revealed in case law that no partnership would arise in clubs and associations,[327] investment trusts,[328] promoters[329] and arrangements with creditors.[330]

When an association is formed with some other predominant motive other than the acquisition of profit, it cannot be a partnership as it lacks the element of 'with a view of profit' that is required by the PAs. Hence, societies, clubs and mutual insurance societies are clearly not partnerships as they are formed without the object of gaining profit.[331]

The word 'profit' within the meaning of the Act refers to net profit. This can be clearly identified by virtue of section 4(b) of the PA (Malaysia) 1961, which provides that 'the sharing of gross returns does not of itself create a partnership, whether the persons sharing such returns have or have not a joint or common right or interest in any property from which or from the use of which the returns are derived'.

In *Re Spanish Prospecting Co. Ltd*, L.J. Fletcher Moulton[332] defined net profits as the net amount remaining after paying out of the receipts of a business, all the expenses incurred in obtaining those receipts. It follows that if the gross return is divided irrespective of profitability, the division involves only an incidental sharing of profits rather than sharing of profits in the true sense. In *Cox v. Coulson*,[333] the parties agreed to share the payment for bills of the business, and in return, they will

324. In *Customs and Excise Comrs v. Morrison's Academy Boarding Houses Association* [1978] *STC* 1, the court held that even if the accommodation was provided on a non-profit making basis to the students or some other group, it may still amount to business.
325. (1879) 15 *Ch.D* 247.
326. *Ibid.*, at p. 276.
327. *Wise v. Perpetual Trustees Co.* (1903) 109 *LT* 219, *Caldicott v. Griffiths* (1853) 8 *Ex* 898, *Re Lead Company's Workmen Fund Society* (1904) 2 *Ch.* 196.
328. *Smith v. Anderson* (1879)15 *Ch.D* 247.
329. *Keith Spicer Ltd v. Mansell* (1970)1 *All ER* 462.
330. *Cox v. Hickman* (1860) 8 *HLC* 268, *Marconi's Wireless Telegraph Co. v. Newman* (1930) 2 *KB* 29.
331. *See also* the judgment of Lord Lindley in: *Wise v. Perpetual Trustee Co.* (1903) *AC* 139 *AC* 149.
332. (1911) 1 *Ch.* 91 at p. 92.
333. (1916) 2 *KB* 177.

share the gross takings. The Court of Appeal held that the parties are not partners as the PAs[334] made it clear that the sharing of gross returns did not create a partnership.

Nevertheless, a partnership, which has been entered into to make a profit, does not cease to be a partnership merely because it fails to generate profit. For example, if a partnership is formed mainly as a mechanism of tax avoidance, the fact that the business does not gain profits is not very relevant to the partners, as long as the profit motive is in existence. In *Newstead (Inspector of Taxes) v. Frost*,[335] the Court of Appeal drew a distinction between transactions entered into wholly to avoid tax and those entered partly for the purposes of commercial operations and partly to avoid tax. The court held that the former did not create a partnership, but, as profit creation was part of the motive of the latter, it resulted in a partnership between the persons.[336]

Profit motive of the persons is said to be the requirement of the PA and not profit-sharing as the words used in the provision is 'business carried on in common with a view of profit'. Although the objective or view of profits may not be realized ultimately, it does not derogate from finding that a partnership subsists so long as the objective to make a profit existed at the time of the formation of that relationship.

Hence, only the business needs to be carried in common and not the profit. In fact, a share of profits is not a conclusive evidence of a partnership.[337]

§2. Nature of Unlimited Liability of Each partner

I. Collective Liability

273. The PA provides that partners are collectively liable for debts and liabilities of the firm as long as they hold the position of partner in the partnership and act within their authority.[338] In fact, the liabilities are extended to a deceased partner as the law provides that the estate of a deceased partner is severally liable for debts of the partnership which was incurred by the firm during his lifetime as a partner.[339] The law also specifically provides that for contractual debts, partners are jointly liable,[340] whereas, for liabilities in torts and other wrongs, the partners are jointly and severally liable.[341]

334. Partnerships Act (UK) 1890, s. 2(2). This provision is *pari materia* to s. 4(b) of PA (Malaysia) 1961.
335. (1979) 2 *All ER* 129.
336. This allows the court to distinguish previous decisions of its own and of the House of Lords that an arrangement entered into to avoid tax did not create a partnership in *Bishop v. Finsbury Securities Ltd* (1966) 1 *WLR* 1402, *HL* and *FA and AB Ltd v. Lupton* (1972) *AC* 634, *HL*.
337. Partnerships Act (UK) 1890; s. 2(3)(a)–(e), PA (Malaysia) 1961, s. 4(c)(i)–(iv). *See also* note 6 at pp. 68–74.
338. Section 11 of the PA 1961.
339. *Ibid. See Bagel v. Miller* (1903) 2 *KB* 212.
340. Section 11 of the PA 1961. *See Kendall v. Hamilton* (1879) 4 *App. Cas*. 504. In UK, by virtue of s. 3 of Civil Liability (Contribution Act) of 1978, the difference between jointly liable and liable

Unlimited liability of partners means that when the partnership's assets are not sufficient to pay the business debts, partners will be personally liable to settle debts of the firm. As such, personal property of partners can be seized to settle the business debts when the firm's fund is insufficient.

A. *Liability of Partners for Contracts*

274. Under the law of partnerships, the principles of agency and contract are recognized as the main actors in regulating the business and structure of the firm. The internal relation between the firm with the partners and partners *inter se* is basically based upon the fundamental principles of contract, while the governing principle in determining liabilities of the firm with the third parties is the general principle of agency. The partnership agreement that forms the relationship between partners constitutes the contractual document which binds both the firm and its partners. On the other hand, provisions of the PA relating to liabilities of the firm to third parties apply the general principles of agency in order to make the firm liable for its partners' actions. Section 7 of the PA provides that 'every partner is agent of the firm for the purpose of the business of the partnership'.

The outsiders are entitled to assume that an agency exists between the individual partners and that what one partner does or says automatically imposes obligations on all others. In *Re Agriculturists Insurance Co.*, L.J. James explained the application of agency rule in partnership:[342]

> As between the partners and the outside world (whatever may be the private arrangements between them), each partner is the unlimited agent of every other in every matter connected with the partnership business, and not being in its nature beyond the scope of the partnership. A partner who may not have a farthing of capital left may take money or assets of the partnership to the value of millions, may bind the partnerships by contracts of any amount, may give the partnership acceptances for any amount, and may even involve his innocent partners in unlimited amounts for fraud which he has craftily concealed from them.

275. Authority is defined as the mandate conferred on an agent by the principal either expressed or implied, to perform a particular act or a series of acts for

jointly is abolished as a judgment creditor is not barred to proceed an action or to continue an action against any person who is jointly liable with the judgment debtor in respect of the same debt or damage.

341. Section 14 of the PA 1961.
342. (1870) LR 5 *Ch. App.* 725 at p. 733.

them.[343] It can also be an incident of the performance of another particular mandate.[344] On the other hand, power lies in the physical or the ability to do the act while authority is found upon the manifestation of consent to do the act.[345] Power is generally described as a legal concept, which basically recognizes the capacity of a person to bind principals in relationships with third parties.[346] It may arise from a mandate, and at the same time, it can be generated through words or conduct by the principal who represents to the third person that authority has been given to the agent. The power will then prohibit the principal from denying the existence of the authority. Therefore, an agent may have the power to bind the principal in a contract with a third party although he may not have the authority to enter into such a transaction.

276. There are two types of authority that may be conferred by a principal to an agent and in the context of a partnership relation by a partner to the other partner:

(a) There is actual authority, which is based upon the partnership agreement. The actual authority is generally described as the authorities which are expressly given to partners. The actual authority of partners may either be expressed or implied. Implicit in the term 'express authority' is the idea that the firm (principal) has made it clear in express and explicit language that the partners can act as provided in the agreement. In *Construction Engineering (Aust) Pty Ltd v. Hexyl Pty Ltd*,[347] the court held that the actual authority of a partner might be negated or qualified by the agreement of the partners.[348] Other than through express provisions of the partnership agreement, the authority of partners may also be implied from the partnership agreement. This type of authority is called implied or usual authority.
(b) There is the apparent authority, i.e., the authority that the agent appears to have in the eyes of the third parties with whom he is dealing. The apparent authority is to be evaluated based on whether there has been any representation made as to whether or not a person being a partner has authority for certain transactions or conduct. Similar to implied authority, apparent authority is based on the idea that the agent looks as though he has the authority to do a particular thing or enter into a particular transaction and the third party relies upon the appearances. It is also implicit that for both implied and apparent authority, the principal will still be bound by the agent's action even though the agent has no actual authority from the principal. The only difference is that implied authority arises from the nature of the agency while apparent authority arises from the representation by the principal such as due to holding out. In *United Bank of*

343. Keith L. Fletcher, *The Law of Partnership in Australia and New Zealand* 151–152 (7th ed., LBC Information Services 1996).
344. *See Australia & New Zealand Bank Ltd v. Ateliers de Constructions Electriques de Charleroi* (1967) 1 *AC* 86 (PC).
345. Harold Gill Reuschlein & William A Gregory, *The Law of Agency and Partnership* 33 (West Publishing Co. 1989).
346. *See Collen v. Gardner* (1856) 21 Bear 560 at 503.
347. (1985) 155 *CLR* 541.
348. *Ibid.*, at p. 547.

Kuwait Ltd v. Hammond,[349] confusion was found in the judgment of the Court of Appeal caused by the terminology. In this case, the Court of Appeal was concerned with the authority of a solicitor to give undertakings to a bank. The money involved was allegedly held by the solicitor firm on behalf of a client which would then be transferred to the bank at a future date. The court held that the solicitor had apparent authority to make such representation. However, in concluding the authority as apparent, the court was in effect applying the usual authority criteria. It was held that the bank had acted reasonably in relying on the authority that the partner represented that he had in such types of business.

277. Every partner is treated as an agent of the firm and therefore permitted to act on behalf of the firm provided that the act is done for the purpose of the partnership business and in the usual way that the business is carried on.[350]

Section 7 of the PA provides for the conditions that must be fulfilled to enable a partner as an agent of the other partners to bind the firm as the principal. Section 7 of the PA provides that the acts of every partner who does any act for carrying on in the usual way business of the kind carried on by the firm of which he is a member binds the firm and his partners.

To enable a partner's conduct to bind the other partners, it must be shown that:

(a) the conduct must relate to the kind of business carried on by the firm or arises from the status of the particular type of business in which the partnership is involved;
(b) the conduct must also be carried on in the usual way for that kind of business; and
(c) the knowledge of the third party of the authority or the fact that he is transacting with a person who is a partner.

278. What amounts to the usual way of carrying on a business may be ascertained by looking at whether or not the business is a trading or a non-trading business. In *Higgins v. Beauchamp*,[351] J. Lush took the view that: 'In my opinion, it would be wrong to say that every business which involves the spending of money is a trading business. To my mind, a trading business is one which depends on the buying and selling of goods'. As for non-trading partnership, in *Higgins v. Beauchamp*,[352] it was held that a partnership conducting cinema business is not a trading partnership as it did not involve the purchase and selling of goods. In this case, the court took the view that selling of service is not sufficient to constitute a trading partnership. Hence, it can be concluded that partnerships which provide services, for example, professional firms such as legal and accounting firms, are non-trading partnerships.

349. (1988) 1 *WLR* 1051 (CA).
350. PA (Malaysia) 1961, s. 7.
351. (1914) 3 *KB* 1192 at p. 1195.
352. (1914) 3 *KB* 1192.

279. The courts have, at times, indicated specific acts that are within the usual authority of a partner in a trading partnership. In *Bank of Australasia v. Breillat,*[353] the Privy Council held that:

> if the partnership is of a general commercial nature, he may pledge or sell the partnership property; he may buy goods on account of the partnership; he may borrow money, contract debts and pay debts on account of the partnership; he may draw, make, sign, endorse, accept, transfer, negotiate and procure to be discounted, promissory notes, bills of exchange, checks [sic] and other negotiable paper, in the name of and on account of the partnership.[354]

Thus, in both *Graham v. Murnin*[355] and *Glass v. Higgins,*[356] the court held that it was in the usual and normal course of such businesses for a partner to borrow money for the purpose of the business. Hence, when an active partner took a loan for the purpose of the partnership, his dormant partner was held liable.

280. A partner's implied authority in non-trading partnerships is more restrictedly applied.[357] Nonetheless, with the commercial developments, modern judges have treated usual authority in non-trading partnerships with more caution. For example, in *United Bank of Kuwait Ltd v. Hammoud*, L.J. Staughton held that:[358] 'the work that solicitors do can be expected to have changed since 1888; it has changed in recent times and is changing now. So I prefer to have regard to the expert evidence of today in deciding what is the ordinary authority of a solicitor'. In *Mandelberg v. Adams,*[359] which concerned a partnership agreement between moneylenders, the court held that where there was no express provision in the partnership agreement which allowed a partner to borrow money on behalf of the partnership, no such power would be implied, because the borrowing of money was not usual in the carrying on of that kind of business. Referring to case law, it can be adduced that the distinction often used by the court to decide 'in the usual way' lies between commercial or trading partnerships, on the one hand, and non-trading partnerships, on the other. In *Polkinghorne v. Holland,*[360] the plaintiff was a client of the defendant's firm of solicitors. After consulting the defendant on investment matters, the plaintiff altered her investment and agreed to act as the guarantor of a bank overdraft of a company in which she was a shareholder and the defendant was the director. The alteration in the investment had resulted in the plaintiff losing a great deal of money. The plaintiff later sought to make other partners in the defendant's firm liable for the loss on investment and payment for the bank guarantee. The court held that although investment analysis was not part of the firm's business, when a solicitor was approached on such questions, he was required by the nature of his business

353. (1847) 6 *Moo PC* 152; 13 *ER* 642.
354. (1847) 6 *Moo PC* 152 at pp. 193–194; 13 *ER* 642 at pp. 657–658.
355. (1862) 1 *SCR (NSW)* 195.
356. (1871) 2 *VR (E)* 28.
357. David Milman et al., *Modern Partnership Law* 66 (Croom Helm 1983).
358. (1988) 1 *WLR* 1051.
359. (1930) 31 *SR (NSW)* 50.
360. (1934) 51 *CLR* 143.

to make inquiries and suggest competent advice. Hence, failure to do so was related to the business of the firm. However, on the second contention, the court took the view that although the plaintiff relied upon her confidence in the defendant as a solicitor, the matter had nothing to do with the firm's business and he had neither given advice as solicitor nor acted on her behalf. The decision to be the guarantor was totally a business arrangement between the plaintiff and the defendant as contracting parties and not as between a solicitor and a client.

281. Section 7 of the PA also highlights the importance of the third party's knowledge of the partner's authority. If the third party knows that the partner has no authority or does not believe that the partner has such authority or does not know or believe that the person is a partner of the firm, then the firm and other partners will not be liable. The requirement of the third party's knowledge as regards the partners' authority is important in relation to the dormant partner. Although the precise identity of the principal, i.e., the other partners, is not required as stated in *Keighley, Maxsted & Co. v. Durant*,[361] the third party must have known or believed that the person with whom the third party is interacting is a partner. If the third party does not believe or know that he was transacting with a person who is a partner, then the other partners cannot be made liable as the third party must have transacted with the 'partner' in his personal capacity.

The effect of section 7 is that if the third party knows that the partner has no authority by having notice regarding any restriction of authority imposed by the firm towards the partner with whom he is dealing, then the firm will not be liable for the transaction. This is supported by section 10, which states that the notice of restriction of authority is effective against persons who have notice of the restriction. Thus, if the third party has notice of the restriction on authority and yet he still entered into the transaction, which is beyond the limit or authority of the respective partner, the firm is not liable. In *Trueman v. Loder*,[362] the court held that a principal could not terminate an agent's power to involve the principal in legal relationships with third parties, merely by notifying the agent that the authority has been withdrawn. In *Waugh v. H B Clifford & Sons Ltd*,[363] the court emphasized that in order to make the agent's power effectively terminated or restricted, notice must be given to third parties.

282. It is obvious that the scope of apparent authority of a partner is more extensive than his actual or implied authority. Provided that there is a representation made by the firm that such a partner has the authority to act, the firm will be liable. The main element required to constitute apparent authority is merely a representation and the act does not need to be done in the usual way that the business is carried on or for the purpose of the partnership business.

283. Section 8 of the PA also provides that whatever is done by a person, whether or not he is a partner if specially authorized by the partners will bind the

361. (1901) *AC* 240 at p. 260.
362. (1840) 113 *ER* 539.
363. [1982] *Ch.* 374.

firm. Thus in *Sithambaram Chetty & Ors v. Hop Hing & Ors,*[364] two persons established a business for the sale of medicated wines. Their connection with the business was not made public and they took no active part in the running of the business. They entrusted the entire control of the business to two managers and the second defendant. The second defendant borrowed money from the plaintiff drawn under the firm's name and later absconded. J. Pritchard held that whatever was the real position of the second defendant, the acknowledged partners did allow him to carry on the particular business as an ostensible principal and therefore clothed him with every authority incidental to a principal in the business. It follows that if there is no authority or where the partner incurred obligations, not within his authority, he has incurred the obligation in his personal capacity and the firm will not be held liable.[365]

284. Where a partner has incurred an obligation by acting within his authority, the firm is liable and thus all the partners are jointly liable to the full extent of the debt.[366] Joint liability means that if judgment is obtained against the firm and remains unsatisfied due to a partner's bankruptcy or otherwise, any other partner who has not been sued in the first instance cannot then be sued in a subsequent proceeding. There is only one cause of action for the recovery of the debts and that having been exhausted, new proceedings cannot be taken involving the same cause of action or action cannot be taken against a partner whom the creditor had failed to sue in the first instance.[367] Thus, a creditor who is suing the firm must make sure that he either uses the firm's name under section 6 of the PA of 1965 or brings the proceedings against all the partners using all the individual partners' names. The use of the firm's name has somewhat been resolved. However, there are several liabilities in relation to the estate of a deceased partner, which means that the estate of a deceased partner may be sued separately in a proceeding involving the firm's contractual obligation.[368]

B. Liability of Partners for Torts and Wrongs

285. The partners may also be liable for wrongful act or omission of a partner if the conduct that causes loss or damage to a third party is authorized by the other partners or if the loss or damage arises out of conduct or omission which is in the ordinary course of the firm's business.[369] The term 'wrongful act or omission' is wide enough to include civil liability in tort as well as conduct that leads to a fine as a punishment although criminal liability that requires *mens rea* (criminal intent)

364. [1928] *SSLR* 52.
365. Section 9 of the PA 1961.
366. Section 11 of the PA 1961.
367. *Guinness Anchor Marketing Sdn Bhd v. Chellam Joe* (1999) 3 *AMR* 2735. Applied in *Ong Guek Siang & Anor v Asset First Sdn. Bhd. & Anor* [2012] *MLJU* 537.
368. Section 11 of the PA 1961. *See Re Hodgson Beckett v Ramsdale* [1885] 31 *Ch D* 177, the Court of Appeal held that a creditor of a partnership firm has concurrent remedies against the estate of a deceased partner and the surviving partners.
369. Section 12 of the PA 1961.

is generally not attributable to other partners merely due to the partnership relation. Where a partner acting within the scope of his authority receives money or property in the ordinary course of the firm's business and misappropriates the money or property, other partners will be jointly liable. Similarly, when the firm receives money or property for example through the conduct of a partner or an employee, and the property is subsequently misappropriated while it is in the firm's custody, all partners would be liable. For torts or wrongs, the partners are jointly and severally liable. This means that the partners may be issued separate writs either contemporaneously or separately.

C. Liability of Non-partner for Credit Given to the Firm

286. The PAs provide that any person who, either expressly or by conduct, represents himself or who knowingly suffers himself to be represented as a partner to anyone, who, on the faith of the representation, gives credit to the firm shall be liable as a partner.[370] This means a person who is not a partner can also be liable as a partner if there is representation, made by himself or by another person, in circumstances where the non-partner allows the representation to be made to the third party that he is a partner. The authority of the non-partner arises from the representation and although he is known as an apparent partner,[371] he is essentially not a partner. His liability is only in relation to the credit given to the firm on the faith of the representation. There is no duty on the third party to inquire as to the correctness of the representation as long as the person giving the credit acted reasonably and there was representation made and the registration could be relied on by a third party if he had relied on it.[372] However, if the third party had verified the representation and found it to be untrue and yet continued to provide credit to the firm, the non-partner cannot be held liable with the other partners for the credit given as the credit was not given based or relying on the representation. There is also no requirement that a partnership actually existed as what is required is that there was representation of the existence of a partnership relationship.[373]

The representation may also arise due to the use of a person's name on the letterheads or the firm's name. There may be difficulties if a partner's name is included on the letterhead or the firm's name. In the event that there is a change of partners, it may appear to an outsider that the outgoing partner is still a partner due to the use of his name as part of the firm's name.[374]

---

370. Section 16 of the PA 1961.
371. *Tower Cabinet v. Ingram* (1949) 2 *KB* 397.
372. *Sivagami Achi v. Ramanathan Chettiar* (1959) 25 *MLJ* 221.
373. *Lynch v. Stiff* (1943) 68 *CLR* 428.
374. Refer to *Tower Cabinet v Ingram* (1949) 2 *KB* 397, where a person who was no longer a partner will not be liable when his name appeared in a notepaper without his knowledge. In this case the court applying s. 14 of PA 1890 held that Ingram was not liable because he had not knowingly suffered himself to be represented as a partner.

D. Liability of Incoming and Outgoing Partners

287. A partner who ceases to be a partner will not cease to be liable for debts incurred before his withdrawal from the partnership.[375] His resignation, retirement, bankruptcy or death will not absolve him from liability of the firm incurred while he was still a partner. However, he will not be liable for any debts or contracts entered after he left the partnership.[376] Thus, under section 38, where a person who is an apparent partner withdraws from the firm (other than due to his death), he has to give sufficient notice of his withdrawal to the public, Notice in the gazette is sufficient for the purpose of informing the public in general, but where there are existing clients of the firm, specific notice must be given to them. In such cases, the fact that a notice was given in widely distributed national newspapers or by informing the Registry of Businesses of the change in partners of the firm will not be sufficient if the intended recipients are persons with whom the firm has had previous dealings; for example, the firm's existing clients.[377] A person whose name continues to be listed by the registry of business may be treated as an apparent partner and P who has resigned was liable for debts incurred after his resignation.[378]

288. An incoming partner will also not be held liable for debts incurred by the firm before he joins as a partner.[379] However, if there is an agreement between the outgoing partner, the creditors and the firm as newly constituted (which may include a new partner), the outgoing partner may cease to be held liable for the firm's debts incurred while he was a partner and the new partner may be held liable for debts incurred before he joins as a partner.

§3. CONTRIBUTIONS AND DIVISION OF PROFITS

289. The capital contribution amongst the partners is to be determined by the agreement of the partners. The division of profit is also determined by agreement and in the absence of express agreement, the division of profit is to follow the ratio of the capital contributed by the partners.

375. Section 19(1) of the PA 1961.
376. Refer *Jasmi Shahdi bin Jasmin Bok v Petron Malaysia Refining & Marketing Bhd* [2016] 10 *MLJ 436*. In this case, the appellant (who was a partner) was sued by the respondent for an agreement which was executed after the appellant left the partnership.
377. *Ang Lay Sim v. Choo Lay Poh* (2004) 8 *CLJ* 7. In: *Tan Sin Moh* (1988) 2 *MLJ* 51, in relation to persons who have had previous dealings with the firm, i.e., the firm's existing clients, a notice to the registry was insufficient.
378. *Hong Kong Printing Co. Sdn Bhd v. Lau Kooi Seng* (1986) 1 *CLJ* 211.
379. Section 19(2) of the PA 1961.

§4. MANAGEMENT AND CONTROL

I. Partnership Agreement

290. One of the obvious advantages of general partnerships is the flexibility of its internal management. The basis of the internal relation of a partnership is mainly agreement by all partners. Similar to ordinary contracts, partnership agreements consist of express and implied terms. The PA itself contains several implied terms[380] to regulate the partnership's internal matters, but these terms can always be amended or excluded either by express terms of the partnership agreement or by conduct of the partners.[381] This is because the Act imposes a largely voluntary framework between the partners themselves.

Under the partnership law, partners are given the freedom to decide measures to regulate their internal matters. This can be seen via provisions of the PA where it is expressly stated that both written terms and those imposed by the Act may be varied by express or implied agreement of the partners.[382] Nevertheless, in the absence of a partnership agreement, the PA provides several rules to regulate the rights and duties of partners amongst each other.[383]

Any fundamental change in the partnership business has to be unanimously agreed upon by the partners[384] while decisions for ordinary matters of the partnership business can be determined by the approval of the majority.[385]

What constitutes ordinary matters of the business is actually a question of fact and determined by referring to the type and actual business of the partnership. In *Highley v. Walker*,[386] the court held that admission of one of the partner's sons as an apprentice was an ordinary matter and should be determined by the majority. Nonetheless, even if a matter can be decided by the majority as provided in the partnership agreement or by the PA, the decision must be exercised in good faith and must not deprive the minority of their rights to participate in the decision making. Furthermore, if the partnership agreement requires a quorum in the partners' meeting to decide ordinary matters of the firm's business, then the prescribed quorum must be fulfilled in order to make the decision valid. In *Re London and Southern Counties Freehold Land Co.*,[387] the court held that as the decision made at the partners' meeting was inquorate as required by the partnership agreement, the decisions made were not valid. In general, the control and decision making of the partnership matters are vested in all partners and not merely in those who have a majority interest in the business.

380. PA 1961 (Malaysia); s. 26.
381. *Ibid.*; s. 21.
382. *Ibid.*; ss 21 and 26.
383. *Ibid.*; s. 26.
384. In the absence of any contrary provision as stated in the partnership agreement. Section 21 of the PA 1961.
385. Section 26(h) of the PA 1961.
386. (1910) 26 *TLR* 685; *see also Donaldson v. Williams* (1833) 1 *Cr. & M*; *Clements v. Norris* (1878) 8 *Ch.D* 129.
387. [1885] *Ch.D* 223.

II. Involvement in Managing the Business

291. Section 26 states that the partners' rights and duties are subject to the rules laid down in the PA 1961 unless there is an agreement, express or implied, stating otherwise. One of the fundamental rights of a partner is that every partner may take part in the management of the firm.[388] No partner can deny other partners' rights in management and control of the firm although some partners may be restricted from performing some management functions such as the signing of cheques or accepting bills of exchange.[389] While the PA provides that every partner may take part in the management of the firm, there might be one or more partners who do not wish to take an active part in the control and management of the firm.[390] Even if there are partners who do not take an active part in the management and control of the firm, the law still emphasizes that no change affecting the nature of the partnership's business can be done without the consent of all partners.[391]

The right to participate in the management of the firm of all partners can be seen in the way internal matters of the firm are decided. Generally, how internal problems of the firm should be resolved depends on the agreement of all partners. However, in the absence of such agreement, the Act provides that ordinary matters can be resolved by a decision of the majority of partners, but any change, which would affect the nature of the partnership business, must get the consent of all partners.[392] Other extraordinary matters will have to be resolved depending on the terms of the agreement. An example is in relation to the expulsion of a partner, where section 27 states that the majority of the partners cannot expel a partner from the firm unless an express agreement to that effect exists between the partners.

The right of partners in management participation is further emphasized by the PA where it is expressly stated that no partner shall be entitled to remuneration for acting in the business.[393] Nonetheless, the partnership agreement may provide circumstances whereby partners who do additional work or have an extra workload compared to other partners are entitled to some remuneration.[394]

---

388. Section 26(e) of the PA 1961.
389. For example, *Kelly v. Tucker* (1907) 5 *CLR* 1.
390. The non-active partner is commonly known as a passive, dormant or sleeping partner. Regardless of the non-active participation the dormant partner is still jointly liable for the debts of the firm, unless a contrary intention is shown in the partnership agreement. *See Watteau v. Fenwick* (1893) 1 *QB* 346, *Bevan v. Webb* (1901) 2, *Ch.* 59; *Mercantile Credit Co. Ltd v. Garrod* (1962) 3 *All ER* 1103.
391. Section 26(h) of the PA 1961. In: *AG v. Great Northern Railway* (1860) 1 *Dr. & Sm.* 154, Lord Lindley held that:

> [N]o majority, however large, can lawfully engage the partnership in matters outside partnership business against the will of even one dissident partner ... . *See also* judgment of Lord Eldon in *Natusch v. Irving* (1824) at p. 398; judgment of Lord Atkin in *Abbatt v. Treasury Solicitor & Others* (1969) 1 *WLR* 1575, *Re A Solicitor's Arbitration* (1962) 1 *WLR* 353; *Nixon v. Wood* (1987) 284 *EG* 1055.

392. Section 26(h) of the PA 1961; *see Tham Kok Cheong v. Low Pui Heng* (1966) 2 *MLJ* 52.
393. Section 26(f) of the PA 1961.
394. *See Re Noonan* [1949] *St R Qd* 62.

292. All partners also have the right to inspect the firm's books[395] and the court has in fact strengthened this right by allowing a partner to appoint an agent to inspect the books on his behalf.[396] This right enables the partners, particularly dormant partners to have direct access to any related information regarding the firm. J. Kan Ting Chin clarified the term 'partnership books' in *Krishinchand Bahjwani & Anor v. Sunil Bhojwani & Anor* as:[397]

> although the term is not defined by the Act or any case that I know of it. It should not be constrained to be limited to accounting records and should include other records kept by the partnership, for example, minutes of partners' meeting.

293. Generally, partners can be assigned their rights or interest in the firm to a third party through voluntary assignment[398] or through a court order (involuntary assignment).[399] In both cases, the assignee only has the right to receive the share of profits to which the assigning partner would otherwise be entitled. As regards rights in the management, the assignee would normally assume the same rights as the assigning partners,[400] but in the case of involuntary assignment, the assignee, who is normally the judgment creditor, may on the application by summons seek for management rights which are necessary for the purpose of settlement of the judgment debts, for example, rights to the partnership books and to appoint a receiver.[401]

III. Managing Financial Affairs

294. One of the main elements required by the PA to constitute a partnership is the sharing of profits.[402] The distribution of profits amongst the partners is basically decided through an agreement of all partners.[403] However, in the absence of any agreement, the PA provides that the partners shall have an equal share in capital and profits of the firm and must contribute equally towards losses of the firm.[404] If any partner advances money beyond the amount of the capital he has agreed to subscribe to, then he will be entitled to a fixed rate of interest upon advances made by him. The rate of interest can be decided in the partnership agreement but in the

395. Section 26(i) of the PA 1961.
396. For example, *Bevan v. Webb* (1901) 2 *Ch.* 59.
397. (1996) 1 *SLR* 29 at p. 33.
398. Section 33(1) of the PA 1961. Refer *TRA Mining (M) Sdn Bhd v. Thien Hong Teck & Ors and another appeal* [2019] 1 *MLJ* 212.
399. Section 25(2) of the PA 1961.
400. Section 33(1) of the PA 1961.
401. Section 25(2) of the PA 1961.
402. Section 3 of the PA 1961.
403. Section 21 of the PA 1961.
404. Section 26(a) of the PA 1961.

absence of such a provision in the agreement, the Act provides that the partner is entitled to an interest of 8% per annum from the date of payment or advance.[405]

295. Other than the advances of loan beyond the agreed capital contribution, partners are also entitled to indemnification in respect of any payment made or for any personal liabilities incurred by him while acting within[406] or outside his authority for the purpose of the partnership business or done for the preservation of the business or property of the firm.[407] In *Matthews v. Ruggles-Brise*,[408] the executors of one of the deceased partner's settled the debt of the firm to the landlord out of the deceased partner's personal estate and later claimed the amount from the other partner's executors. The court held that the plaintiff was entitled to the indemnification, as the liability was a partnership debt.

IV. Duties Owed to Other Partners

296. The main fiduciary duty of partners is to render true accounts and full information of all things affecting the partnership.[409] Partners have the duty to account for any profit they have made derived where the profit is derived from the use of the firm's assets, name or business connection without the other partners' consent, even if the dealings are outside the scope of the partnership's business.[410] They cannot allow themselves to use their positions, knowledge or influence in the firm to gain personal profits. Lord Lindley explained:[411]

> Good faith requires that a partner shall not obtain a private advantage at the expense of the firm. He is bound in all transactions affecting the partnership, to do his best for the common body and to share with his co-partners any benefit which he may have been able to obtain from other people and in which the firm is in honour and conscience entitled to participate. The element of fraud or negligence is not necessary in order to invoke a breach of good faith.[412]

In *Pathirana v. Pathirana*,[413] the parties were partners in a service station in Sri Lanka. The station belonged to Caltex (Ceylon) Ltd, which had appointed them as agents. The respondent gave the appellant three months' notice to dissolve the partnership and during that period he obtained a new agreement with Caltex, which

405. Section 26(c) of the PA 1961.
406. Section 26(b)(i) of the PA 1961.
407. Section 26(b)(ii) of the PA 1961.
408. (1911) 1 *Ch.* 194.
409. Section 30 of the PA 1961.
410. Section 31(1) of the PA 1961.
411. Lindley and Banks on Partnerships at p. 412.
412. *Tham Kim Fai @Tham Kim Fay v Ng Kon Seong* [2006] 7 MLJ 1 at 9. In *Hogar Estates Ltd v. Shebron Holdings Ltd* [1980] 101 *DLR* (3d) 509, the court held that there was no misrepresentation and no proof of dishonesty in this case, however, the fiduciary obligation to disclose all material facts requires neither of these ingredients.
413. (1967) 1 *AC* 233.

transferred the agency into his name alone. The Privy Council held that the agency agreement was a partnership asset and the respondent's unauthorized use of it was a clear breach of fiduciary duty.[414]

297. Partners cannot allow themselves to be in situations where their duties and interests outside the partnership conflict with any of their duties and interest as partners.[415] Thus, a partner cannot engage in a business that is of the same nature and in competition with the partnership business without the consent of the other partners. Whether a business, which is carried on by a partner, is different from a partnership business is to be proven based on the circumstances. In *Aas v. Benham*,[416] the defendant who was a partner in a firm of shipbrokers used information which he had acquired from the firm to set up a new shipbuilding company, for which he had received both remuneration and a salaried directorship. The other partners sought an account of both the remuneration and salary received by the defendant as director in the new company. The court held that as the company's business was entirely beyond the scope of the firm's business, the other partners were not entitled to claim the benefits received by the defendant from the company.

If partners fail to observe the fiduciary obligations, without having obtained their fellow partners' consent, they will be liable to account for any benefit that they receive in consequence of the breach. For example in *Bentley v. Craven*,[417] the defendant was a partner who was employed to purchase sugar on the firm's behalf. Unknown to the other partners, the defendant had bought the sugar at lower than the market price but charged the firm for full market value. The court held that although the firm did not incur any loss as it paid the sugar at market price, the defendant was accountable to the firm for the profits, which he had made.

As long as there is a tendency for conflict of interest between a partner's interests in the firm with his personal activities, then he is obliged to disclose it to the other partners.

§5. Transferability of a Partner's Interest

298. Without the other partner's consent, a partner cannot transfer his interest in the partnership to someone who is outside the firm, so as to make the transferee a new partner. This characteristic is found essential to the relation of partners *inter se* as trust and confidence can only exist amongst the partners when they are free to select and decide on who can become their partners. In *Sturgeon v. Salmon*,[418] Lord Darling took the view that a unilateral assignment of a partner's shares affected an automatic dissolution of the partnership. Nevertheless, like most other features of

414. Applied in *Barber and others v. Rasco International Ltd and another* [2012] *EWHC* 269 (QB).
415. Section 32 of the PA 1961.
416. (1891) 2 *Ch.* 244.
417. (1853) 18 *Beav. 75. See also Dunne v. English* (1874) 18 *Eq* 524, *Boston Deep Sea Fishing & Ice Co. v. Ansell* (1888) 39 *Ch.D* 339 and *Kuhlirz v. Lambert* (1913) 108 *LT* 560.
418. (1906) 22 *TLR* 584 at p. 585.

partnership, the characteristics of non-transferability of a partner's interest can be dispensed with by unanimous consent of all partners.[419]

299. A partner's interest is his share of the partnership property and profits. Partnership property refers to any property which belongs to the firm and all the partners are entitled to deal with it in the performance of the partnership business. Under the PA, partnership property may exist if:[420]

(a) it is originally brought into the partnership stock, i.e., brought as the capital;
(b) acquired by purchase or otherwise on the firm's account; or
(c) acquired by purchase or otherwise for the purpose and in the course of partnership business.

In *Miles v. Clark*,[421] the plaintiff and defendants were photographers and partners in a business. Both of them contributed to the stock in trade. The leasehold premises, furniture and studio equipment belonged to the defendant. They intended to enter into an agreement to treat the above as a partnership but failed. Upon dissolution, the court held that no terms ought to be implied as partnership property other than those essential to the business efficacy. Therefore only the consumable items of stock in trade were to be regarded as partnership property.

The partnership name may also be considered partnership property especially if there is goodwill in the name.[422] Thus, where a partner's name appears in the firm's name, it is prudent for the partners to consider in their agreement whether the firm's name is partnership property or not and whether the partners who continue with the business, where some partners have retired or ceased to be partners, are entitled to use the firm's name.[423] The test of whether a partner can use the name of the partnership after the dissolution of the firm depends on whether the goodwill of the partnership has been assigned.[424]

In *N.B. Menon v. Abdullah Kutty*,[425] the plaintiff and defendant were partners running a restaurant in Kelantan. The defendant was the tenant of the restaurant, but he lived in Johore while the plaintiff managed the restaurant. Later there was a dissolution and a question arose on who was the actual tenant. The court held that as the defendant had not assigned the tenancy to the partnership, it stayed as a personal asset of the defendant and cannot be treated as the partnership property.

---

419. Section 26(g) of the PA 1961. *See also Thompson v. Thompson* [1962] *HL* 29.
420. Section 22(1) of the PA 1961.
421. (1953) 1 *WLR* 537.
422. *Teoh Swee Here v. Tio Hock Thye* (1997) 1 *CLJ Supp* 413; *Colin Ng Teck Sim v. Engelin The & Young* (1995) 2 *SLR* 380. *Tan Peng Chin v. Sunny Wong Fook Choy* (unreported) cited in: H.Y. Yeo, *Partnership Law in Singapore* (Butterworths 2000).
423. *Sukhinderjit Singh Mulker v. Arumugam Deva Rajah* (1998) 2 *CLJ* 110.
424. Court of Appeal in *Tai Foong Lam v. Hamdi Abdullah & Ors* [2013] 5 *CLJ* 89. Applied in *Mohd Ghazali Ahmad Nasaruddin v. Chok Kai Kuang & Ors* [2017] *MLJU* 1258.
425. (1974) 2 *MLJ* 189.

In *Ponnukon v. Jebaratnam*,[426] the appellant and respondent formed a partnership to develop a piece of land. The firm failed to obtain a bank loan to buy the land. Later, the respondent bought the land with his own money. The appellant sought a declaration that the land was held in trust for the partnership. The court held that the land was paid by the respondent and it was clearly his separate property. The fact that the object of partnership was land development did not necessarily mean that the land must be owned by the firm. Furthermore, there was no agreement between the partners that the land was to be purchased and treated as partnership property.

300. The PA also provides that where partners are co-owners of a piece of land that is not partnership property, but share the profits from the land as partners and later buy other land using the shared profits and used in the same manner, the presumption is that the subsequent land is not partnership property.[427] By analogy, this also applies to improvement on land done out of profit. In *Davis v. Davis*,[428] a father left freehold business premises to his sons. The sons carried on the business and borrowed money by mortgaging the premises and used it to expand the workshop. The court held that there was a partnership in the business, but not on the premises.

§6. Dissolution of Partnerships

301. The main basis of a partnership is the agreement which forms the relationship between the partners. Once the relationship can no longer sustain, the partnership will not be able to continue and has to be dissolved.

I. Contractual Dissolution

302. Partnership is basically a contractual relationship between the partners. In *Wong Peng Yuen v. Senanayake*,[429] J. Wee Chong Jin clearly stated that the word 'relation' as provided in the PA is a relation resulting from a contract.[430] Hence, it is common for the methods and grounds for dissolution to be provided in the partnership agreement. The PA itself is obvious in this fact as it provides that 'subject to any agreement between the partners, a partnership is dissolved'.[431] The Act also highlighted the circumvent events as grounds for dissolution which are normally prescribed in the partnership agreement, namely, expiration of a certain period for

426. (1980) 1 *MLJ* 282. . Referred by the Court of Appeal in *Soo Boon Siong v. Saw Fatt Seong and Soo Hock Seang & Ors* [2008] 1 *MLJ* 27, paras 59–62.
427. Section 22(2) of the PA 1961.
428. (1887) 36 *Ch.D* 359.
429. (1962) 28 *MLJ* 204.
430. *Ibid.* at p. 206.
431. Section 34(1) of the PA 1961.

fixed-term partnership,[432] termination of an undertaking or adventure for partnerships which are formed for one particular undertaking or adventure[433] and involuntary assignment of any partner's shares to his personal creditors.[434] There can also be a dissolution of a partnership upon the death of a partner unless otherwise provided in the partnership agreement.[435] Other than these express dissolution clauses, there are also many other examples of dissolution events, which are expanded and included in the partnership agreement. For example, in *Clifford v. Timms*,[436] the partnership deed provided that one of the grounds for dissolution of the firm is 'professional misconduct'. For professional partnerships, observing professional ethics are very important and therefore when partners committed professional misconduct such as destroying clients' and public confidence in the firm, it could amount to the dissolution of the partnership.

303. Despite being included in the partnership agreement, contractual grounds for dissolution can be contracted out by the partners through an agreement of all partners. For example, upon expiration of a fixed-term partnership, if the partners agreed to still continue trading under the same partnership, then it shall continue despite the express provision of the agreement which states that the partnership shall be dissolved upon expiration of the agreed term. Nevertheless, the continued partnership shall have the nature of a partnership at will.[437]

II. Dissolution due to Illegality

304. The main ground for automatic dissolution is illegality. The PA expressly provides that a partnership shall be dissolved by the happening of any event, which makes it unlawful for the business of the firm to be carried on.[438] Most cases of automatic dissolution involve enemy aliens in times of war[439] and carrying on business, which is illegal.[440]

432. Section 34(1)(a) of the PA 1961.
433. Section 34(1)(b) of the PA 1961.
434. Section 35(2) of the PA 1961. Nonetheless, this provision only provides an option for partners other than the involuntary assignee to dissolve the firm.
435. Section 35 of the PA 1961.
436. [1908] *AC* 112. *See also Carmichael v. Evans* (1904) 1 *Ch.* 486.
437. Section 29 of the PA PA1961.
438. Section 36 of the PA 1961.
439. *See R v. Knupfer* (1915) 2 *KB* 321, *Re Alexander & Co.* (1915) 19 *CLR* 533 and *Stoll v. Patterson & Co. Ltd* (1915) 18 *WALR* 42.
440. *See Hudgell Yeates & Co. v. Watson* [1978] *QB* 451.

III. Dissolution by Court Order

305. As emphasized by the PA, the right to dissolve the partnership belongs to the partners. Even if the partnership agreement does not provide grounds for dissolution, any partner may apply to the court for a dissolution order under one of the six grounds provided by the PA:[441]

(a) *Insanity*:[442] Application to dissolve partnership under this ground will be entertained by the court if the petitioning partner can prove that the state of incapacity is permanent and not temporary.[443]
(b) *Permanent incapacity*:[444] This provision covers all forms of incapacity, which must be permanent. What constitutes such disability is a question of fact, which depends upon the kind of business carried on by the partnership.[445]
(c) *Prejudicial conduct*:[446] A partner who applies for dissolution under this ground does not have to prove that the prejudicial conduct of another partner occurred in the course or is connected with the firm's business.[447] He also does not need to prove that the firm suffered a loss due to the conduct.[448] As long as the conduct of a partner is considered to be prejudicial against the firm, then it can become a ground for dissolution by the court.
(d) *Wilful or persistent breach of trust*:[449] This provision constitutes two separate grounds upon which dissolution may be sought.[450] The first requires a partner to be wilfully or persistently in breach of the partnership agreement.[451] The second circumstance requires misconduct of a partner, which renders the continuation of the partnership impractical.[452] The court would be reluctant to order a dissolution if the breach or misconduct is trivial.[453]
(e) *Carrying on business at a loss*:[454] A partner who applies for dissolution under this ground must prove that the loss suffered by the firm is continuous and making a profit is impossible in practice. The court would be reluctant to order dissolution if the loss suffered by the business is temporary or due to certain circumstances which can be remedied.[455]
(f) *Just and equitable ground*:[456] This provision may be regarded as the general-purpose ground authorizing a court to dissolve a partnership. It basically

441. Section 37 of the PA 1961.
442. Section 37(a) of the PA 1961.
443. *See Sayer v. Bennet* (1833) 29 *ER* 1084; *Jones v. Noy* (1833) 39 *ER* 892.
444. Section 35(b) of the PA 1961.
445. *See Whitwell v. Arthur* (1865) 55 *ER* 848; *Peyton v. Midham* (1972) 1 *WLR* 8.
446. Section 37(c) of the PA 1961.
447. *See Carmichael v. Evans* (1904) 1 *Ch.* 486.
448. *See Pearce v. Foster* (1886) 17 *QBD* 536.
449. Section 37(d) of the PA 1961.
450. Terence Prime & Gary Scanlan, *The Law of Partnerships* 269 (Butterworths 1995).
451. *See Smith v. Jeyes* (1841) 4 *Beav* 503; *Re John Thomson* (1893) 1 *SLT* 59.
452. *See Cheesman v. Price* (1865) 35 *Beav* 142.
453. *See* judgment of V.C. Shadwell in: *Loscombe v. Russell* (1830) 4 *Sim* 8 at p. 11.
454. Section 37(e) of the PA 1961.
455. *See Handyside v. Campbell* (1901) 17 *TLR* 623; *Jennings v. Baddeley* (1856) 69 *ER* 1029.
456. Section 37(d) of the PA 1961.

involves the exercise of judicial discretion.[457] Nevertheless, the court in interpreting this provision is not prepared to restrict its future application.[458] Generally, the court will make an order of dissolution under this ground from whatever causes resulted in the objects of the partnership that can no longer be achieved.

---

457. *Oliver v. Hillier* (1959) 1 *WLR* 551.
458. *See Re Amalgamated Syndicate* (1897) 2 *Ch.* 600; *Ebrahimi v. Westbourne Galleries Ltd* [1973] *AC* 60.

Chapter 3. LLPs in Malaysia

§1. Introduction and Historical Background

306. In Malaysia, the initiative to expand the option of business entities was made by the Companies Commission of Malaysia (CCM) under its Corporate Law Reform Programme. One of the outcomes of the CLRC is the 2003 consultative document for an alternative business vehicle for small businesses and venture capital arrangements. The second consultative document was issued in April 2008. Pursuant to the feedback received from public consultations in 2003 and 2008, SSM published the discussion draft bill for Limited Liability Partnerships in March 2009. Subsequently, the Limited Liability Partnerships Act 2012 (LLP Act 2012) was passed by the Parliament on 9 February 2012, gazetted on 12 February 2012 and came into force on 26 December 2012. Under the LLP Act 2012, names for all LLPs shall end with the words 'Perkongsian Liabiliti Terhad' or the abbreviation 'PLT' (in Bahasa Melayu which is the national language).[459]

307. An LLP can also be established as a Labuan Limited Liability Partnerships (Labuan LLP) operating in the Federal Territory of Labuan.

However, Labuan LLP may only be registered in Labuan and is regulated by the Labuan LP and LLPA 2010. This is a unique legislation as it regulates two business vehicles, LP and LLPs, under one statute.

I. Registration under the LLP Act 2012

308. Section 3(1) of the LLPs Act 2012 provides that LLP is a body corporate and is a legal entity distinct from its partners. Having the status of a body corporate, LLPs enjoy all attributes of a corporation namely, perpetual succession, rights to enter legal proceedings under its own name, and power to acquire, own, hold, develop or dispose of the property.[460] Despite its name which bears the term partnerships, LLP is not a partnership and all provisions of the PA 1961, the rules of equity and of common law applicable to partnerships, shall not be applicable to the LLP.[461]

459. Section 13(1) of the Limited Liability Partnerships Act 2012. Failure to use the abbreviation PLT is an offence and upon conviction shall be liable to a fine not exceeding MYR 250,000 or to imprisonment for a term not exceeding three years or both.
460. Section 3(2), 3(4) (a)-(c) of Limited Liability Partnerships Act 2012.
461. Section 4 of Limited Liability Partnerships Act 2012.

309. Formal registration is required for the establishment of an LLP.[462] A person may apply for registration of an LLP to the Registrar[463] and the application shall be accompanied by the prescribed fee[464] and documents as may be specified by the Registrar. For the professional LLP, the application for registration of LLP must also be accompanied by an approval letter from the relevant governing body of the profession.[465] The Registrar has the power to refuse the application for registration of LLP if he is satisfied that:[466]

(a) the registration of the LLP would be contrary to the national security or interest; or
(b) the proposed business is likely to be used for:
   (i) a charitable purpose;
   (ii) an unlawful purpose; or
   (iii) purposes prejudicial to public peace, welfare or good order or morality in Malaysia.

310. The LLP Act 2012 requires all foreign LLPs to be registered with the Registrar of LLP. A foreign LLP shall have a registered office in Malaysia to which all communications and notices may be addressed. Similar to the local LLPs, foreign LLPs must appoint at least one compliance officer from amongst their partners or persons qualified to act as secretaries under the companies Act who is a citizen or permanent resident of Malaysia and ordinarily resides in Malaysia. If the foreign LLP ceases to have a place of business or carry on business in Malaysia, it must lodge with the Registrar a notice of cessation of business within seven days after the date of cessation. The cessation of business shall take effect upon the lodgement of the notice.

311. The LLP Act 2012 has a specific provision for professional LLPs.[467] Under the First Schedule of LLP Act 2012, there are only three professions, namely the advocate and solicitors, accountants and company secretaries, which are allowed to be carried out in the form of LLP. These professions are clearly stated under the

---

462. Section 10–12 of Limited Liability Partnerships Act 2012. Regulation 2 of the Limited Liability Partnerships Regulations 2012 provides for 'electronic filing system' which allows lodgment of documents for LLP via electronic filing. Regulation 3 the Limited Liability Partnerships Regulations 2012 provides that all applications or lodgments by electronic filing shall be made to the Registrar in the forms provided by the Registrar in the electronic filing system and shall be accompanied by a prescribed fee, where applicable. The Registrar may make any amendment to any form for the purpose of facilitating the application or lodgment of any document required under the LLP Act (Regulation 5(4)).
463. Section 2 of LLP (Amendment) Act 2015, provides that reference to Registrar under the LLP Act 2012 is amended to a person designated under subs. 20(A1) of Companies Commission of Malaysia Act 2001.
464. Regulation 4 of Limited Liability Partnerships Regulations 2012.
465. Section 10(3) of Limited Liability Partnerships Act 2012.
466. Section 12(1) of Limited Liability Partnerships Act 2012.
467. Section 8 Limited Liability Partnerships Act 2012.

First Schedule of the Act. To date, the advocates and solicitors under the Legal Profession Act 1976 are not yet able to establish their business via an LLP as the Bar Council rulings only recognize a sole proprietor or a partnership.[468]

312. Section 92, LLP Act 2012 provides the Minister with the power to add or alter the First Schedule. This indicates that other professionals who are interested to form LLP may request the minister to add their respective professions to be included in the First Schedule.

FIRST SCHEDULE: *[section 2]*

Professional practice	**Governing law**	**Governing body**
1. Chartered Accountant	**Accountants Act 1967** *[Act 94]*	Malaysian Institute of Accountants
2. Advocate and Solicitor	(i) **Legal Profession Act 1976** *[Act 166]* (ii) **Advocates Ordinance of Sabah** *[Sabah Cap. 2]* (iii) **Advocates Ordinance of Sarawak** *[Sarawak Cap. 110]*	(i) Malaysian Bar (ii) Sabah Law Association (iii) Association of Sarawak
3. Company Secretary	**Companies Act 1965** *[Act 125]*	-Nil-

The main difference between professional LLPs and other LLPs lies in the requirement of membership. In a professional LLP, the members shall only be from the same professions such as all accountants or all advocates and solicitors.[469] The partners shall regulate their activities by way of an agreement amongst themselves[470] which should incorporate the requirement of the professionals' ethics and regulation. The professional LLPs also need to have professional insurance coverage which cannot be below the compulsory level of insurance which shall be approved by the Registrar upon consultation with the governing body of respective professions.[471]

There are requirements imposed on the LLP to display its name at its registered office and place of business, on letterheads invoices, etc., including electronic

468. The Legal Profession Bill 2019 was mooted to replace the Legal Profession Act 1976 and the Advocates Ordinances of Sabah and Sarawak but the Bill did not come to fruition. The Advocates Ordinance (Sabah) (Amendment) Act 2021 was passed but did not contain any provision dealing with alternative business forms or the use of the LLP.

469. Section 8(a) Limited Liability Partnerships Act 2012.

470. Section 9 of Limited Liability Partnerships Act 2012.

471. Section 8(b)(i) and (ii) of Limited Liability Partnerships Act 2012.

medium. The LLP must also keep and maintain certain documents including a copy of any instrument relating to any charge created by the LLP.

II. Requirements Relating to Partners

313. LLP must have a minimum number of two partners and if the number of partners is less than two, the LLP is allowed to carry on business not exceeding six months or a longer period as may be determined by the Registrar.[472] The partners of LLPs can be both natural and artificial persons.[473] A partner of the LLP may cease to be a partner according to the LLP agreement[474] or in the absence of such agreement, by giving thirty days' notice to the other partners of that partner's intention to resign as a partner.[475] A partner shall also cease to be a partner upon the death or dissolution of the partner[476] and for a professional LLP, a partner shall cease to be a partner if he has been disqualified from carrying out the professional practice under the relevant governing law of the profession.[477] Under the LLP Act, bankruptcy shall not by itself cause a person to cease being a partner of the LLP[478] The Act also states that in the absence of any notice that a partner has ceased to be a partner of the LLP, the third party is entitled to assume that such partner is still a partner of the LLP.

III. Annual Declaration and Accounting Records

314. LLP is required by the LLP Act 2012 to lodge with the Registrar a declaration that the LLP is to be able to pay its debts as they become due in the normal course of business or does not appear as at that date to be able to pay its debts as they become due in the normal course of business.[479] The first annual declaration must be lodged with the Registrar not later than eighteen months from the date of the registration of the LLP[480] while subsequent annual declaration must be within ninety days from the end of the financial year of the LLP.[481]

315. Failure of the LLP to submit the annual declaration is an offence under the LLP Act 2012 and upon conviction could be liable to a fine not exceeding twenty thousand ringgit and, in the case of a continuing offence, to a further fine not exceeding five hundred ringgit for each day during which the offence continues after

472. Section 7(1) of Limited Liability Partnerships Act 2012. The application for extension must be made by the remaining partner, provided that the period so extended by the Registrar does not exceed one year.
473. Section 6 of Limited Liability Partnerships Act 2012.
474. Section 24(1)(a) of Limited Liability Partnerships Act 2012.
475. Section 24(1) (b) of Limited Liability Partnerships Act 2012.
476. Section 24(2)(a) of Limited Liability Partnerships Act 2012.
477. Section 24(2)(b) of Limited Liability Partnerships Act 2012.
478. Section 25 of Limited Liability Partnerships Act 2012.
479. Section 68(1) Limited Liability Partnerships Act 2012.
480. Section 68(3) Limited Liability Partnerships Act 2012.
481. Section 68(2) Limited Liability Partnerships Act 2012.

conviction.[482] The LLP Act 2012 also provides personal liability for any person who makes a declaration without having reasonable grounds for his opinion and upon conviction shall be liable to a fine not exceeding two hundred and fifty thousand ringgit or to imprisonment for a term not exceeding two years or to both.[483] The LLP Act 2012 prescribes a criminal liability for any person who made a declaration which contained a statement or information, that is directly or indirectly false or misleading, when he knows or ought to have known that the statement or information is false or misleading in a material particular[484] and if any person committed with intent to defraud creditors of the LLP for a fraudulent purpose.[485]

316. LLPs are required to keep accounting and other records that will sufficiently explain the transactions and financial position of the LLP and enable profit and loss accounts and balance sheets to be prepared from time to time which give a true and fair view of the state of affairs of the LLP. The accounting records must be kept by LLPs at the registered office for a period of not less than seven years from the end of the financial year in which the transactions or operations to which those records relate are completed.[486] Failure of the LLP to keep the accounting records shall be an offence under the LLP Act 2012 and upon conviction, the LLP, including all partners, shall be liable to a fine not exceeding MYR 50,000 or to imprisonment for a term not exceeding six months or to both.[487]

The accounting records are not required to be audited[488] but the Registrar may by notice in writing to the LLP or any of its partners, require the accounting and other records for his inspection within such time and at such place as may be specified in that notice.[489]

§2. Nature of the Liability

317. As regards internal arrangement, the LLP Act 2012 provides that except as otherwise provided by the Act, rights and duties of the partners in the LLP shall be governed partners by the partners' agreement which the partners may draft and agreed between themselves.[490] However, in the absence of the partners' agreement, default rules as provided in the Second Schedule of the LLP Act 2012 shall be applicable.[491]

482. Section 68(5) Limited Liability Partnerships Act 2012.
483. Section 68(6) Limited Liability Partnerships Act 2012.
484. Section 68(7) Limited Liability Partnerships Act 2012.
485. Section 68(8) Limited Liability Partnerships Act 2012.
486. Section 69(2) Limited Liability Partnerships Act 2012.
487. Section 69 (6). For a continuing offence, the LLP and every partner shall be liable to a further fine not exceeding MYR 500 for each day during which the offence continues after conviction; s. 69(7).
488. Section 69(5) Limited Liability Partnerships Act 2012.
489. Section 69(4) Limited Liability Partnerships Act 2012.
490. Section 9(1)(a) of Limited Liability Partnerships Act 2012.
491. Section 9(1)(b) and the Second Schedule Limited Liability Partnerships Act 2012.

318. As regards the liability of partners, the LLP Act 2012 provides that every partner of LLPs is the agent of the LLP and has limited liability in respect of claims against the LLP.[492,493] Limited liability is available to all partners as the LLP can incur its own obligations due to its separate legal entity. Any obligation of an LLP whether arising in contract, tort or otherwise, is solely the obligation of the LLP. The protection of limited liability is available to innocent partners in relation to any loss or damage suffered by a third party due to the wrongful act or omission of a partner in the course of the LLP's business while the errant partner shall be jointly liable with the LLP for the damage, loss or injury suffered by the third party.[494] The liability of the LLP is to be borne out of the assets of the LLP.

The LLP is liable provided the partner is acting with authority. As far as third parties are concerned, the LLP is liable unless the partner is acting without authority and the person with whom the partner is dealing knows that the partner has no authority or does not know that he is a partner of the LLP: section 23(20) of the LLP Act.

§3. Contributions and Division of Profits

319. The LLP agreement sets out the amount of capital contribution of each partner, the second schedule provides that all partners are entitled to share equally in the capital and profits of the LLP.

§4. Management

320. Section 23(1) of the LLP Act states that every partner of the LLP is the agent of the LLP. The LLP must have a compliance officer who can either be one of its members or any person qualified to act as company secretary under the Companies Act.[495] The job scope of the compliance officer is akin to a company secretary, where the compliance officer is obliged to submit all documents required to be lodged with the Registrar by the partners of the LLP.[496] The LLP Act 2012 clearly stated that the compliance officer must be a natural person and resides in Malaysia.[497] The compliance officer may be disqualified from acting if he is an undischarged bankrupt or is disqualified to act as director or secretary under the Companies Act.

The LLP agreement is the primary document regulating and determining the mutual rights and duties of the LLP and its partners. In the absence of any agreement setting out the matters specified in the second schedule of the LLP Act, the provisions in the second schedule shall apply. The second schedule provides that:

---

492. Section 23(1) of Limited Liability Partnerships Act 2012.
493. Section 21 of Limited Liability Partnerships Act 2012.
494. Section 21 of Limited Liability Partnerships Act 2012.
495. Regulation 6((2): Where a limited liability partnership has appointed more than one compliance officer, only one of them shall be named for the purpose of lodgment under these Regulations.
496. Regulation 6 of LLP Regulations 2012.
497. Section 27 of Limited Liability Partnerships Act 2012.

(a) every partner may take part in the management of the LLP;
(b) no partner shall be entitled to remuneration for acting in the business or management of the LLP;
(c) no new partner may be introduced without the consent of all existing partners;
(d) any matters relating to the LLP shall be decided by resolution passed by a majority in the number of partners and each partner shall have one vote;
(e) no partner shall assign all or part of his interest in the LLP without the consent of all existing partners;
(f) each partner owes a duty to account to the LLP for any benefit derived without the consent of the LLP from any transaction concerning the LLP or form any use by that partner of the LLP property, name or any business connection;
(g) no majority of partners can expel any partner unless the power to do so has been conferred by express agreement between the partners.

§5. Transferability of Partnership Interests

321. The interest in the LLP may be transferred in accordance with the partnership agreement. Section 24 of the LLP Act provides that a partner may cease to be a partner of the LLP:

(a) in accordance with the LLP agreement;
(b) in the absence of the agreement, by giving a thirty days' notice of his intention to resign as a partner.

When a person ceases to be a partner, the person shall be entitled to receive from the LLP an amount:

(a) Equal to the former partner's capital contribution and accumulated profits after deduction of the losses.
(b) Determined at the date the former partner ceases to be a partner.

The interest of a partner in an LLP cannot be transferred without the consent of all existing partners, nor can the interest be assigned without all existing partners' consent. The interest may be transferred by a sale and purchase agreement as the interest is the property of each partner. Where there is an assignment of interest, this does not automatically cause the partner to cease being a partner. The assignment also does not entitle the assignee to interfere in the management of the LLP.

§6. Dissolution, Liquidation and Striking Off of the LLP

322. Generally, when the LLP ceased to operate and discharged all its debts and liabilities, a partner of the LLP may, after giving notice to Registrar on the intention to dissolve the LLP,[498] apply in writing to the Registrar for a declaration of dissolution of the LLP.[499] An application for a declaration of dissolution shall be made within seven days from the date of the publication or notification and must be accompanied by the statutory declaration.[500] A partner or creditor of the LLP may make a written objection against the proposed dissolution of the LLP to the Registrar within thirty days of the date of publication or posting of the notice, whichever is the latter.[501]

323. The Registrar may, by notice in writing, declare that the LLP is dissolved if there is no objection received for the proposed dissolution or if there was a withdrawal of the objection or if the Registrar decides that the objection made by a partner or creditor of the LLP is without justification.[502] Upon declaration of dissolution of the LLP, the Registrar shall notify the LLP that, subject to the LLP agreement, the partners are entitled to surplus assets according to their respective rights and interests.[503] The declaration of dissolution shall only take effect upon receipt of the notification by the Registrar.[504] Notwithstanding the declaration of dissolution and the distribution of assets of the LLP, the liability of the LLP shall continue and may be enforced as if the LLP had not been dissolved.[505]

324. In addition to the voluntary winding-up, LLP agreement, the LLP Act 2012 provides that the procedures for receivership and winding-up of the LLP shall be subjected to the Companies Act and the company (Winding-up) Rules.[506]

The LLP act 2012 provides power to the Registrar to strike off the LLP from the register if he believes that:[507]

(a) an LLP is not carrying on business or is not in operation;
(b) an LLP has contravened this Act;
(c) it is prejudicial to the national interests for an LLP to remain on the register;
(d) there is no liquidator acting in cases of winding-up by the court as specified under paragraph 49(1)(b); or
(e) the affairs of an LLP are fully wound up under section 49 or 50 and there are no assets or the assets available are not sufficient to pay the costs of obtaining an order of the court dissolving the LLP, he may serve a notice on the LLP notifying that its name may be struck off the register unless the LLP gives reasons why its name should not be struck off the register within thirty days of the date specified in the notice or a longer period as extended by the Registrar.

---

498. Section 50(4) of Limited Liability Partnerships Act 2012.
499. Section 50 of Limited Liability Partnerships Act 2012.
500. Section 50(3) of Limited Liability Partnerships Act 2012.
501. Section 50(5) of Limited Liability Partnerships Act 2012.
502. Section 50(7) of Limited Liability Partnerships Act 2012.
503. Section 50(8) of Limited Liability Partnerships Act 2012.
504. Section 50(10) of Limited Liability Partnerships Act 2012.
505. Section 50(11) of Limited Liability Partnerships Act 2012.
506. Section 49 of Limited Liability Partnerships Act 2012.
507. Section 51(1) of Limited Liability Partnerships Act 2012.

325. The Registrar may also strike off the LLP from the register after the expiration of the period specified in the notice or such longer period if he:[508]

(a) receives a confirmation from the LLP or its partner that the LLP is no longer carrying on business or is not in operation;
(b) receives no reply from the LLP to the notice referred to in subsection 51(1); or
(c) is not satisfied with the reasons as to why the name of the LLP should not be struck off.

326. Where the name of an LLP has been struck off the register, the LLP is deemed to have been dissolved[509] but the liability of every partner continues and may be enforced as if the name of the LLP had not been struck off.[510]

327. The LLP Act 2012 gives rights to any partner, creditor or an aggrieved person who is affected by the dissolution of the LLP, to apply to the court for revocation of the dissolution at any time within two years from the date of the dissolution, on the grounds that:[511]

(a) the LLP has not discharged all its debts and liabilities; or
(b) it is just and reasonable that the dissolution of the LLP be revoked.

328. If the court is satisfied with the application, the court may order that the dissolution of the LLP be revoked and upon a sealed copy of the order being delivered to the Registrar for registration.[512] In such a case, the LLP shall be deemed to have continued in existence as if it had not been dissolved[513] and give directions to place the LLP and all other persons affected by the dissolution in the same position as nearly as may be as if the LLP had not been dissolved.[514]

For the foreign LLP in Malaysia, which incorporation was liquidated or dissolved at the place of origin, section 48 of the LLP Act 2012 requires certain notices to be submitted to the Registrar.

§7. Tax Status

329. Under the Finance Act 2013, section 8(1A) is inserted into the Income Tax Act (ITA) 1967 which recognized LLP as a taxable entity under the ITA 1967. The Finance Act 2013 also clearly stated that the word LLP shall be added after the word company in section 21(1A) of the ITA 1967, which provides for the basis period for a company. As such, it is clear that by virtue of the Finance Act 2013, the tax status

508. Section 51(2) of Limited Liability Partnerships Act 2012.
509. Section 51(3)(b) of Limited Liability Partnerships Act 2012.
510. Section 51(3)(a) of Limited Liability Partnerships Act 2012.
511. Section 52 (1) of Limited Liability Partnerships Act 2012.
512. Section 52(2) of Limited Liability Partnerships Act 2012.
513. Section 52(2) of Limited Liability Partnerships Act 2012.
514. Section 52(3) of Limited Liability Partnerships Act 2012.

of the Malaysian PLT is similar to a company. Such an approach diverges totally from approaches of LLPs in other countries, which recognized LLP tax status as a partnership albeit its body corporate status.

The Finance Act 2013 also provides that a new provision of section 75B is inserted in ITA 1967, which imposes the responsibility for doing all acts and things required to be done by or on behalf of the LLP for the purposes of the ITA, including the payment of tax shall lie jointly and severally on the compliance officer and in the case where there is no compliance officer being appointed in the PLT, all partners shall be treated as compliance officers and shall be responsible under the ITA 1967.

Chapter 4. Labuan Limited Liability Partnerships

§1. Introduction

330. On 16 April 1984 Labuan was declared a Federal Territory and subsequently on 1 October 1990, the Government of Malaysia declared the Federal Territory of Labuan as an IOFC. As an integrated IOFC, Labuan offers a wide range of offshore financial products and services to customers worldwide, including banking and investment banking, insurance, captives, trust business, fund management, investment holding, company management and Islamic financing. In 1996, the LOFSA was established as a one-stop agency and sole independent authority responsible for the administration of the offshore industry in Labuan.

331. In 2009, new legal frameworks were tabled and approved by the Parliament of Malaysia. Four legislation are retained with amendments; the LFSA, Labuan Companies Act 1990, Labuan Trust Act 1996 and Labuan Business Activity Tax Act 1990. in addition, four new legislation were introduced: Labuan LP and LLPA 2010, LFSSA, Labuan Foundations Act 2010, LIFSSA and Labuan Foundations Act 2010. The new framework provides Labuan IBFC with updated legislation that is flexible and conducive to the conduct of international business. Amongst the highlights of the new legislation is the name change from LOFSA to Labuan Financial Services Authority (LFSA).

332. This transformation was in line with the strategic direction to reposition Labuan as an IBFC. Consequently, all reference to the term 'offshore' was deleted from Labuan laws and the distinction between Labuan and domestic markets was made through the term 'Labuan' with clear provisions on the applicability of relevant law, domestic or otherwise. The new laws allowed for a wider range of entities that may be established in Labuan IBFC, such as Labuan PCCs, Labuan Special Trusts and Labuan Foundations.

§2. Nature of Liability

333. Under the Labuan LP and LLPA 2010, any two or more persons may form a Labuan limited liability partnership for any lawful purpose.[515] An individual or a corporation may be a partner in an LLPA.[516] To register an LLLP, the designated partner shall submit all relevant documents to the Authority and be accompanied by the prescribed fee as may be specified by the Authority.[517] The name of an LLLP shall end with the words 'Labuan Limited Liability Partnership' in full or the abbreviation '(Labuan) L.L.P.' or '(Labuan) LLP' or any other form of abbreviation in

515. LLP and LLPA 2010; s. 29(1).
516. LLP and LLPA 2010; s. 29(2).
517. LLP and LLPA 2010; s. 30(1).

Romanized character or words in the national language of a country which connotes an LLP or any abbreviation thereof as may be approved by the Authority.[518]

334. A Labuan LP may convert to a Labuan LLP provided that the partners are all existing partners of the LP and consist of no new partner.[519] A Labuan company may also convert to a Labuan LLP provided that there is no security interest in its assets subsisting or in force at the time of application and the partners of the LLLP to which it is to be converted comprises all the shareholders of the Labuan company and consists of no new shareholders.[520]

335. Upon registration, the LLLP shall be a body corporate and has a legal personality separate from that of its partners.[521] It shall also enjoy perpetual succession[522] and have all the powers of a natural person.[523] Similar to a company, Labuan LLP is capable of suing and being sued,[524] acquiring, owning, holding and developing or disposing of property, both movable and immovable[525] and having a common seal[526] under its own name. Any change in the partners of an LLLP shall not affect the existence, rights or liabilities of the LLLP.[527]

336. As a legal entity, Labuan LLP shall be liable for its own debts arising in contract, tort or otherwise.[528] The liabilities of Labuan LLP shall be met out of the property of Labuan LLP.[529]

A partner is not personally liable, directly or indirectly solely by reason of being a partner of Labuan LLP.[530] However, the protection of limited liability shall not be applicable to the personal liability of a partner in tort for his own wrongful act or omission.[531] In such a case, Labuan LLP is liable to the same extent as the defaulted partner.[532] This means the third party can make a claim against the defaulted partner and Labuan LLP.

In the Labuan LLP, every partner is the agent of the LLP and accordingly, the acts of a partner in the partner's capacity as a partner shall bind it.[533] However, the LLP shall not be bound by any act of a partner with the third party if the partner has, in

518. LLP and LLPA 2010; s. 32(1).
519. LLP and LLPA 2010; s. 34(1).
520. LLP and LLPA 2010; s. 35(1)(a) and (b).
521. LLP and LLPA 2010; s. 55(1).
522. Labuan LP and LLPA 2010; s. 55(2).
523. Labuan LP and LLPA 2010; s. 55(3).
524. Labuan LP and LLPA 2010; s. 55(4)(a).
525. Labuan LP and LLPA 2010; s. 55(1)(b).
526. Labuan LP and LLPA 2010; s. 55(1)(c).
527. Labuan LP and LLPA 2010; s. 55(4).
528. Labuan LP and LLPA 2010; s. 56(1).
529. Labuan LP and LLPA 2010; s. 56(5).
530. Labuan LP and LLPA 2010; s. 56(2).
531. Labuan LP and LLPA 2010; s. 56(3). The other partner shall not be personally liable for the wrongful act or omission of any other partner of the LLP.
532. Labuan LP and LLPA 2010; s. 56(4).
533. Labuan LP and LLPA 2010; s. 57(1).

fact, no authority to act for the LLP[534] and the person knows that the partner has no authority or does not know or believe that partner to be a partner LLP.[535]

§3. Contributions and Division of Profits

337. Similar to the LLP operating in other parts of Malaysia, the interest of a partner in an LLP cannot be transferred without the consent of all existing partners, nor can the interest be assigned without all existing partners' consent. The interest may be transferred by a sale and purchase agreement as the interest is the property of each partner. Where there is an assignment of interest, this does not automatically cause the partner to cease being a partner. The assignment also does not entitle the assignee to interfere in the management of the LLP.

§4. Management

338. The mutual rights and duties of the partners *inter se* and between the LLP with its partners are mainly governed by the partnership agreement.[536] Only in the absence of an agreement that such matter shall be referred to the Labuan LP and LLP Act 2010.[537]

In Labuan LLP, there must be at least one designated partner.[538] A partner may become or cease to be a designated partner by and in accordance with an agreement with the other partners.[539] A designated partner shall be responsible for all acts required to be done by him under the Act[540] and shall be personally liable for all penalties imposed on Labuan LLP for any contravention of Parts IV and V of the Act unless the court decided that he should not be liable.[541]

§5. Transferability of Partners' Interests

339. The interest of a partner in an LLP cannot be transferred without the consent of all existing partners, nor can the interest be assigned without all existing partners' consent. The interest may be transferred by a sale and purchase agreement as the interest is the property of each partner. Where there is an assignment of interest, this does not automatically cause the partner to cease being a partner. The assignment also does not entitle the assignee to interfere in the management of the LLP.

534. Labuan LP and LLPA 2010; s. 57(2)(a).
535. Labuan LP and LLPA 2010; s. 57(2)(b).
536. Labuan LP and LLPA 2010; s. 58(1).
537. Labuan LP and LLPA 2010; s. 58(2)(a)–(j).
538. Labuan LP and LLPA 2010; s. 64(3).
539. Labuan LP and LLPA 2010; s. 64(2).
540. Labuan LP and LLPA 2010; s. 65(a).
541. Labuan LP and LLPA 2010; s. 65(b).

§6. LIQUIDATION

340. The Labuan LP and LLPA 2010 clearly states that in the case of receivership of an LLLP, the provisions of Part VIII (in so far as they relate to a company limited by shares) of the CA shall apply[542] and in the case of winding-up of an LLLP, the provisions of Part X (in so far as they relate to a company limited by shares) of the CA and the Companies (Winding-Up) Rules 1972, or section 68 shall apply.[543] As such, it is apparent that laws applicable to receivership and winding-up of Labuan LLP are the company law. However, different from a company, a partner in Labuan LLP may dissolve the LLP by giving notice of dissolution provided that the LLP has ceased to operate and has discharged all its debts and liabilities.[544] This method is akin to a partnership structure.

Nonetheless, the notice of dissolution is not an absolute method of dissolution as in a partnership[545] but a ground to apply for dissolution by the authority.[546]

§7. TAXATION

341. In 2002, when the Labuan Offshore Business Activities Tax Act (LOBATA) 1990 was amended, the Labuan LP were included in the definition of offshore companies and as such has a tax status as a company. However, with the amendment of the LBATA 1990 in 2010, LLLPs is categorized as Labuan entity and therefore shall be the person assessable and chargeable to tax under the Act.

342. In Labuan, tax shall be charged at the rate of 3% for a year of assessment upon the chargeable profits of a Labuan entity carrying on a trading activity for the basis period for that year of assessment[547] while a Labuan entity carrying on a non-trading activity for the basis period for a year of assessment shall not be charged to tax for that year of assessment.[548] As Labuan LLP is categorized as a Labuan entity, it shall be the person assessable and chargeable to tax under the Act.

542. Labuan LP and LLPA 2010; s. 67(1)(a).
543. Labuan LP and LLPA 2010; s. 67(1)(b).
544. Labuan LP and LLPA 2010; s. 68(1).
545. *See* PA 1961; ss 34(1)(c) and 28(1).
546. Labuan LP and LLPA 2010; s. 68(1).
547. LOBATA 1990; s. 4(1).
548. LOBATA 1990; s. 9.

Chapter 5. Labuan Limited Partnership

§1. Introduction

343. The Labuan LP in Labuan is the only LP entity offered in Malaysia. Under the Labuan LP and LLPA 2010, Labuan LP must consist of not fewer than two and not more than fifty partners.[549] There must be at least one general partner.[550] Where a Labuan LP is formed for the purpose of carrying on any professional practice, the Labuan LP shall consist of partners none of whom is a corporation and shall have in force professional indemnity insurance cover for an amount not less than the prescribed amount with any insurer approved by the Labuan Financial Services Authority (LFSA).[551]

344. The Labuan LP can be formed for the purposes of a specific project[552] or for carrying on an offshore professional partnership.[553] The offshore LP can also be formed to carry on an offshore general LP.[554]

345. Under the Labuan LP and LLPA 2010, a LP must be formally registered with Labuan Financial Services Authority (LFSA).[555] LFSA shall not register an offshore LP unless a partnership agreement which is duly executed has been submitted to the authority.[556] Upon compliance with the registration requirement, LOFSA will issue a certificate which shall be conclusive evidence that an offshore

549. Section 4(2) of the Labuan LP and LLPA 2010.
550. Section 4(2) of the Labuan LP and LLPA 2010.
551. Section 4(4) of the Labuan LP and LLPA 2010.
552. LOLPA 1997; s. 3(5). Where an offshore LP is formed for the purpose of carrying on an offshore project partnership, the offshore project partnership:
    (a) shall be established solely for the purpose of undertaking the project or business specified in its partnership agreement, being the only project or business to be undertaken by the offshore project partnership;
    (b) shall incorporate in its partnership agreement a provision providing that the offshore project partnership shall be dissolved after the completion of the project or business specified in the agreement; and
    (c) shall consist of partners each of whom is a body corporate.
553. LOLPA 1997; s. 3(4): Where an offshore LP is formed for the purpose of carrying on an offshore professional partnership, the offshore professional partnership:
    (a) shall not carry on practice except in one or more of the following fields:
        (i) accounting;
        (ii) actuarial science;
        (ii i) engineering;
        (iv) law; or
        (v) such other fields as may be prescribed by the Authority.
    (b) shall have in force professional indemnity insurance coverage for not less than the prescribed amount with any insurer approved by the Authority; and
    (c) shall consist of partners none of whom is a body corporate.
554. LOLPA 1997; s. 3(6): Where an offshore LP is formed for the purpose of carrying on an offshore general LP, the offshore general LP may consist of any persons as partners.
555. LLP and LLPA 2010; s. 5(1).
556. LLP and LLPA 2010; s. 5(2)(a)-(f).

LP has been legally registered.[557] Nonetheless, the certificate shall be valid and effective for a period not exceeding one year from the date of registration or as may be specified in the certificate.[558] This means that the certificate of registration for offshore LP must be renewed annually.[559] Upon registration, the name Labuan limited partnership shall end with the words 'Limited Partnership' in full or the abbreviation 'Ltd.P.', 'LP', 'L.P' or any other form of abbreviation in Romanised character or words in the national language of a country which connotes a LP or any abbreviation thereof as may be approved by the Authority. The words 'Limited Partnership' in full or the abbreviation 'Ltd.P.'.[560] The name of a limited partner or a body corporate shall not appear in the name of a Labuan LP unless it is also the name of one of the general partners or the Labuan LP has been carried on under that name before the admission of that partner or corporate partner as a limited partner.[561]

I. Formations – Type of Partners

346. There must be two types of partners, i.e., general partners and limited partners.[562] A general partner in an offshore LP essentially has all the rights and powers and shall be subject to all the restrictions and liabilities similar to a partner in a general partnership.[563] This means general partners have the management rights and decision-making power in the firm. However, despite the vast authority given to them, general partners cannot act without the written consent or ratification of all limited partners, in certain matters, namely:[564]

(a) do an act which makes it impossible to carry on the activities of the Labuan LP;
(b) possess any Labuan LP property, or dispose of any rights in any Labuan LP property, for other than a partnership purpose; or
(c) admit a person as a general partner or a limited partner, unless the right to do so is given in the partnership agreement.

347. As for the limited partners, the Act clearly states that a limited partner has the same right as a general partner during business hours, to inspect and make copies of or take extracts from the Labuan LP books, documents and records and to be given, on demand, true and full information of all things affecting the Labuan LP and to be given a formal account of partnership affairs whenever circumstances render it just and reasonable to do so.[565] However, a limited partner shall not have management rights in the LP and shall not be entitled to dissolve a Labuan LP by notice

557. LOLPA 1997; s. 4(7).
558. LOLPA 1997; s. 4(8).
559. Section 4(9) of the Labuan LP and LLPA 2010.
560. Section 7(1) of the Labuan LP and LLPA 2010.
561. Section 7(3) and (4) of the Labuan LP and LLPA 2010.
562. Section 4(2) of the Labuan LP and LLPA 2010.
563. Section 11(1) of the Labuan LP and LLPA 2010.
564. Section 11(1) (a)–(c) of the Labuan LP and LLPA 2010.
565. Section 13(1) (a) and (b) of the Labuan LP and LLPA 2010.

except as expressly provided in the partnership.[566] If a limited partner participates in the management[567] of the Labuan LP in its dealings with persons who are not partners, that limited partner shall be liable, in the event of the insolvency of the Labuan LP, for all debts and obligations of the Labuan LP incurred during the period that the limited partner participated in the management of the Labuan LP as though the limited partner were for that period a general partner.[568]

§2. Nature of the Liability of Partners

348. The general partners have unlimited liability towards the business debts similar to partners in general partnerships. On the other hand, the limited partners have limited liability to contribute towards the business debts. Generally, the limited partner shall only be liable to the Labuan LP for the difference, if any, between the value of money or other property contributed by that limited partner to the Labuan LP or the statutory value and the value of money or other property specified in the documents to be contributed by that limited partner to the Labuan LP.[569] The Act also clearly provides that if limited partners participate in the management of the firm, they will lose their limited liability shield and become liable as general partners.[570]

566. Section 13(2) of the Labuan LP and LLPA 2010.
567. Section 19(5) of the Labuan LP and LLPA 2010; A limited partner shall not be deemed to participate in the management of a Labuan LP within the meaning of this section by doing one or more of the following:
    - (a) being a contractor for or an agent or employee of the Labuan LP or of a general partner or acting as a director, officer or shareholder of a corporate general partner;
    - (b) consulting with and advising a general partner with respect to the activities of the Labuan LP;
    - (c) investigating, reviewing, approving or being advised as to the accounts or affairs of the Labuan LP or exercising any right conferred by this Act;
    - (d) acting as surety or guarantor for the Labuan LP either generally or in respect of specific obligations;
    - (e) approving or disapproving an amendment to the partnership agreement;
    - (f) voting on, or otherwise signifying approval or disapproval of, one or more of the following:
        - (i) the dissolution and winding-up of the Labuan LP;
        - (ii) the purchase, sale, exchange, lease, pledge, hypothecation, or creation of a security interest, or any other dealing in any asset by or of the Labuan LP;
        - (iii) the creation or renewal of an obligation by the Labuan LP;
        - (iv) a change in the nature of the activities of the Labuan LP;
        - (v) the admission, removal or withdrawal of a general or a limited partner and the continuation of the Labuan LP thereafter;
        - (vi) transactions in which one or more of the general partners have an actual or potential conflict of interest with one or more of the limited partners;
    - (g) bringing an action on behalf of the Labuan LP pursuant to subs. 22(3).
568. Section 19(3) of the Labuan LP and LLPA 2010.
569. Section 18 of the Labuan LP and LLPA 2010.
570. Section 19(2) of the Labuan LP and LLPA 2010.

§3. CONTRIBUTIONS AND DIVISION OF PROFITS

349. The partners share in the contribution of capital and the profits of the Labuan LP as predetermined portions agreed in the partnership agreement or in accordance with the Labuan LP and LLP Act.

§4. MANAGEMENT

I. The Internal Relation Between Partners

350. The internal regulation of LP is generally similar to general partnerships except for the composition of partners. As the general partners in a LP have similar rights and terms as partners in the general partnerships, the LPA does not specify any provision to regulate internal relations between the general partners.[571] On the other hand, the Act clearly provides for a relation between the limited partners.[572]

§5. LIQUIDATION

351. Generally, the power to dissolve the LP is only vested in the general partners as it forms part of the management rights.[573] The LP and LLPA 2010 clearly provides that in the event of the dissolution of a Labuan LP, its affairs shall be wound up by the general partners. The Act also expressly stated that a limited partner shall not be entitled to dissolve a Labuan LP by notice except as expressly provided in the partnership agreement.[574] As for the general partners, they have the right to dissolve by notice but the notice would not take effect until it is filed with the authority.[575]

352. The LP and LLPA 2010 also provides that the LP shall be dissolved:[576]

---

571. In absence of a specific statute on the offshore Partnerships Act, reference on the relation between general partners *inter se* should be made to the PA (Malaysia) of 1961.
572. Section 16(1) of the Labuan LP and LLPA 2010; Relations of limited partners with one another, shall rank:

    (1) (a) *pari passu* in respect of the return of their contributions; and
    (b) pro rata to those contributions in respect of profits.
    (2) Where there is more than one limited partner, the partnership agreement may provide that one or more of the limited partners is to have greater rights than the other limited partners as to:
    (a) the return of contributions;
    (b) profits; and
    (c) any other matter.

573. Section 25(1) of the Labuan LP and LLPA 2010.
574. Section 13(2) of the Labuan LP and LLPA 2010.
575. Section 24(1) of the Labuan LP and LLPA 2010.
576. Section 26(1) of the Labuan LP and LLPA 2010.

(a) where the sole or last remaining general partner is an individual, his death, legal incapacity, bankruptcy, retirement or withdrawal from the Labuan LP; and
(b) where the sole or last remaining general partner is a corporation, its winding-up or dissolution in other forms, bankruptcy or withdrawal from the Labuan LP, shall cause the immediate dissolution of the Labuan LP which shall forthwith be wound up:
  (i) in accordance with the partnership agreement; or
  (ii) in accordance with the directions of the court on the application of a limited partner or a creditor of the Labuan LP.

353. Other than the giving rights of dissolution to the general partners, the Act also provides that upon application of any partner (this means either general or limited partners), the LP may be dissolved by the order of the court.[577]

§6. Taxation

354. Similar to Labuan LLP, Labuan LPs is categorized as a Labuan entity[578] and therefore shall be the person assessable and chargeable to tax under the Act.[579] In Labuan, tax shall be charged at the rate of 3% for a year of assessment upon the chargeable profits of a Labuan entity carrying on a trading activity for the basis period for that year of assessment[580] while a Labuan entity carrying on a non-trading activity for the basis period for a year of assessment shall not be charged to tax for that year of assessment.[581]

577. Section 27(1) of the Labuan LP and LLPA 2010-The court may, on the application of a partner, order the dissolution of a Labuan LP if it is satisfied that:(a) the Labuan LP is being conducted in a manner contrary to the terms of the partnership agreement of the Labuan LP;(b) the Labuan LP is being conducted in a manner oppressive to one or more of the limited partners; or (c) circumstances have arisen which render it just and equitable that the Labuan LPw be dissolved.
578. Labuan Business Activities Tax Act (LBATA)1990; Schedule Section 2B. Under s. 11 of LBATA 1990, **11.** A Labuan entity shall (a) at the time of filing of the statutory declaration and return of its profits for a year of assessment under s. 5, make full payment on account of (i) tax to be charged for that year of assessment; or (ii) tax to be charged for that year of assessment after reduction of rebate under s. 8A; or (b) at the time of filing of the statutory declaration under s. 7 or 8, make full payment of (i) the tax charged for that year of assessment; or (ii) the tax charged for that year of assessment after reduction of rebate under s. 8A.
579. LBATA 1990; s. 15.
580. LBATA 1990; s. 4(1).
581. LBATA 1990; s. 9.

Selected Bibliography

Cheang, L.S. *Corporate Powers and Accountability*, 2nd ed. (Kuala Lumpur: Malayan Law Journal *Sdn Bhd*, 2002).

Khan, M.A. 'An Analysis of the Malaysian Corporate Disclosure Regime', *IIUM Law Journal* 12 (2004): 259.

Khan, M.A. 'Compulsory Share Acquisitions: Australian Lessons for Malaysia Regulation', *MLJ* 1 (2004): i.

Khan, M.A. 'Defensive Tactics and Strategies in Company Takeovers'. *MLJA* 4 (2005): 53.

Khan, M.A. 'Minority Shareholders: Proposal for Reform in Malaysia'. *Current Law Journal* 1 (2003): vii.

Rachagan, S., J. Pascoe & A. Joshi. *Concise Principles of Company Law in Malaysia* (Kuala Lumpur, Malayan Law Journal *Sdn Bhd*, 2005).

Mohd-Sulaiman, A.N.. 'Construing Preference Shareholders' Rights: Implications on Redeemable Preference Shares'. *Australian Journal of Corporate Law* 15, no. 2 (2003): 169.

Mohd-Sulaiman, A.N.. 'A Cross-Jurisdictional Study of Financial Assistance Provisions and Proposals – Convergence of Concepts?'. *LAWASIA J* (2005): 157.

Mohd-Sulaiman, A.N.. 'Duty of Care, Skill and Diligence: A Survey on Non-executive Directors in Public Listed Companies in Malaysia'. *The Corporate Governance Law Review* 1, no. 2 (2005): 205–327.

Mohd-Sulaiman, A.N.. 'Defining Financial Assistance and Ascertaining Locus Standi: A Case Review for Section 67 of the Companies Act 1965'. *CLJ* (2007): I-xxiii.

Mohd-Sulaiman, A.N.. 'Encouraging Shareholders' Participation in Company's Decision Making: A Reflection on Existing Law and Reform Issues'. *MLJ* 1 (2003): cxlviii.

Mohd-Sulaiman, A.N.. 'Legitimate Expectation, the Oppression Provision and Shareholders' Agreement'. *Australian Journal of Corporate Law* 12 (2001): 1–17.

Mohd-Sulaiman, A.N.. 'Revising Directors' Duty of Care, Skill and Diligence in Malaysia'. *Australian Journal of Corporate Law* 17, no. 2 (2004): 196–217.

Mohd-Sulaiman, A.N.. 'Shares in the Modern Corporation: A Comparison between Malaysian Companies Act 1965 and the Islamic Perspective'. *IIUM Law Journal* 13 (2005): 1–25.

Mohd-Sulaiman A. N. and Othman E. *Malaysia Company Law-Principles and Practice. 3rd Ed* (Wolters Kluwer, Singapore).

Selected Bibliography

Index

The numbers here refer to paragraph numbers.

www.ingramcontent.com/pod-product-compliance
Ingram Content Group UK Ltd.
Pitfield, Milton Keynes, MK11 3LW, UK
UKHW020143290926
15471UKWH00004B/667

9 789403 549453